More Outstanding Books for the College Bound

Young Adult Library Services Association

AMERICAN LIBRARY ASSOCIATION
Chicago   2006

While extensive effort has gone into ensuring the reliability of information appearing in this book, the publisher makes no warranty, express or implied, on the accuracy or reliability of the information, and does not assume and hereby disclaims any liability to any person for any loss or damage caused by errors or omissions in this publication.

The paper used in this publication meets the minimum requirements of American National Standard for Information Sciences—Permanence of Paper for Printed Library Materials, ANSI Z39.48-1992. ∞

Library of Congress Cataloging-in-Publication Data

More outstanding books for the college bound / Young Adult Library
   Services Association, editor.
      p.   cm.
Includes bibliographical references and index.
ISBN 0-8389-3553-2 (alk. paper)
   1. College students—Books and reading—United States. 2. Best books—
United States. I. Young Adult Library Services Association.

Z1039.C65M67 2005
028'.9—dc22   2005013078

Printed in the United States of America

10   09   08   07   06   5   4   3   2   1

CONTENTS

PART TWO

Lists by Year, 2004–1959

PART THREE

Special Lists

PREFACE

"What should I read?" That question was often stamped plainly on the faces of the young people who came into the libraries where I used to work. Daunted by the rows and rows of books, young adults would wander timidly through the stacks. Oftentimes, if left to their own devices, they would locate a section of books that held some interest for them, grab the thinnest book from the shelf without so much as a peek between the covers, and head quickly for the circulation desk. *More Outstanding Books for the College Bound* is meant to be a resource that librarians, educators, and concerned adults can use to help young adults find great books that are right for them. But between these pages is also a little something for anyone who might wander into a library or classroom. There is recommended reading for that budding history buff, for the future actor, for the poetry lover, for the environmental activist, for the lifelong learner, for the star gazer, and for many others.

As the world leader in creating and disseminating book lists for young adults, the Young Adult Library Services Association (YALSA) strives to promote young adult literature as well as to increase the number of teens who are competent, avid readers. The lists presented in this book are the product of a labor of love by dozens of dedicated members of YALSA, the fastest growing division of the American Library Association. When evaluating and selecting the titles that appear in this book, these members have strived to keep the needs and interests of teens and lifelong learners in mind. With lists of required reading as much a part of the classroom today as in the past, we hope that *More Outstanding Books for the College Bound* will help librarians, educators, and concerned adults offer a wider selection of recommended reading to the young adults in their lives. YALSA, then, is proud to present this work to you.

Beth Yoke
YALSA Executive Director

INTRODUCTION

Is reading falling by the wayside? Are the books that students carry around in their backpacks giving them pleasure or pain? Has reading been overtaken by the electronic media that seems to be dominant in our lives? The concern about technology and its impact on reading is not new. Eighty years ago, Ida E. Melson had this to say:

> To arouse a taste for good reading is admittedly half of the province of the teacher of English, but that the present time furnishes particular obstacles to general and earnest reading among young people, no one can deny. Our chief recreations are automobile-riding and moving pictures. With the building of more garages than homes in the United States during the past year, reading has inevitably lost some tricks in the game. As for movies, whatever they may be as an educational force (and strong claims have often been set forth) frequent attendance upon them fails to increase a child's power to read with understanding—and consequently with pleasure.[1]

Although reading may have lost a few more tricks since 1924, there's still hope. Even though television, video games, and the Internet have been added to cars and movies, reading still has a place in our lives, thanks to people and organizations working to help us develop fluent readers. Book discussion groups abound, and there has been a proliferation of recommended reading lists from secondary schools and colleges. Interest in rereading favorite books is growing, and an avalanche of new books is being published each year.

And, of course, today's students know the importance of reading. How could they not? The emphasis on reading at the elementary and secondary school levels has escalated thanks to the No Child Left Behind Act. Nonetheless, a National Endowment for the Arts survey reports a decline in leisure reading, especially among adults between the ages of eighteen and thirty-four.[2] This distressing news comes at a time when a great deal of attention is focused on adolescent literacy. Even though the International Reading Association, the National Council of Teachers of English, and the National Middle School Association have all issued statements that support the importance of reading in the years of adolescent development, the attention may not be enough to stem the lack of interest in reading among younger adults.

Along with the associations named above, the Young Adult Library Services Association (YALSA), a division of the American Library Association (ALA), has joined in the effort to support the adolescent literacy movement. Adolescent literacy is one of YALSA's ten core values, as outlined in *New Directions for Library Service to Young Adults*.[3] The Teen Read Week initiative is another way YALSA encourages reading for pleasure. And lists of recommended books, including *Outstanding Books for the College Bound* (OBCB), are still another.

HISTORY

OBCB lists have been produced by YALSA since 1959. The last two lists (1999 and 2004) have been the result of a collaborative effort with the Association for College and Research Libraries (ACRL), another division of ALA. The target audience has always been young adults, ages twelve through eighteen, who are planning on continuing their education after high school. In later years, the lists have found a secondary audience. They are useful for anyone, of whatever age, who seeks a postsecondary education or who is a lifelong learner.

The lists were first produced at the request of the National Education Association and were published in the *NEA Journal* in 1959. They have also been published in a brochure format by ALA each time a new list has been created.

Since 1959, fifteen OBCB lists have been produced. In 1984 and 1996, the existing lists were compiled in books published by ALA. This edition supersedes those publications.

Librarians, teachers, guidance counselors, and youth development workers have found the lists especially useful because, unlike many recommended reading lists, they are annotated by youth-oriented librarians in a lively style that will appeal to young adults.

WHO SELECTS THE BOOKS?

Titles for OBCB lists are selected by a fifteen-member committee of YALSA and ACRL members who have been appointed by the YALSA president. The committee members are librarians who serve young adults in various capacities in school, public, and college libraries. Committee members read book reviews, review lists of recommended books, check annual book awards, solicit recommendations from young adults, and collect opinions from teachers in middle schools, high schools, and colleges. They meet at the ALA annual and midwinter conferences over the course of two years. After extensive reading and intensive discussion, they vote to select twenty to twenty-five titles in each of the genres or subjects they have selected. Committee members also write the annotations, describing special characteristics and content that will tempt and intrigue young adult users of the list. For more committee guidelines, see appendix A.

WHAT CRITERIA ARE USED?

The basic criteria for inclusion on an OBCB list were established by YALSA and are very general in nature. In addition to meeting standard selection criteria consonant with the ALA Bill of Rights, titles should be published in English and should be widely available, though out-of-print as well as in-print titles are considered. Also considered are titles that have appeared on previous OBCB lists.

In addition, each category may have a special set of criteria, and the criteria for the committees have changed over the years to reflect societal changes as well as changes in the publishing industry. Additional criteria considered by the committee for the 2004 OBCB list included readability, cultural and ethnic diversity, and balance of viewpoints, with a focus on books published within the last five years. Classic and modern literature is represented on all the lists; however, the lists for 1999 and 2004 feature more modern literature than classics. Young adult literature is particularly well represented on the 2004 list. The abundance of new books suitable for the lists has ballooned in recent years, and the 2004 list has very few repeats from previous lists.

WHO ARE THE COLLEGE BOUND?

Undergraduates who attend the country's colleges and universities are a varied group. In 1999–2000, close to a third were nonwhite, and more than half were women. Students in the traditional age range (younger than twenty-three) made up just over half—or 57 percent—of all undergraduates.

Variations among students have changed little over the past ten years, but there are two notable differences. The proportion of white students has decreased, while the number of students in other racial/ethnic groups has increased. The proportion of minority students in 1999–2000—close to a third—represented an increase of about 25 percent from 1989–1990.[4]

ORGANIZATION OF THE BOOK

The lists are arranged in two ways, by genre or subject and by year of appearance on a list. In part 1, all of the books selected over the years are combined. Literature is subdivided into Fiction, Poetry, and Drama. Nonfiction contains ten separate categories, including Biography, Dance, and Music. Each major section and secondary subsection begins with a quote about the subject, usually from one of the books included in that genre.

Within each section in part 1, the books are listed alphabetically by title. The date in parentheses after each title is the original date of publication or composition. The years of appearance on the lists are also given for each title. Each title is annotated; the annotations are from the original lists and were written by the OBCB committee members and make this part most suitable for browsing. Apart from the original date of publication, the only bibliographic information given is the title and the author or editor. Many of the titles are available in several editions; some are out of print. For complete bibliographic information and for copies of the books, check your local school, public, or college library.

Part 2 is a historical record of the lists by year, without annotations, beginning with the latest list (2004) and ending with the earliest list (1959). The titles for each year are further organized by genre or subject selected by that committee, with titles listed alphabetically by author or editor.

Part 3 contains two special lists. The Top Twenty-Four chart lists titles most frequently selected over the years. The Now/Current list is a combination of the Now list from 1971 and the Current list from 1976 and serves as a snapshot of tense, turbulent times.

Because parts 1 and part 2 serve different purposes, using the index will be the quickest way to fnd a specific title.

THE APPENDIXES

The appendixes include committee guidelines for the 2004 OBCB Committee for those users who want more detail about the selection of titles. "Tips for Using *More Outstanding Books for the College Bound*" will provide strategies for encouraging readers to use the book. The "Reading Action Plan" can be used by students and lifelong learners to systematically create reading goals and to record progress toward those goals. The bibliography includes print and electronic resources for more information on related topics.

NOTES

1. Ida E. Melson, "Current Reading as a Stimulus," *English Journal* 13, no. 6 (1924): 389–96; excerpted in "EJ 80 Years Ago," *English Journal* 93, no. 5 (2004): 23.

2. National Endowment for the Arts, *Reading at Risk: A Survey of Literary Reading in America* (Washington, DC: NEA, 2004), http://www.nea.gov/pub/ReadingAtRisk.pdf.

3. Patrick Jones, *New Directions for Library Service to Young Adults* (Chicago: American Library Association, 2002).

4. National Center for Education Statistics, *The Condition of Education 2004* (June 2004), http://nces.ed.gov/pubs2004/2004077.pdf.

PART ONE

Outstanding Books
by Genre or Subject

LITERATURE

How simple the writing of literature would be
if it were only necessary to write in another way
what has been well written. It is because we have
had such great writers in the past that a writer
is driven far out past where he can go, out to
where no one can help him.

Ernest Hemingway,
Nobel Prize Acceptance Speech (1954)

Great writers of the past as well as writers who have "driven far out past" are present in these lists of poetry and prose. All these writers have demonstrated excellence in expression and a grasp of the human condition, regardless of the time when they were writing. Of course, the selection of categories and titles for a literature section is always open to debate. There are more questions than answers whenever the subject is discussed. What makes a book good literature? Is a best seller literature? Have these titles stood the test of time? Isn't nonfiction literature? These lists provide fuel for the fodder for that discussion.

FICTION

*For a long time I thought the eagle and the serpent on
the Mexican flag were the United States and Mexico
fighting. And then, afterward, I thought of the eagle
and serpent as the story of Mother and Father.*

From *Caramelo*, by Sandra Cisneros

1984, George Orwell **(1948),** 1971

In a society of the future, individual privacy is invaded as the Thought Police persuade the people that "War is Peace—Freedom is Slavery—Ignorance is Strength."

The Accidental Tourist, Anne Tyler **(1985),** 1991

Recently divorced Macon Leary, author of a series of guide books for businessmen who hate to travel, chronicles his journey from lonely self-absorption to an accidental new life with a dog trainer from the Meow Bow Animal Hospital.

The Adventures of Augie March, Saul Bellow **(1953),** 1971

Born out of wedlock, brought up in the poverty of Chicago, Augie takes life as it comes and wherever he can get it.

The Adventures of Huckleberry Finn, Mark Twain **(1884),** 1959, 1963, 1965, 1967, 1971, 1976, 1982, 1988, 1991, 1994

A Missouri boy tells of adventure on the Mississippi.

All Quiet on the Western Front, Erich Maria Remarque **(1930),** 1959, 1963, 1965, 1967, 1971, 1976, 1982, 1988, 1994

Through the eyes and mind of a German private, the reader shares life on the battlefield during World War I.

The Ambassadors, Henry James **(1902),** 1967

The struggle between the old-fashioned New England conscience and the cultured maturity of Paris is told with subtle irony.

An American Tragedy, Theodore Dreiser **(1925),** 1959, 1963, 1965, 1967

Ambitious Clyde Griffiths has an affair with Roberta. But Roberta's pregnancy does not fit into Clyde's plan for success, so he murders her.

Animal Dreams, Barbara Kingsolver **(1990),** 1994

Codi Noline learns secrets about her past that change her future when she returns home to care for her ailing father and to teach high school biology.

Animal Farm, George Orwell **(1946),** 1959, 1963, 1965, 1967, 1982, 1988, 1994

> A satire on communism and the totalitarian state.

Anna Karenina, Leo Tolstoy **(1875),** 1971

> Anna forsakes her husband for dashing Count Vronsky and brief happiness.

Arrowsmith, Sinclair Lewis **(1924),** 1959, 1963, 1965

> A young doctor must decide between worldly success and money and his own desire to devote his life to scientific research.

The Autobiography of Miss Jane Pittman, Ernest J. Gaines **(1971),** 1988, 1994

> This fictional autobiography tells the story of a remarkable African American woman born in slavery on a Louisiana plantation who is freed after the Civil War and lives another 100 years to see the second emancipation.

The Awakening, Kate Chopin **(1899),** 1999

> Edna Pontellier, an unhappy wife and mother, discovers new qualities in herself when she visits Grand Isle, a resort for the Creole elite of New Orleans.

Bastard Out of Carolina, Dorothy Allison **(1992),** 1999, 2004

> Bone confronts poverty, the troubled marriage of her mother and stepfather, and the stigma of being considered "white trash" as she comes of age in South Carolina.

The Bean Trees, Barbara Kingsolver **(1998),** 2004

> Taylor Greer leaves Kentucky and heads west to find a new life. When a baby is abandoned in her car, she learns that responsibilities and independence are not mutually exclusive in this story of family and community.

The Bear, William Faulkner **(1931),** 1982, 1999

> Ike McCaslin's hunting trips for the legendary bear, Old Ben, are played out against opposing ideas of corruption and innocence.

Beauty: A Retelling of the Story of Beauty and the Beast, Robin McKinley **(1978),** 1988, 1994, 1999

> Love is the only key to unlocking a curse and transforming the Beast into a man.

Bee Season, Myla Goldberg **(2000),** 2004

> Eliza's extraordinary gift for spelling leads her to understand the sounds of the alphabet, in a way that echoes the teachings of the mystical Kabbal.

The Beekeeper's Apprentice; or, On the Segregation of the Queen, Laurie R. King **(1994),** 1999

> Retired Sherlock Holmes meets his intellectual match in fifteen-year-old Mary Russell, who challenges him to investigate yet another case.

A Bell for Adano, John Hersey **(1944),** 1967

> In the Italian village of Adano, Major Joppolo tries to replace the town's bell and gain the respect of the villagers.

Beloved, Toni Morrison **(1987)**, 1991, 1999

> Preferring death over slavery for her children, Sethe murders her infant daughter who later mysteriously returns and almost destroys the lives of her mother and sister.

Betsey Brown, Ntozake Shange **(1985)**, 1988

> Betsey Brown, full of dreams to change the world, struggles with her loving but conflict-torn family in this enchanting lyrical portrait of three generations of African American women.

Birdy, William Wharton **(1979)**, 1982

> Under the strain of war, Birdy's boyhood obsession with canaries evolves into madness and the conviction that he himself is a bird.

Bleak House, Charles Dickens **(1852)**, 1971

> A woman who is not what she seems, a lawyer who becomes a corpse, and a girl with no past are all part of Dickens' engrossing literary riddle.

Bless Me, Ultima, Rudolfo A. Anaya **(1972)**, 1991, 1999

> Ultima, a wise old mystic, helps a young Hispanic boy resolve personal dilemmas caused by the differing backgrounds and aspirations of his parents and society.

The Bluest Eye, Toni Morrison **(1970)**, 1994

> Pecola yearns to have beautiful blue eyes like the little white girls she sees.

The Bounty Trilogy: Comprising the Three Volumes, *Mutiny on the Bounty,* **Men** *against the Sea,* **and** *Pitcairn's Island,* Charles B. Nordhoff and James Norman Hall **(1936)**, 1959, 1963, 1965, 1967

> This great trilogy tells of men who mutiny against an insufferable sea captain.

Brave New World, Aldous Huxley **(1932)**, 1967, 1971, 1976, 1982, 1988, 1999

> In a chilling vision of the future, babies are produced in bottles and exist in a mechanized world without soul.

Briar Rose, Jane Yolen **(1992)**, 1999

> Disturbed by her grandmother Gemma's unique version of *Sleeping Beauty,* Rebecca seeks the truth behind the fairy tale.

The Bride Price, Buchi Emecheta **(1976)**, 1988, 1999

> Aku-nna, a very young Ibo girl, and Chike, her teacher, fall in love despite tribal custom forbidding their romance.

The Bridge of San Luis Rey, Thornton Wilder **(1927)**, 1959, 1963, 1965, 1967, 1971

> The story of five travelers who are victims of the collapse of a bridge built over a deep chasm in Peru.

The Caine Mutiny, Herman Wouk **(1951)**, 1967

Under the command of tyrannical Captain Queeg, Willie Keith develops from a carefree college boy to a captain distinguished for bravery.

The Call of the Wild, Jack London **(1903)**, 1991

Stolen from his life as a beloved pet, Buck must learn to adapt to abuse as a Klondike sled dog, to life with a loving master, John Thornton, and finally, when Thornton dies, to life in the wild as a leader of the wolfpack.

Caramelo, Sandra Cisneros **(2002)**, 2004

LaLa learns the stories of her Awful Grandmother and weaves them into a colorful family history. The "caramelo," a striped shawl begun by her Great-Grandmother, symbolizes their traditions.

Catch-22, Joseph Heller **(1961)**, 1971, 1976, 1982, 1988, 1999

In this satirical novel, Captain Yossarian confronts the hypocrisy of war and bureaucracy as he frantically attempts to survive.

The Catcher in the Rye, J. D. Salinger **(1951)**, 1967, 1971, 1976, 1982, 1988, 1991, 1994

A ribald, hilarious, and touching tale of a sixteen-year-old's wanderings in New York for three days after he is dropped from his school.

Cat's Cradle, Kurt Vonnegut **(1963)**, 1971

Finding themselves on the imaginary island of San Lorenzo, a gallery of grotesque people learn about ice-nine and espouse a new religion, Bokonism.

Caucasia, Danzy Senna **(1998)**, 2004

Separated when their parents' interracial marriage ends in divorce, light-skinned Birdie and her dark-skinned sister Cole lead very different lives while hoping for a reunion with one another.

The Chant of Jimmie Blacksmith, Thomas Keneally **(1972)**, 1991

Mixed-race Australian Jimmie Blacksmith is brutally betrayed by white society and embarks on a murderous rampage.

China Boy, Gus Lee **(1991)**, 1994

Kai Ting enters the boxing program at the YMCA and learns how to survive in the tough Tenderloin section of San Francisco.

The Chocolate War, Robert Cormier **(1974)**, 1976, 1988, 1994

When Jerry refuses to sell chocolates for a fund-raising drive, he upsets the power structure of his school and becomes the object of a "war" of intimidation and violence.

The Chosen, Chaim Potok **(1982)**, 1988, 1991, 1994, 1999

A baseball injury brings together two Jewish boys, one Hasidic, the other Orthodox, first in hostility but finally in friendship.

Cold Mountain, Charles Frazier **(1997),** 1999

Inman, a wounded Civil War soldier, endures the elements, The Guard, and his own weakness and infirmity to return to his sweetheart, Ada, who is fighting her own battle to survive while farming the mountainous North Carolina terrain.

The Collected Stories of Isaac Bashevis Singer, Isaac Bashevis Singer **(1982),** 1988

Short stories that glow with irony, humor, mysticism, and strength from the renowned Yiddish writer.

The Color Purple, Alice Walker **(1982),** 1994

In a series of letters to God and her sister, Celie reveals her struggle to overcome the violence and brutality in her life.

The Complete Tales and Poems, Edgar Allan Poe **(1938),** 1959, 1963, 1965, 1967

Outstanding tales of mystery and suspense rise from the pen of one of the great mystery writers of all times.

The Count of Monte Cristo, Alexandre Dumas **(1888),** 1959, 1963, 1965

An adventure story of a man's unjust imprisonment, escape, and return to a new life.

Crime and Punishment, Fyodor Dostoyevsky **(1917),** 1959, 1963, 1965, 1967, 1971, 1976, 1982, 1988, 1999

A sensitive intellectual is driven by poverty to believe himself exempt from moral law.

The Cruel Sea, Nicholas Monsarrat **(1951),** 1959, 1963, 1965

The story of the courageous crew aboard the Compass Rose in the North Atlantic during World War II.

Cry, the Beloved Country: A Story of Comfort in Desolation, Alan Paton **(1948),** 1959, 1963, 1965, 1967, 1971, 1976, 1982, 1988, 1991, 1994

The personal tragedy of a humble Zulu parson seeking his son and sister in Johannesburg.

The Curious Incident of the Dog in the Night-Time, Mark Haddon **(2003),** 2004

Christopher has two mysteries to solve: who killed Wellington the dog, and what happened to his mother. But Christopher, who has Asperger Syndrome, a form of autism, approaches these mysteries and the world itself in a unique and special way.

David Copperfield, Charles Dickens **(1849),** 1959, 1963, 1965, 1967

An autobiographical novel reflecting the life of England in the early nineteenth century.

A Death in the Family, James Agee **(1957),** 1971, 1999

The enchanted childhood summer of 1915 suddenly becomes a baffling experience for Rufus Follet when his father dies.

Death in Venice, Thomas Mann **(1925)**, 1976

A successful author, proud of his work and self-discipline, is forced to confront the mysterious and decadent potential in himself when he becomes infatuated with a frail boy.

Don Quixote de la Mancha, Miguel de Cervantes Saavedra **(1605)**, 1959, 1963, 1965, 1967, 1971, 1976

The adventures of a mad Spaniard who imagines he lives in the age of heroic knights.

Dracula, Bram Stoker **(1899)**, 1982, 1988

Count Dracula's nasty practice of drinking the blood of his victim is finally ended by a group of stalwart English.

Dune, Frank Herbert **(1965)**, 1982

A desert planet is the exotic scene of a richly detailed space fantasy in which the freemen of Dune battle the Emperor of the known universe.

East of Eden, John Steinbeck **(1952)**, 1991

The lives of two California families intertwine as good clashes against evil.

Ellen Foster, Kaye Gibbons **(1987)**, 1999

Casting an unflinching yet humorous eye on her situation, eleven-year-old Ellen survives her mother's death, an abusive father, and uncaring relatives to find for herself a loving home and a new mama.

Ender's Game, Orson Scott Card **(1985)**, 1999

In a world decimated by alien attacks, the government trains young geniuses like Ender Wiggin in military strategy with increasingly complex computer games.

Ethan Frome, Edith Wharton **(1911)**, 1959, 1963, 1965, 1967, 1971

A bitter, stark story of people trapped in a marriage from which they can't escape though love has long since gone.

Everything That Rises Must Converge, Flannery O'Connor **(1965)**, 1991, 1999

Stories about misfits in small southern towns force the reader to confront hypocrisy and complacency.

Fahrenheit 451, Ray Bradbury **(1953)**, 1988, 1991, 1994

Books are for burning in this future society in which thinking and reading are crimes.

The Fall of the House of Usher, and Other Tales, Edgar Allan Poe **(1960)**, 1976, 1982

Desolation and impending doom press heavily on these splendid tales of physical horror and psychological terror.

Far from the Madding Crowd, Thomas Hardy **(1887),** 1982

> Three men seek the love of Bathsheba Everdene in this novel of betrayal and murder in rural England.

A Farewell to Arms, Ernest Hemingway **(1929),** 1982, 1991, 1999

> World War I is the setting for this love story of an English nurse and a wounded American ambulance officer.

The Farming of Bones, Edwidge Danticat **(1998),** 2004

> A Caribbean holocaust story, when nationalist madness and ethnic hatred turn island neighbors into executioners. Amid the rumors of terror, Annabelle and Sebastien hold on to love, to dignity—and struggle to survive.

Fathers and Sons, Ivan Turgenev **(1862),** 1959, 1963, 1965, 1967

> A straightforward novel which dramatizes the conflict and differences between generations in Russia.

Feed, M. T. Anderson **(2002),** 2004

> In this society your brain cyberfeed provides an endless stream of information, entertainment, and advertising. When Violet's feed is disrupted, she's cast adrift and everyone is forced to examine the power of the feed in his/her life.

The Fixer, Bernard Malamud **(1966),** 1971, 1976, 1982, 1988, 1991, 1999

> Victim of a vicious anti-Semitic conspiracy, Yakov Bok is in a Russian prison with only his indomitable will to sustain him.

Flowers for Algernon, Daniel Keyes **(1966),** 1971

> After an experiment on a mouse named Algernon triples its intelligence, the same operation is performed on Charlie, a thirty-two-year-old.

Fools Crow, James Welch **(1986),** 1988

> Fools Crow, an eighteen-year-old Blackfoot in nineteenth-century Montana, tries to help his people understand the significance of the white "seizers" who threaten the traditional Native American way of life.

For Whom the Bell Tolls, Ernest Hemingway **(1940),** 1971, 1976

> Robert Jordan, a young American professor fighting for the Loyalist cause in Spain, discovers love, destroys a bridge as assigned, and faces his final test alone.

Forgotten Fire, Adam Bagdasarian **(2000),** 2004

> Based on a true story from the Armenian Holocaust, this is an eloquent, touching, and heart-wrenching portrait of pain and triumph during a time of tragedy.

The Forsyte Saga, John Galsworthy **(1922),** 1959, 1963, 1965, 1967

> The chronicle of three generations of an upper-middle-class English family.

A Gathering of Old Men, Ernest J. Gaines **(1983),** 1991, 1994

> More than a dozen aging African American men claim to be the sole murderer of a southern white farmer and welcome a chance to confound the law after lifetimes of oppression.

Giants in the Earth, O. E. Rolvaag **(1927),** 1959, 1963, 1965, 1967, 1971

> The lives of Norwegian settlers in South Dakota.

Girl with a Pearl Earring, Tracy Chevalier **(2003),** 2004

> Sixteen-year-old Griet is hired as a maid in the household of Delft painter Johannes Vermeer, where she becomes an assistant and muse to the famous artist.

Go and Come Back, Joan Abelove **(2002),** 2004

> In a story of mutual culture shock, Alicia, a young Isabo girl in a remote area of Peru, is just as fascinated by the American anthropologists, Joanna and Margarita, as they are with the ways of her people.

Go Tell It on the Mountain, James Baldwin **(1953),** 1976, 1988

> Fourteen-year-old John struggles against the sins of his forefathers and the sensuous evils of Harlem to attain a religious conversion that reflects man's battle for inner peace.

Going after Cacciato, Tim O'Brien **(1978),** 1982, 1988

> Private Cacciato takes off from the Vietnam War to walk to Paris, and his company follows him in a real/surreal journey.

The Golden Compass, Philip Pullman **(1996),** 2004

> Lyra Belacqua, a young girl living in an alternate Oxford, and her daimon, Pantalaimon, set out to find her kidnapped playmate and uncover a sinister plot. Now Lyra must use her special powers to thwart evil and redeem the world.

Gone with the Wind, Margaret Mitchell **(1936),** 1959, 1963, 1965, 1967, 1971

> Scheming, beautiful Scarlett O'Hara and unscrupulous Rhett Butler make this story of the Civil War adventurous and absorbing.

The Good Earth, Pearl S. Buck **(1931),** 1959, 1963, 1965, 1967, 1971

> The trials and problems of a Chinese peasant and his wife.

A Gracious Plenty, Sheri Reynolds **(1997),** 2004

> What happens to us when we die? Finch Nobles, a cemetery keeper with horrible burn scars, talks to the dead and helps them examine what keeps them tied to the earth.

The Grapes of Wrath, John Steinbeck **(1939),** 1959, 1963, 1965, 1967, 1971, 1976, 1988, 1999

> An Oklahoma farmer and his family leave the Dust Bowl during the Great Depression to go to the promised land of California.

The Grass Dancer, Susan Power **(1994),** 1999

> Ending in the 1980s with the love story of Charlene Thunder and grass dancer Harley Wind Soldier, this multigenerational tale of a Sioux family is told in the voices of the living and the dead.

Great Expectations, Charles Dickens **(1861),** 1976, 1994

> The hero Pip, reared by humble relatives, is informed he is to be made a gentleman of "great expectations" by a mysterious unknown patron.

The Great Gatsby, F. Scott Fitzgerald **(1925),** 1959, 1963, 1965, 1967, 1971, 1976, 1982, 1988, 1991, 1994

> Lives of wealthy persons in the New York area during the "roaring twenties" are carefully portrayed.

Great Short Works of Joseph Conrad, Joseph Conrad **(1966),** 1976

> Guilt and honor, conscience and moral justice are explored in these tales of sea adventure and unknown lands.

Green Mansions, W. H. Hudson **(1904),** 1959, 1963, 1965, 1967

> A romantic fantasy is set in a South American jungle.

Grendel, John Gardner **(1971),** 1976, 1988, 1999

> In a unique interpretation of the Beowulf legend, the monster Grendel relates his struggle to understand the ugliness in himself and mankind in the brutal world of fourteenth-century Denmark.

The Gulag Archipelago, 1918–1956: An Experiment in Literary Investigation, Aleksandr I. Solzhenitsyn **(1974),** 1976

> Solzhenitsyn examines what life was like for the millions of prisoners in the vast network of penal institutions across Stalin's Russia.

Gulliver's Travels, Jonathan Swift **(1794),** 1976

> Adventures among the miniature inhabitants of Lilliput, the giants of Brobdingnag, the immortal Struldbrugs, and the reasoning Houyhnhnms form a masterful satire on man and human institutions.

The Handmaid's Tale, Margaret Atwood **(1985),** 1999

> In Gilead, a Christian fundamentalist dystopia, fertile lower-class women serve as birthmothers for the upper class.

The Heart Is a Lonely Hunter, Carson McCullers **(1940),** 1982, 1988

> The deaf-mute John Singer becomes the talisman for the dreams and yearnings of four people in a small southern town.

The House on Mango Street, Sandra Cisneros **(1983),** 1999

> In short, poetic stories, Esperanza describes life in a low-income, predominantly Hispanic neighborhood in Chicago.

How Green Was My Valley, Richard Llewellyn **(1941),** 1959, 1963, 1965, 1967

> A young Welsh miner watches his idyllic village become a scene of tragedy.

How the Garcia Girls Lost Their Accents, Julia Alvarez **(1991),** 1994

> The four Garcia girls face a strange new life in America when they are forced to flee the Dominican Republic.

The Human Comedy, William Saroyan **(1943),** 1959, 1963, 1965, 1967

> Saroyan poignantly relates incidents in the life of a family during World War II.

I Never Promised You a Rose Garden, Joanne Greenberg **(1964),** 1971, 1976

> A sixteen-year-old girl struggles out of the seductive kingdom of her madness and reenters the real world.

If Beale Street Could Talk, James Baldwin **(1974),** 1982

> When Fonny is jailed on a frame-up, he and his girlfriend, Tish, are supported by a loyal family.

In Country, Bobbie Ann Mason **(1985),** 1991, 1999

> After her father is killed in the Vietnam War, Sam Hughes lives with an uncle whom she suspects suffers from the effects of Agent Orange, and struggles to come to terms with the war's impact on her family.

In the Time of the Butterflies, Julia Alvarez **(1994),** 1999, 2004

> Dede, the only survivor of the four Mirabel sisters, code named Mariposas or butterflies, reveals their role in the liberation of the Dominican Republic from the dictator Trujillo.

Invisible Man, Ralph Ellison **(1952),** 1971, 1976, 1982, 1999

> A young African American seeking identity during his high school and college days, and later in New York's Harlem, relates his terrifying experiences.

Ivanhoe, Sir Walter Scott **(1819),** 1959, 1963, 1965, 1967

> The days of Robin Hood and of Saxon and Norman feuds come alive in this story of medieval England.

Jane Eyre, Charlotte Brontë **(1847),** 1959, 1963, 1965, 1967, 1971, 1982, 1988, 1991, 1994

> An unassuming English orphan becomes a governess and falls in love with her employer.

The Joy Luck Club, Amy Tan **(1989),** 1991, 1994

> A young Chinese American woman realizes her mother's early life in China is an important reason for the rift between them.

The Jungle, Upton Sinclair **(1906),** 1988

> This gritty description of urban life at the turn of the century shows the moral and physical degradation of a "jungle" in which humans barely live better than animals.

Kidnapped, Robert Louis Stevenson **(1886),** 1959, 1963, 1965

Scotland after the rising of Prince Charlie is the background for this adventure story.

The Killer Angels, Michael Shaara **(1974),** 1994, 1999

Officers and foot soldiers from both the Union and Confederacy steel themselves for the bloody Battle of Gettysburg.

Kim, Rudyard Kipling **(1901),** 1959, 1963, 1965

Kipling recounts the adventures of an orphan son of an Irish soldier during days of British rule in India.

The King Must Die, Mary Renault **(1958),** 1991

The myth of Theseus and the minotaur of Crete comes to life in the form of a novel.

The Kite Runner, Khaled Hosseini **(2003),** 2004

Years after he flees Afghanistan, Amir, now an American citizen, returns to his native land and attempts to atone for the betrayal of his best friend before he fled Kabul and the Taliban.

Kristin Lavransdatter, Sigrid Undset **(1922),** 1959, 1963, 1965, 1967, 1971

A vivid description of Scandinavian life during the fourteenth century.

The Left Hand of Darkness, Ursula K. Le Guin **(1969),** 1976, 1982, 1988, 1999

First envoy to the technologically primitive world of Winter, Al must deal with a hostile climate, a suspicious bickering government, and his own conventional sexual mores.

Les Misérables, Victor Hugo **(1862),** 1959, 1963, 1965, 1967, 1971

A powerful story of an unfortunate thief in the underworld of Paris.

A Lesson before Dying, Ernest J. Gaines **(1993),** 1999

When Jefferson's attorney states, "I would just as soon put a hog in the electric chair as this," disillusioned teacher Grant Wiggins is sent into the penitentiary to help this slow learner gain a sense of dignity and self-esteem before his execution.

Life Is Funny, E. R. Frank **(2000),** 2004

Growing up in New York can be agonizing, humorous, and always a challenge for these teens who tell their stories.

Like Water for Chocolate: A Novel in Monthly Installments with Recipes, Romance and Home Remedies, Laura Esquivel **(1992),** 1994

As the youngest of three daughters in a turn-of-the-century Mexican family, Tita may not marry but must remain at home to care for her mother.

Lincoln: A Novel, Gore Vidal **(1984),** 1991

>The mosaic of other people's lives in Lincoln's Washington renders a complete picture of the man and his times.

The Little Prince, Antoine de Saint-Exupéry **(1943),** 1971

>A strange and mysterious small boy greets a pilot whose plane is forced down in the Sahara, and tells him of his own journey to earth.

The Little World of Don Camillo, Giovanni Guareschi **(1950),** 1959, 1963, 1965

>The half-humorous, half-serious feud between an Italian village priest and a communist mayor.

Look Homeward, Angel: A Story of the Buried Life, Thomas Wolfe **(1929),** 1967, 1971, 1976

>Hemmed in by the hatreds, jealousies, pretenses, and limited horizons of his family, Gene Gant realizes that he must leave home in order to survive as an individual.

Looking Backward: 2000–1887, Edward Bellamy **(1888),** 1959, 1963, 1965

>The author's idea of what life will be like in the year 2000.

The Loon Feather, Iola Fuller **(1940),** 1959, 1963, 1965

>Oneta tells of the decline of her Native American Indian world.

Lord Jim, Joseph Conrad **(1900),** 1959, 1963, 1965, 1967, 1971, 1982

>A man attempts to live with himself after an act of cowardice.

Lord of the Flies, William Golding **(1954),** 1967, 1971, 1976, 1982, 1988, 1991, 1994

>Innocence ends and savagery begins when English school boys are marooned on an ocean island and they attempt to set up a society of their own.

The Lord of the Rings, J. R. R. Tolkien **(1954),** 1971, 1976, 1982, 1988, 1991, 1994

>Frodo, a young hobbit, descends to the depths of Middle Earth to keep the magic ring from falling into evil hands.

Love Is Eternal, Irving Stone **(1954),** 1959, 1963, 1965

>The misunderstandings, sorrows, and devotion are revealed in this novel about Abraham Lincoln and Mary Todd.

Lucky, Alice Sebold **(1999),** 2004

>"You save yourself or you remain unsaved." With these words, Sebold recounts the brutal rape that she was "lucky" to survive. Tragedy and hope combine as she makes her way through a survivor's maze of emotions.

Lust for Life: A Novel of Vincent van Gogh, Irving Stone **(1934),** 1967

>This autobiographical novel reveals the tortured life of Vincent van Gogh.

Madame Bovary, Gustave Flaubert **(1856),** 1971, 1991

Emma Bovary seeks escape from a dull marriage in a novel showing the effect of narrow-mindedness and squalor on a woman's life.

The Magic Mountain, Thomas Mann **(1927),** 1971

A tuberculosis sanatorium visited by Hans Castorp becomes a symbol of the diseased pre-war Europe that made World War I inevitable.

Main Street, Sinclair Lewis **(1920),** 1967, 1971, 1976

A young doctor's wife tries to change the ugliness, dullness, and ignorance which prevail in the small town of Gopher Prairie.

Man's Fate, André Malraux **(1934),** 1971

A small group of revolutionaries struggle to free the Chinese workers during the conspiracy, bombing, and bloodshed of the Shanghai Insurrection of 1927.

The Martian Chronicles, Ray Bradbury **(1950),** 1982

Earthlings gain and lose Mars in these short tales about the colonization of another planet.

Me and Orson Welles, Robert Kaplow **(2003),** 2004

What would it be like to spend a week with the great Orson Welles, even sleeping in his pajamas? Richard Samuels, a budding teenage actor, gets the opportunity to see what life on stage, and behind the stage, is really like on Broadway in 1937.

The Member of the Wedding, Carson McCullers **(1946),** 1966, 1968, 1971, 1976, 1991, 1994, 1999

A young southern girl is determined to be the third party on a honeymoon, despite all advice. The novel was published in 1946; the author dramatized it in 1950.

The Metamorphosis, Franz Kafka **(1916),** 1976

Gregor Samsa becomes a cockroach.

The Mill on the Floss, George Eliot **(1860),** 1959, 1963, 1965, 1967

Impulsive, loving Maggie and her plodding brother, Tom, find in death the solution to their emotional conflicts.

Moby-Dick, Herman Melville **(1851),** 1959, 1963, 1965, 1967, 1971, 1976

Sea captain vows revenge on the white whale that caused him to lose his leg.

Monster, Walter Dean Myers **(1999),** 2004

Steve Harmon is accused of being an accomplice to murder. He creates a screenplay of his wrenching experiences at the crime scene, in jail, and on trial.

Montana 1948, Larry Watson **(1993),** 1999

> The summer he is 12, David watches as his family and small town are shattered by scandal and tragedy.

The Moonstone, Wilkie Collins **(1868),** 1959, 1963, 1965, 1971

> A celebrated jewel is stolen from an idol in a Buddhist temple.

My Ántonia, Willa Cather **(1918),** 1959, 1963, 1965, 1967, 1971, 1976, 1982, 1988

> A Bohemian immigrant girl faces hardships in pioneer Nebraska.

My Heartbeat, Garret Freymann-Weyr **(2002),** 2004

> Can Ellen get the boy who loves her brother?

Native Son, Richard Wright **(1940),** 1971, 1976, 1988, 1999

> For Bigger Thomas, an African American man accused of a crime in the white man's world, there can be no extenuating circumstances, no explanations, and only death.

Nectar in a Sieve, Kamala Markandaya **(1954),** 1971, 1988, 1999

> Natural disasters, an arranged marriage, and industrialization of her village are the challenges Rukmani must face as the bride of a peasant farmer in southern India.

Northwest Passage, Kenneth Roberts **(1937),** 1959, 1963, 1965, 1967

> Major Robert Rogers' tough expedition in 1759 searches for an overland passage to the Pacific.

Nothing but the Truth, Avi **(1991),** 1994

> When Philip Malloy hums along with "The Star-Spangled Banner" in homeroom, no one expects a national media event.

Of Human Bondage, W. Somerset Maugham **(1915),** 1959, 1963, 1965, 1967, 1971, 1976

> A young man searches for a way of life.

Of Mice and Men, John Steinbeck **(1937),** 1982, 1994

> When he accidentally kills a woman, Lennie, a retarded migrant worker, is protected by his friend George.

Of Such Small Differences, Joanne Greenberg **(1988),** 1991

> Falling in love with an actress propels deaf and blind John into a whole new world of experiences.

The Old Man and the Sea, Ernest Hemingway **(1952),** 1959, 1963, 1965, 1967, 1994

> Santiago, an old Gulf fisherman, battles with a monster marlin.

The Once and Future King, T. H. White **(1958),** 1991

> King Arthur learns his lessons from Merlin the Magician, creates Camelot and the knights of the Round Table, and loves and loses Guinevere.

One Day in the Life of Ivan Denisovich, Aleksandr I. Solzhenitsyn **(1963),** 1971, 1976, 1982, 1988, 1991, 1994

> An inmate lives one day at a time in a Siberian prison camp.

One Flew over the Cuckoo's Nest, Ken Kesey **(1962),** 1976, 1982

> An irrepressible rebel leads fellow inmates of a mental hospital in a struggle with tyrannical Head Nurse Ratched.

Ordinary Love and Good Will: Two Novellas, Jane Smiley **(1989),** 1994

> Two modern families in turmoil come to terms with their problems.

Ordinary People, Judith Guest **(1976),** 1988

> Seventeen-year-old Conrad Jarrett returns home after an attempted suicide and finds his journey back to normal life slow and painful.

The Painted Bird, Jerzy N. Kosinski **(1965),** 1976, 1999

> An abandoned dark-haired child wanders alone through isolated villages of Eastern Europe in World War II.

Parable of the Sower, Octavia E. Butler **(1993),** 1999

> Lauren Olamina, who suffers from a hereditary trait called "hyperempathy" that causes her to feel others' pain physically, journeys north along the dangerous highways of twenty-first-century California.

A Passage to India, E. M. Forster **(1924),** 1971

> East and West clash in India when an English woman accuses an Indian man of attacking her.

The Passion of Artemisia, Susan Vreeland **(2002),** 2004

> This eloquent rendering of the story of Artemisia Gentileschi evokes appreciation of both her magnificent art and her struggles to succeed as an artist, a story that mirrors the experiences of young women today.

Père Goriot, Honoré de Balzac **(1835),** 1959, 1963, 1965, 1967

> Paris transforms Eugene de Rastignac from a naive provincial to a Parisian gentleman.

Picture Bride, Yoshiko Uchida **(1987),** 1994, 1999

> Taro journeys to America in the early 1900s to marry a man she has never met.

The Picture of Dorian Gray, Oscar Wilde **(1891),** 1967, 1971

> A handsome young man's portrait becomes a mirror, increasingly grotesque, of his true inner self.

The Plague, Albert Camus **(1948),** 1971, 1982

> A small group of people react to the catastrophe of bubonic plague at the Algerian fort of Oran.

The Portable Faulkner, William Faulkner. Ed. Malcolm Cowley **(1946)**, 1991, 1994

>A group of southern families living in an imaginary Mississippi county form a network of relationships with one another.

Portrait of the Artist as a Young Dog, Dylan Thomas **(1940)**, 1988

>A famous poet's youthful escape from the realities of provincial life.

A Portrait of the Artist as a Young Man, James Joyce **(1916)**, 1976, 1982, 1991

>A young Irish student struggles to become a writer.

Postcards from No Man's Land, Aidan Chambers **(2002)**, 2004

>Seventeen is an age of self-discovery, and Jacob has gone to Amsterdam to explore his life. His quest strangely parallels discoveries about his grandfather's life there during World War II.

The Postman, David Brin **(1985)**, 1988

>Gordon Krantz finds an old, worn postman's uniform after a nuclear holocaust and becomes a symbol of hope to the communities of the American Northwest.

Pride and Prejudice, Jane Austen **(1813)**, 1959, 1963, 1965, 1967, 1971, 1976, 1982, 1988, 1991, 1994

>The romances of the Bennett girls and the ardent desire of their mother to have them all well married.

Prince of Foxes, Samuel Shellabarger **(1947)**, 1959, 1963, 1965

>Italian princes live a life of suspicion and intrigue during the Renaissance.

Push, Sapphire **(1996)**, 2004

>Precious Jones is a survivor. She had her father's baby at 12 and now, at 16, she is pregnant by him again. But an alternative school, a dedicated teacher, and classmates who understand help her fight back.

The Queen's Gambit, Walter S. Tevis **(1983)**, 1991

>Beth Harmon is taught to play chess by the janitor in her orphanage. She jeopardizes her achievements by personal doubts and dependence on drugs and alcohol.

Quo Vadis, Henryk Sienkiewicz **(1896)**, 1959, 1963, 1965, 1967

>The immorality of the first-century Romans is a contrast to the purity of the Christians in ancient Rome.

Ragtime, E. L. Doctorow **(1975)**, 1991

>Real and fictional people from widely different economic and ethnic groups interact in nineteenth-century America.

Rebecca, Daphne du Maurier **(1938)**, 1982

>The timid new mistress of Manderley is haunted by the shadow of her predecessor, the vibrant Rebecca.

The Red Badge of Courage, Stephen Crane **(1885),** 1959, 1963, 1965, 1967, 1971, 1976, 1982, 1988

>A boy moves from cowardice to courage in the Civil War.

The Reivers: A Reminiscence, William Faulkner **(1962),** 1988

>In 1905, eleven-year-old Lucius and two other "reivers," or plunderers, steal his grandfather's car and set off for Memphis and misadventure.

The Return of the Native, Thomas Hardy **(1878),** 1959, 1963, 1965, 1967, 1976

>The powerful influence of Egdon Heath turns to tragedy the love of Clym and Eustacia and brings ruin to others as well.

The Sand-Reckoner, Gillian Bradshaw **(2000),** 2004

>A youthful Archimedes comes into his own as a mathematician, an engineer, and a fascinating human being in this engaging novel.

Sarah, Orson Scott Card **(2001),** 2004

>The character of Sarah, Abraham's beloved wife, illuminates this rendering of a pivotal story from the Old Testament.

The Scarlet Letter, Nathaniel Hawthorne **(1850),** 1959, 1963, 1965, 1967, 1976, 1982, 1988

>Hester Prynne and her lover feel the effects of sin in Puritan New England.

Schindler's List, Thomas Keneally **(1982),** 1988, 1999

>Oskar Schindler, a rich factory owner, risks his life and spends his personal fortune to save Jews listed as his workers during World War II.

The Sea of Grass, Conrad Richter **(1936),** 1959, 1963, 1965, 1967

>Cattlemen and homesteaders fight for land and grazing rights.

Selected Tales of Edgar Allan Poe, Edgar Allan Poe **(1980),** 1994

>These chilling tales of the supernatural are not for the nervous.

A Separate Peace, John Knowles **(1959),** 1967, 1971, 1976, 1982

>Against the backdrop of World War II, the rivalry of two roommates at a boys' school turns into a private war.

Sherlock Holmes: Selected Stories, Arthur Conan Doyle **(1902),** 1982, 1988, 1991

>The brilliant, analytical detective Sherlock Holmes and his friend, Dr. Watson, put Scotland yard to shame as they outwit the villainous Moriarty.

Shizuko's Daughter, Kyoko Mori **(1993),** 1999

>In the years following her mother's suicide, Yuki develops the inner strength to cope with her distant father, her resentful stepmother, and her haunting, painful memories.

Siddhartha, Hermann Hesse **(1951),** 1971, 1976, 1982, 1988, 1991, 1994, 1999

Emerging from a kaleidoscope of experiences and tasted pleasures, Siddhartha transcends to a state of peace and mystic holiness in this strangely simple story.

A Single Pebble, John Hersey **(1956),** 1959, 1963, 1965

An American engineer finds Oriental philosophy a greater obstacle than the wild Yangtze River.

Slaughterhouse-Five; or, The Children's Crusade, Kurt Vonnegut **(1969),** 1976, 1982, 1988, 1994

Billy Pilgrim, an optometrist from Ilium, New York, shuttles between the cellars of Dresden smoldering from Allied bombardment and a luxurious zoo on the planet Tralfamadore.

The Slave, Isaac Bashevis Singer **(1962),** 1982

Forbidden love and suffering teach Jacob wisdom and strength.

Sons and Lovers, D. H. Lawrence **(1913),** 1971, 1976

Neither of Paul Morel's two lovers can wean him away from the stifling influence of excessive mother love.

The Sound and the Fury, William Faulkner **(1929),** 1967, 1971, 1976

The tragic life of the Compsons, a degenerate Southern family, is described by Benjy, a thirty-three-year-old idiot.

The Sound of Waves, Yukio Mishima **(1956),** 1971, 1988

This work delicately traces the lives of two young lovers on a small, traditional Japanese island untouched by modern civilization.

Speak, Laurie Halse Anderson **(1999),** 2004

Calling the police to a party is a tough choice, but what made Melinda call is the devastating secret that keeps her locked in silence.

Spring Moon: A Novel of China, Bette B. Lord **(1981),** 1988

Spring Moon's pampered easy life changes as China changes.

Steppenwolf, Hermann Hesse **(1921),** 1971

Considering himself half-man, half-wolf of the steppes, Harry Haller faces the conflict between nature and spirit.

Stone Heart: A Novel of Sacajawea, Diane Glancy **(2003),** 2004

You are there on the epic journey of Lewis and Clark that opened the West to the call of manifest destiny. Contrasts between the explorers' actual journals and the young Shoshone woman's own records reveal the inherent clash of cultures in this vast new land.

Storm, George R. Stewart **(1941),** 1959, 1963, 1965

> A hurricane forms at sea.

The Strange Case of Dr. Jekyll and Mr. Hyde, Robert Louis Stevenson **(1886),** 1967

> Dr. Jekyll discovers a drug that will create a separate personality that will absorb all of his evil characteristics. He calls him Mr. Hyde.

The Stranger, Albert Camus **(1946),** 1967, 1976, 1991, 1994

> An ordinary little clerk lives quietly and unemotionally until he becomes involved in another man's passions, commits an absurd murder, and is sentenced to death.

A Tale of Two Cities, Charles Dickens **(1859),** 1982, 1988

> The lives of Alexander Manette and his daughter Lucie and those of Charles Darnay and Sydney Carton become entangled during the French Revolution.

Tales of Terror: Ten Short Stories, Edgar Allan Poe **(1985),** 1988

> Ten of Poe's terrifying tales are told in this collection.

Tell Me a Riddle, Tillie Olsen **(1960),** 1982

> Four stories about the very young, the mature, the dying, and the poor are told without pretense.

Things Fall Apart, Chinua Achebe **(1959),** 1991, 1994

> European missionaries and colonial officials disrupt the patterns and rituals of traditional Nigerian Ibo society at the end of the nineteenth century.

Things Invisible to See, Nancy Willard **(1985),** 1988

> In Paradise, on the banks of the River of Time, the Lord of the Universe is playing ball with his archangels; and in Ann Arbor, Michigan, Ben Harkissan is hitting a baseball that strikes Clare Bishop, paralyzing her—an act that entwines the characters.

The Things They Carried: A Work of Fiction, Tim O'Brien **(1998),** 1999

> These stories follow Tim O'Brien's platoon of American soldiers through a variety of personal and military encounters during the Vietnam War.

Time and Again, Jack Finney **(1970),** 1982, 1988

> Simon Morley travels back in time to New York of the 1880s.

The Tin Drum, Günter Grass **(1961),** 1971

> Oskar, who stops growing when he is three, describes life in Germany during and after World War II.

To Kill a Mockingbird, Harper Lee **(1960),** 1967, 1971, 1982, 1988, 1991, 1994, 1999

> A young girl tells of life in a small Alabama town in the 1930s and her father's defense in court of an African American accused of raping a white woman.

The Tree of Liberty, Elizabeth Page **(1939),** 1959, 1963, 1965, 1967

Page provides a saga of an American family from the days of the colonies to the Western plains.

The Trial, Franz Kafka **(1925),** 1971

Joseph K., a bank official, is arrested, tried, and convicted of an unnamed crime of which he knows nothing.

Troy, Adèle Geras **(2001),** 2004

A city under siege, epic battles and heroes, powerful supernatural forces—it's the story of the Trojan War seen through the eyes of its women in one of our oldest stories of the cruelty of war.

The Turn of the Screw, Henry James **(1891),** 1971

A governess tries to break the spell she believes evil spirits have cast over the two innocent children in her care.

Vanity Fair: A Novel without a Hero, William Makepeace Thackeray **(1847),** 1959, 1963, 1965, 1967

Becky Sharp is an ambitious social climber in Victorian London.

Vein of Iron, Ellen Glasgow **(1935),** 1959, 1963, 1965

A family "vein of iron" runs in Ada, indomitable daughter of a Virginia family.

The Wall, John Hersey **(1950),** 1982

The doomed Jews of the Warsaw ghetto turn and face their oppressors.

War and Peace, Leo Tolstoy **(1869),** 1959, 1963, 1965, 1967, 1976, 1982

When Napoleon invades Russia, characters both real and fictional find their lives changed.

The Way of All Flesh, Samuel Butler **(1903),** 1959, 1963, 1965, 1967

The son of a strict clergyman breaks parental ties, thereby freeing himself to make his own way of life.

Way Past Cool: A Novel, Jess Mowry **(1992),** 1994

Thirteen-year-old Gordon is the leader of a gang of African American boys struggling to hold a few blocks of bleak turf in Oakland, California.

Whale Talk, Chris Crutcher **(2001),** 2004

What does a guy do when he has all the talents to be a star athlete, but hates his high school athletic program?

When the Legends Die, Hal Borland **(1963),** 1982

Embittered by the white man's deceits, Thomas Black Bull punishes the rodeo horses he rides until a crushing accident sends him back to the mountains of his Indiana boyhood.

White Teeth, Zadie Smith **(2000),** 2004

Archie and Samad, two unlikely friends, are brought together by bizarre twists of fate and near-death experiences in this epic novel of family, culture, love, and loss set in post–World War II London.

Wuthering Heights, Emily Brontë **(1848),** 1959, 1963, 1965, 1967, 1971, 1982

A story of intense and frustrated love, of hate and revenge, takes place in the wild moors of England.

The Yearling, Marjorie Kinnan Rawlings **(1938),** 1959, 1963, 1965

Life is hard for crippled Jody who lives in the Florida back country.

A Yellow Raft in Blue Water, Michael Dorris **(1987),** 1991, 1994

At times separated by hardships and angry secrets but always bonded by kinship, three generations of Native American women tell their stories in their search for self-identity.

Zorba the Greek, Nikos Kazantzakis **(1952),** 1971

As manager of a mine in Crete, Zorba—philosopher and roué—accomplishes fantastic feats of physical prowess, tells wild stories of his erotic adventures, misbehaves badly with the owner's money, sings, dances, and talks of the world.

POETRY

What is striking about Native American poetry is not the bitterness or anger, though they are there. Nor is it the sense of loss, of living divided in two worlds, or alienation, though they are there too. What is impressive is the courage to continue, to write poetry that uses all the resources of the English language, a language clearly loved for its "beauty and poetic power."

From *Harper's Anthology of 20th Century Native American Poetry,* edited by Duane Niatum

19 Varieties of Gazelle: Poems of the Middle East, Naomi Shihab Nye **(2002),** 2004

Another world, another culture—poems that personalize the conflicts and people, deepening understanding of the impact of September 11th.

50 Modern American and British Poets, 1920–1970, Louis Untermeyer (ed.) **(1973),** 1988

> From Robert Frost to Erica Jong, Untermeyer discusses fifty years of radical change, new tones, new techniques, and a diversity of voices.

100 Best-Loved Poems, Philip Smith (ed.) **(1993),** 1999

> Shakespeare, English and American ballads, and the classics most of us remember and love are part of the treasure found in this publication.

The Best American Poetry, Donald Hall and David Lehman (eds.) **(1989),** 1991

> Well-known and beginning poets present their poetry.

The Black Poets, Dudley Randall (ed.) **(1971),** 1988

> An anthology encompassing the range of African American poets from singers of slave songs to Nikki Giovanni.

A Book of Love Poetry, Jon Stallworthy (ed.) **(1987),** 1999

> You can experience love throughout the ages, as expressed in the past 2000 years of poetry.

Cool Salsa: Bilingual Poems on Growing Up Latino in the United States, Lori M. Carlson (ed.) **(1994),** 1999

> Party times, hard times, memories, and dreams come to life in these English, Spanish, and Spanglish poems.

Crazy to Be Alive in Such a Strange World: Poems about People, Nancy Larrick (sel.) **(1977),** 1982

> A spirited collection of American poetry.

Earth-Shattering Poems, Liz Rosenberg (ed.) **(1998),** 1999

> Poets from around the world and through the centuries express the emotional intensity of life's experiences.

Final Harvest: Emily Dickinson's Poems, Emily Dickinson **(1961),** 1988

> In love with words, in love with brevity, Emily Dickinson's poems are like her life—enigmatic, intensely felt, and unforgettable.

A Fire in My Hands: A Book of Poems, Gary Soto **(1990),** 1994

> Poems by a Mexican American poet explore the universal themes of growth, family, friendship, and first love.

Going Over to Your Place: Poems for Each Other, Paul B. Janeczko (sel.) **(1987),** 1991

> These poems celebrate everyday feelings—from the first kiss to the wonder of a parade.

Harper's Anthology of 20th Century Native American Poetry, Duane Niatum (ed.) **(1988),** 1999

> The century's best native American poets capture their cultural heritage through powerful poetry.

Heart to Heart: New Poems Inspired by Twentieth Century American Art, Jan Greenberg **(2001),** 2004

> Can a painting speak? This collection of lyrical responses to famous American works of art will make you a believer.

How Does a Poem Mean? John Ciardi **(1960),** 1971, 1976, 1999

> A poet and critic discusses the value and nature of poetry, using selections from six centuries of American and English poems.

How to Read and Interpret Poetry, Carole Kiler Doreski and William Doreski **(1988),** 1991

> A valuable handbook that helps to evaluate, read, and appreciate poetry in relation to the poet's life.

I Feel a Little Jumpy around You: A Book of Her Poems and His Poems Collected in Pairs, Naomi Shihab Nye and Paul B. Janeczko (eds.) **(1996),** 1999

> In this anthology of thought-provoking poems, male and female writers view life from gender perspectives.

In Search of Color Everywhere: A Collection of African-American Poetry, E. Ethelbert Miller (ed.) **(1994),** 1999

> From spirituals, to rap, to classic works by famous poets, this presentation delights the senses.

New and Selected Poems, Mary Oliver **(1992),** 1999

> Pulitzer Prize–winning poet presents a smorgasbord of her poems, composed and published over the last three decades, about life, death, and humanity's relationship to the natural world.

The New Oxford Book of Light Verse, Kingsley Amis (ed.) **(1978),** 1988

> The self-appointed curmudgeon of the British literary world displays editorial quirkiness in his selection of humorous poetry.

The Odyssey of Homer: A Modern Translation, Homer. Trans. Richard Lattimore **(1967),** 1976, 1982, 1999

> A Greek epic tells of the adventures of the hero Odysseus during his perilous and protracted journey home from the Trojan War.

One Hundred Poems from the Japanese, Kenneth Rexroth (trans.) **(1955),** 1988

> A sampler of sensitively translated poems that preserve the beauty and spirit of the original.

Pierced by a Ray of Sun: Poems about the Times We Feel Alone, Ruth Gordon (ed.) **(1995),** 1999

> World famous poets reflect on solitude and loneliness.

Poems (Everyman's Library Pocket Poets), Emily Dickinson **(1993),** 1999

> A compact collection of the best known works of an eminent American poet proves that good things come in small packages.

Poems for a Small Planet: Contemporary American Nature Poetry, Robert Pack and Jay Parini (eds.) **(1993)**, 1994

> Eighty-three of America's most accomplished poets respond to the plight of nature today.

The Poetry of Yevgeny Yevtushenko, Yevgeny Yevtushenko **(1981)**, 1988

> Yevtushenko's poetry is presented in two languages.

Poetry Out Loud, Robert Alden Rubin (ed.) **(1993)**, 1999

> Poems from the world's greatest poets, as well as suggestions for reading them aloud, are found in the backpack-sized gem.

Poets of World War II, Harvey Shapiro (ed.) **(2003)**, 2004

> They have been called the Greatest Generation, and in their own voices they reveal the true price of their call to arms.

The Rattle Bag, Seamus Heaney and Ted Hughes (eds.) **(1982)**, 1994, 1999

> This compilation of poetry includes poems from the oral tradition.

Reflections on a Gift of Watermelon Pickle . . . and Other Modern Verse, Stephen Dunning, Edward Lueders, and Hugh Smith (eds.) **(1995)**, 1999

> Photographs complement or illustrate 114 poems that range from sharp and biting to easygoing and optimistic.

The Rose That Grew from Concrete, Tupac Shakur **(1999)**, 2004

> Written when Tupac was nineteen and not yet a star, these poems bring emotion, power, and passion to the experience of becoming you.

Singing America, Neil Philip (ed.) **(1995)**, 1999

> Experience American poetic heritage through dramatic black-and-white drawings that illustrate a wealth of poetry from Walt Whitman to spirituals, songs of the Sioux, the National Anthem, and Woody Guthrie.

Sleeping on the Wing: An Anthology of Modern Poetry, with Essays on Reading and Writing, Kenneth Koch and Kate Farrell **(1981)**, 1994

> Essays on the reading and writing of modern poetry complement this contemporary anthology.

The Tree Is Older Than You Are: A Bilingual Gathering of Poems and Stories from Mexico, with Paintings by Mexican Artists, Naomi Shihab Nye (sel.) **(1995)**, 1999

> Modern and ancient Mexican poetry, prose, and paintings come alive in this lavish anthology.

Under 35: The New Generation of American Poets, Nicholas Christopher (ed.) **(1989)**, 1991

> Many young poets present poems in a variety of themes and forms.

The United States of Poetry, Joshua Blum, Bob Holman, and Mark Pellington (eds.) **(1996),** 1999

> Contemporary poems enhanced by outstanding photographs highlight poets ranging from Nobel laureates to rappers.

Unsettling America: An Anthology of Contemporary Multicultural Poetry, Maria Mazziotti Gillan and Jennifer Gillan (eds.) **(1994),** 1999

> This poetry feast challenges stereotypes about who or what is American.

The Vintage Book of Contemporary American Poetry, J. D. McClatchy (ed.) **(1990),** 1994

> Sixty-five of America's greatest contemporary poets contribute to this comprehensive collection.

The War Poets, Robert Giddings (ed.) **(1988),** 1999

> The work of a variety of World War I poets, many of whom died in the conflict, is reinforced with illustrations, biographical notes, and a brief history of "the war to end all wars."

DRAMA

Drama—what literature does at night.

From *Testament of a Critic,*
by George Jean Nathan

Plays

Abe Lincoln in Illinois, Robert E. Sherwood **(1939),** 1966, 1968

> Sherwood dramatizes Lincoln's life from the time of his romance with Ann Rutledge until he leaves Springfield to become president.

Agamemnon, Aeschylus **(c. 458 B.C.),** 1991

> After the Trojan War, Agamemnon is murdered by his wife and her lover.

Ah, Wilderness! Eugene O'Neill **(1933),** 1966, 1994

> In this comedy a seventeen-year-old faces his first temptations, and his parents try to understand him.

The Amen Corner: A Play, James Baldwin **(1968),** 1968, 1991

> Love is a necessity in the African American family, church, and community.

Angel Street: A Victorian Thriller in Three Acts, Patrick Hamilton **(1942),** 1966

> A scheming husband's nearly successful effort to drive his wife insane and obtain her fortune.

Angels in America: A Gay Fantasia on National Themes. Part 1: Millennium Approaches; Part 2: Perestroika, Tony Kushner **(1992),** 1994, 1999

> Kushner chronicles AIDS in America during the Reagan era.

Antigone, Sophocles **(440 B.C.),** 1966, 1968

> A young girl defies the decrees of her uncle, King Creon, and attempts to bury the body of her dead brother.

Antigone, Jean Anouilh **(1944),** 1991

> Antigone chooses death because of her fear that compromise will distort and defame life in this contemporary version of the Sophocles tragedy.

Arms and the Man, George Bernard Shaw **(1894),** 1988

> The ugly reality of war intrudes into the life of a romantic young woman.

Arsenic and Old Lace: A Play in Three Acts, Joseph Kesselring **(1941),** 1966

> A comedy about two spinster sisters who quietly do away with old gentlemen who answer their ads for boarders.

The Barretts of Wimpole Street: A Comedy in Five Acts, Rudolf Besier **(1930),** 1966

> The romantic courtship and elopement of Elizabeth Barrett and Robert Browning against the wishes of her tyrannical father.

Betrayal, Harold Pinter **(1978),** 1994

> Beginning in the present and moving gradually backwards, Pinter brings subtlety and insight to the eternal triangle.

The Belle of Amherst, William Luce **(1976),** 1994

> Luce's one-act play is based upon the poetry of Emily Dickinson.

Billy Budd, Louis O. Coxe and Robert Chapman **(1951),** 1966

> Adapted from the Herman Melville story of a young sailor condemned to die by a captain who knows that the young sailor is spiritually guiltless.

The Birthday Party, Harold Pinter **(1959),** 1971, 1976, 1991

> A birthday party destroys a lazy pianist.

The Blacks: A Clown Show, Jean Genet **(1960),** 1976

> African Americans, as caricatures of whites, act out the murder of a white man in a play within a play which hovers between illusion and reality.

Blithe Spirit, Noël Coward **(1941),** 1988, 1991, 1994, 1999

> A ghost troubles a novelist's second marriage.

Blood Wedding, Federico García Lorca **(1932),** 1968, 1971, 1976, 1991

> A Castilian wedding ends in tragedy when the bride runs away with her lover.

The Boys Next Door: A Play in Two Acts, Tom Griffin **(1988),** 1994

> A social worker supervising four men in a group home finds them touching, funny, poignant, and frustrating, but always human.

Brighton Beach Memoirs, Neil Simon **(1982),** 1988

> First of an autobiographical trilogy about Eugene Jerome and his family in Depression-era Brooklyn.

Buried Child and Seduced and Suicide in B-flat, Sam Shepard **(1979),** 1994

> With these three plays, Shepard probes deeply into the disintegration of the American Dream.

Caught in the Act: New York Actors Face to Face, Don Shewey and Susan Shacter **(1986),** 1988

> Today's finest actors speaking candidly about their craft in an inside analysis of the pressure, fame, and struggle for perfection.

Cavalcade, Noël Coward **(1932),** 1966

> A pageant of English life from 1899 to 1930.

The Cherry Orchard: A Comedy in Four Acts, Anton Chekhov **(1923),** 1966, 1968, 1971, 1976, 1988, 1991

> The ineffectual Ranevskys exemplify the passing of the Russian aristocracy.

Children of a Lesser God, Mark Medoff **(1980),** 1988, 1991, 1994

> A young deaf woman falls in love with a hearing man.

The Children's Hour, Lillian Hellman **(1934),** 1988, 1991, 1994

> The sly suggestions of a vicious teenager destroy the tranquility of a girls' boarding school.

Crimes of the Heart, Beth Henley **(1982),** 1991, 1994

> Three unhappy sisters have strong family ties that see them through their many troubles.

The Crucible, Arthur Miller **(1953),** 1971, 1991

> Teenage girls accused of being witches come to trial in seventeenth-century Salem, Massachusetts.

Cyrano de Bergerac, Edmond Rostand **(1898),** 1966, 1971, 1988, 1991

> A soldier who is witty and writes poetry is hindered by his own nose.

Death of a Salesman, Arthur Miller **(1949),** 1966, 1968, 1976, 1999

> When an ordinary man faces his failure as husband, father, and human being, the only solution he sees is suicide.

The Deputy, Rolf Hochhuth **(1964),** 1971, 1976

> Pope Pius XII, Christ's deputy on earth, fails to voice a fundamental Christian principle when he does not publicly condemn Hitler's pogrom, which results in the extermination of six million Jews.

Doctor Faustus, Christopher Marlowe **(1588),** 1966, 1968, 1971, 1976

> In return for pleasure, knowledge, and power beyond the human limit, a learned man sells his soul to the devil and ultimately pays his debt.

A Doll's House, Henrik Ibsen **(1889),** 1976, 1988, 1991, 1994, 1999

> Nora, one of feminism's great heroines, steps off her pedestal and encounters the real world.

Dream on Monkey Mountain, and Other Plays, Derek Walcott **(1970),** 1994

> An old man in the West Indies searches for meaning, identity, and relevance.

Driving Miss Daisy, Alfred Uhry **(1988),** 1999

> Over the years, the Southern and headstrong Miss Daisy and her black chauffeur, Hoke, develop a deep and abiding friendship.

The Effect of Gamma Rays on Man-in-the-Moon Marigolds: A Drama in Two Acts, Paul Zindel **(1970),** 1976, 1991

> Tillie escapes a nightmarish life by burying herself in a scientific experiment in school.

The Elephant Man, Bernard Pomerance **(1979),** 1991

> Victorian society exploits John Merrick, a grotesquely deformed man.

An Enemy of the People: A Play in Five Acts, Henrik Ibsen **(1939),** 1971

> The advanced ideas of a Norwegian town doctor put him in conflict with town authorities and public opinion, causing him to lose job, home, and friends.

Equus, Peter Shaffer **(1973),** 1991

> A psychiatrist helps a juvenile delinquent who has blinded six horses and, in the process, finds himself facing complex and disturbing questions.

Everyman, Anonymous **(1485),** 1971, 1976

> In the best of the medieval morality plays, Everyman is summoned by Death, and finds that of all his friends (Fellowship, Knowledge, Beauty, Strength, etc.) only Good Deeds will accompany him.

The Father, August Strindberg **(1907),** 1971

> Sexual conflicts are subtly and thoroughly explored in this naturalistic drama of a destructive marriage.

Fences, August Wilson **(1986),** 1994, 1999

> A garbage man recalls his career as a Negro League baseball star.

For Colored Girls Who Have Considered Suicide / When the Rainbow Is Enuf, Ntozake Shange **(1977),** 1994

> The inner feelings of young African American women are captured in this passionate feminist spellbinder.

The Foreigner, Larry Shue **(1985),** 1994

> Nonstop hilarity demonstrates what can happen when a group of devious characters deal with a stranger who supposedly knows no English.

Foxfire, Susan Cooper and Hume Cronyn **(1979),** 1994

> A seventy-nine-year-old Appalachian widow fights to determine her own future as she lives on a mountain farm with the acerbic ghost of her husband.

The Front Page, Ben Hecht and Charles MacArthur **(1928),** 1994

This comedy of a big city newspaper brings thrills and excitement to reporters and reporting.

The Glass Menagerie, Tennessee Williams **(1945),** 1966, 1968, 1971, 1976, 1991, 1994, 1999

A brother is haunted by the memory of his teenage sister who takes refuge from the world in her collection of glass animal figurines.

The Great White Hope, Howard Sackler **(1968),** 1971

Based loosely on the life of African American heavyweight champion Jack Johnson, this prizewinning play serves primarily to illuminate and comment on the prevailing racial attitudes of Johnson's time and today.

The Green Pastures: A Fable, Marc Connelly **(1929),** 1966

A fable based on Roark Brandford's novel, *Ol' Man Adam an' His Chillun,* that is a moving African American folk interpretation of the Bible.

Hadrian VII: A Play, Peter Luke **(1968),** 1971

An unsuccessful candidate for the Catholic priesthood is later visited by bishops who summon him belatedly to Holy Orders from which point, through a bizarre set of circumstances, he rises meteorically to the eminence of pope.

Hamlet, William Shakespeare **(1603),** 1966, 1968

A prince is tormented by uncertainty over whether he should avenge his father's murder.

Harvey: A Comedy in Three Acts, Mary Chase **(1952),** 1966

A middle-aged bachelor's friendship with a six-foot imaginary rabbit.

The Hasty Heart: A Play in Three Acts, John Patrick (pseud.) **(1945),** 1966

A proud and aloof Scottish soldier who does not know that he is dying rebuffs the friendship of five other wounded patients in an Army hospital.

Hedda Gabler, Henrik Ibsen **(1890),** 1966, 1968

This character study shows a woman of good taste and culture who is spiritually a monster.

The Heidi Chronicles, Wendy Wasserstein **(1990),** 1994

This hilarious coming-of-age story tells of a successful art historian in a rapidly changing world.

The Heiress, Ruth Goetz and Augustus Goetz **(1948),** 1966, 1968

This exciting story tells of a plain girl's conflict with her austere father and a handsome, fortune-hunting suitor.

The Hostage, Brendan Behan **(1958)**, 1971

> A hilarious play about a British soldier who is held hostage in a Dublin brothel in order to prevent the execution of an Irish rebel.

House of Atreus: Adapted from the Oresteia, John Lewin **(1966)**, 1971

> Each of three classical Greek tragedies by Aeschylus is compressed into one act in this re-creation in modern verse of murder and retribution within a family.

How I Learned to Drive, Paula Vogel **(1998)**, 1999

> Li'l Bit learns about more than driving when her relationship with Uncle Peck moves from friendship to betrayal.

I Remember Mama: A Play in Two Acts, John Van Druten **(1945)**, 1966

> Based on the novel *Mama's Bank Account*, this is a portrayal of a Norwegian immigrant family living in San Francisco at the turn of the century.

I'm Not Rappaport, Herb Gardner **(1986)**, 1994

> Two octogenarians in New York City are determined not to be "put out to pasture."

The Importance of Being Earnest, Oscar Wilde **(1895)**, 1966, 1968, 1971, 1976, 1988, 1991, 1994, 1999

> Can a baby, abandoned in Victoria Station, grow up to find love, romance, identity, and the importance of being earnest?

Inherit the Wind, Jerome Lawrence and Robert E. Lee **(1955)**, 1966, 1968, 1971, 1976, 1994

> The famous Scopes "Monkey" Trial, argued by a celebrated pair of antagonists, William Jennings Bryan and Clarence Darrow, involves a young teacher in America's "Bible belt" charged with blasphemy for teaching Darwin's theory of evolution.

J. B., Archibald MacLeish **(1958)**, 1966, 1968, 1971, 1976, 1991

> The biblical story of Job is set in a worn, tattered circus, which symbolizes the modern world.

Juno and the Paycock: A Tragedy in Three Acts, Sean O'Casey **(1954)**, 1971, 1976

> The misfortunes of the idle "Paycock" and his strong wife Juno reflect the Irish dramatist's hatred of war, misery, and death.

King Lear, William Shakespeare **(1605)**, 1991, 1999

> An arrogant old man goes insane after his daughters strip him of every dignity and possession.

The Lady's Not for Burning: A Comedy, Christopher Fry **(1949)**, 1976

> Condemned to burn as a witch, the pretty heroine enchants everybody.

The Lark, Jean Anouilh **(1956),** 1991

    The story of Joan of Arc is retold using flashbacks.

Le Bourgeois Gentilhomme, Molière **(1670),** 1988

    Sudden wealth turns M. Jordan's head and his household into turmoil.

Life with Father, Howard Lindsay and Russel Crouse **(1940),** 1966, 1968

    Based on Clarence Day's amusing book about his family, especially Father.

The Lion in Winter, James Goldman **(1966),** 1971

    Henry II, his wife, Eleanor of Aquitaine, and their three sons clash in rip-roaring fashion in this interpretation of royal domestic life in twelfth-century Britain.

The Little Foxes, Lillian Hellman **(1939),** 1968, 1971, 1976, 1999

    Members of the greedy and treacherous Hubbard family compete with each other for control of the mill that will bring them riches in the post–Civil War South.

Long Day's Journey into Night, Eugene O'Neill **(1955),** 1968, 1971, 1976, 1988, 1991, 1999

    This painfully autobiographical play reveals the illusions and delusions of the Tyrone family.

Look Back in Anger: A Play in Three Acts, John Osborne **(1957),** 1971, 1976

    Marriage, friendship, rebellion against a stultifying society, and affirmation of life lived lustily are explored by the first of Britain's "angry young men."

Look Homeward, Angel, Ketti Frings **(1958),** 1966

    Adaptation of the Thomas Wolfe novel about a young man seeking to break away from the stifling world of his youth.

Lost in Yonkers, Neil Simon **(1991),** 1994

    Two brothers must live with their harsh grandmother when the Great Depression escalates family problems in this bittersweet comedy.

The Lower Depths, Maxim Gorky **(1902),** 1976

    A motley group of derelicts, whose faith in themselves is beyond restoration, huddle together in a basement enduring the misery and despair from which they will never escape.

Lysistrata, Aristophanes **(c. 416 B.C.),** 1971, 1976, 1988, 1991, 1994

    Is this the ultimate anti-war weapon? Women say "no" to sex in an attempt to end the Athens-Sparta War.

M. Butterfly, David Henry Hwang **(1988),** 1994

    A brilliant tour de force of a twenty-year liaison between a French diplomat and a Chinese opera star—with a startling climax.

Macbeth, William Shakespeare **(1606),** 1976

> The consequences of unscrupulous ambition ultimately destroy Macbeth and his lady after they perpetrate an evil crime to gain the Scottish throne.

The Madwoman of Chaillot, Jean Giraudoux **(1946),** 1966, 1968, 1971, 1976, 1991

> A madwoman who wants to enjoy the pleasures of daily living devises a plan to save Paris from destruction.

A Man for All Seasons, Robert Bolt **(1962),** 1971, 1976

> As a result of his controversy with Henry VIII, Sir Thomas More, a devout Catholic, goes to his death rather than violate his conscience.

"Master Harold". . . and the Boys, Athol Fugard **(1982),** 1991, 1994, 1999

> Hally, a precocious white South African teenager, lashes out at two older black friends who are substitute figures for his alcoholic father.

The Matchmaker, Thornton Wilder **(1954),** 1991, 1994

> A marriage broker attempts to snare another woman's intended husband for herself.

The Member of the Wedding, Carson McCullers **(1946),** 1966, 1968, 1971, 1976, 1991, 1994, 1999

> A young southern girl is determined to be the third party on a honeymoon, despite all advice. The novel was published in 1946; the author dramatized it in 1950.

A Midsummer Night's Dream, William Shakespeare **(1595),** 1971, 1976

> Thwarted but determined lovers escape to the enchanted forest where fairies are problem solvers.

The Miracle Worker: A Play for Television, William Gibson **(1957),** 1966, 1968, 1971, 1976

> Annie Sullivan's patience and firmness produce a miracle when she frees the brilliant mind of blind and deaf Helen Keller by teaching her to speak.

The Misanthrope, Molière **(1666),** 1976, 1991

> The hypocrisy of seventeenth-century Parisian society causes Alceste to become a hermit.

The Miser, Molière **(1668),** 1971, 1994

> Satire, humor, and romance combine in a drama of greed versus love.

Miss Julie, August Strindberg **(1888),** 1976, 1991

> Parental, personal, and social pressures force Miss Julie to commit suicide.

Mister Roberts: A Play, Thomas Heggen and Joshua Logan **(1948),** 1966, 1968

> Comic adventures of a crew of a U.S. Navy cargo ship fighting boredom and a stiffnecked captain in World War II.

Moon on a Rainbow Shawl: A Play in Three Acts, Errol John **(1958),** 1994

Ambition and betrayal lurk in a Trinidad tenement yard.

Mother Courage and Her Children: A Chronicle of the Thirty Years' War, Bertolt Brecht **(1941),** 1968, 1971, 1976, 1991, 1994

A mother gives up her three children to the Thirty Years' War, yet continues to survive because of the war.

The Mousetrap, Agatha Christie **(1954),** 1994, 1999

Stranded in a boarding house during a snowstorm, a group of strangers discovers a murderer in their midst.

Murder in the Cathedral, T. S. Eliot **(1935),** 1971, 1988

Friendship, ambition, loyalty, and morality are in conflict in this poetic drama about Henry II and Thomas à Becket.

No Exit, Jean-Paul Sartre **(1944),** 1968, 1971, 1988, 1991, 1999

In this existential drama, we learn that Hell is other people.

The Noh Drama: Ten Plays from the Japanese 14th and 15th Centuries, Arthur Waley **(1960),** 1988

A collection of classic Japanese plays.

The Odd Couple, Neil Simon **(1966),** 1971, 1991

Can two men who are as different as day and night, and who will not change or compromise, live happily together?

Oedipus the King, Sophocles **(c.409 B.C.),** 1971, 1976, 1988, 1991

Here's the original Freudian dilemma. A prophecy is fulfilled when Oedipus kills his father and marries his mother.

Othello, William Shakespeare **(1604),** 1971

Jealousy and passion torment a Moorish army commander who loves his wife too much.

Our Town, Thornton Wilder **(1938),** 1966, 1968, 1971, 1976, 1988, 1999

Love and death in a small town are seen through the eyes of the Stage Manager.

Phaedra, Jean Racine **(1677),** 1971, 1976

A great French dramatist gives new dimensions to a Greek myth about a mother's tragic love for her son.

The Piano Lesson, August Wilson **(1990),** 1994

An African American family sells an heirloom piano for a plot of land in Mississippi.

The Playboy of the Western World, J. M. Synge **(1907),** 1966, 1968, 1971, 1976

Believing he has killed his father, a timid Irish peasant boy runs away from home.

Playing for Time: A Screenplay, Arthur Miller **(1980),** 1994

A French Jewish singer describes her escape from Auschwitz in this dramatized memoir.

The Price, Arthur Miller **(1968),** 1988

Two brothers come to grips with the meaning of family, sacrifice, and happiness.

Purlie Victorious: A Commemorative, Ossie Davis **(1993),** 1994

To save his people's church, a southern African American preacher must go head-to-head with rich local whites.

Pygmalion, George Bernard Shaw **(1913),** 1966, 1968, 1988, 1991, 1994, 1999

Professor Higgins bets a friend he can turn common Eliza Doolittle into a duchess.

A Raisin in the Sun, Lorraine Hansberry **(1959),** 1966, 1968, 1971, 1976, 1991, 1999

The sudden appearance of money tears an African American family apart.

Restoration Plays, Robert G. Lawrence (ed.) **(1966),** 1991

The Restoration period in England was a great age for drama, especially comedies of manners.

Rhinoceros, Eugène Ionesco **(1959),** 1971, 1976, 1991, 1994, 1999

The subject is conformity; the treatment is comedy and terror.

Riders to the Sea, J. M. Synge **(1903),** 1991

The relentless activity of the sea tragically influences the lives of Irish fisherfolk.

Romeo and Juliet, William Shakespeare **(c. 1595),** 1994

Ill-fated lovers from feuding families experience tragedy.

Rosencrantz and Guildenstern Are Dead, Tom Stoppard **(1966),** 1971, 1991, 1994, 1999

Two bit players from Shakespeare's *Hamlet* are thrust into a terrifying new situation.

Saint Joan, George Bernard Shaw **(1923),** 1971, 1976, 1991

A teenage girl shows great innocence in political and religious matters and great genius in military affairs.

The School for Scandal, Richard Brinsley Sheridan **(1777),** 1966, 1968, 1971, 1976, 1988, 1991

Wit rivals sincerity and hypocrisy rivals true love as Lady Sneerwell, Sir Benjamin Backbite, and Mrs. Candor get their just desserts.

The Sheep Well, Lope de Vega **(1619),** 1991

The peasant class clashes with the feudal landlords who rule their lives.

Six Characters in Search of an Author, Luigi Pirandello **(1921),** 1971, 1976, 1988, 1991

> In this avant-garde play within a play, the technique is as important as the plot.

A Soldier's Play, Charles Fuller **(1981),** 1994

> An African American sergeant's 1944 murder in a Louisiana army camp is investigated by his white captain and a black outsider, with shocking results.

A Streetcar Named Desire, Tennessee Williams **(1947),** 1988

> This is a steamy look at the seamy side of life in New Orleans.

The Tempest, William Shakespeare **(1611),** 1988

> A shipwreck catapults Ferdinand, the duke's son, into romance with the magician's daughter Miranda.

Three Tall Women, Edward Albee **(1994),** 1999

> A frustrated 92-year-old woman reveals three arduous and painful stages of her life.

The Tooth of Crime; Geography of a Horse Dreamer: Two Plays, Sam Shepard **(1974),** 1991

> A rising rock musician challenges the reigning star.

Torch Song Trilogy: Three Plays, Harvey Fierstein **(1979),** 1994

> These plays provide a funny, touching story of a drag queen's desire for a happy, middle-class existence.

Twelfth Night, William Shakespeare **(1601),** 1988

> In Shakespeare's own words, "If music be the food of love, play on."

The Visit: A Tragi-comedy, Friedrich Durrenmatt **(1956),** 1976

> The population's conscience is tested when a rich woman offers her destitute hometown a fortune to murder the man who seduced and betrayed her.

Volpone, Ben Jonson **(1606),** 1976

> In this satire on greed a rich, childless nobleman pretends to be dying so that those expecting to become his heir will bring gifts.

Waiting for Godot: A Tragicomedy in Two Acts, Samuel Beckett **(1952),** 1966, 1968, 1971, 1976, 1991, 1999

> Two tramps wait eternally for the elusive Godot in this first success of the Theater of the Absurd.

The Way of the World, William Congreve **(1700),** 1971, 1976

> Mirabell and Millamont overcome obstacles on the path toward marriage in this unequaled Restoration comedy which satirizes society and manners.

The Winslow Boy, Terence Rattigan **(1946),** 1966, 1968, 1971

> An ordinary English family takes the problems of its son's expulsion from school all the way to Parliament.

Winterset: A Play in Three Acts, Maxwell Anderson **(1936)**, 1966, 1968, 1971

In depicting the anguish of a young Italian American whose radical father was executed for a murder he did not commit, Anderson is influenced by the Sacco and Vanzetti murder trial.

The Wisteria Trees, Joshua Logan **(1950)**, 1966

An American play in which a member of the southern aristocracy cannot grasp the idea that her Louisiana plantation is doomed.

Woza Afrika! An Anthology of South African Plays, Duma Ndlovu (ed.) **(1986)**, 1988

These six plays represent the first anthology of recent black South African theater. Each play is built around the political and emotional horror of apartheid.

You Can't Take It with You, George S. Kaufman and Moss Hart **(1937)**, 1966, 1968, 1971, 1988, 1991

The staid, stuffy parents of Alice's fiancé come to meet her eccentric family on the wrong night.

The Zoo Story: A Play, Edward Albee **(1958)**, 1971, 1976, 1988

A terrifying encounter unfolds between two strangers who finally "communicate" through violence.

Musicals

Cabaret, John Kander **(1967)**, 1988

Decadent prewar Berlin as seen through the eyes of free-living Sally Bowles.

Cats, Andrew Lloyd Webber **(1981)**, 1991, 1994

Felines from T. S. Eliot's *Old Possum's Book of Practical Cats* portray life from their vantage point on a rubbish heap.

The Fantasticks, Tom Jones and Harvey Schmidt **(1964)**, 1991, 1994

A teenage couple meet secretly while falsely believing their fathers would disapprove.

Fiddler on the Roof, Joseph Stein **(1965)**, 1968, 1971

A musical, illustrating the pathos of Jewish life in a Russian village, based on Sholom Aleichem's stories.

Hair, Galt MacDermot **(1969)**, 1971, 1988

This production was the first tribal rock musical on Broadway.

Hello, Dolly! Jerry Herman and Michael Stewart **(1964)**, 1994

This musical based on a Thornton Wilder play follows a marriage broker's attempts to snare another woman's intended husband for herself.

Into the Woods, Stephen Sondheim and James Lapine **(1987)**, 1994

Cleverly interwoven storybook characters lead a trip of growth and self-discovery.

Jesus Christ Superstar: A Rock Opera, Tim Rice and Andrew Lloyd Webber **(1970)**, 1976

An age-old story is retold in this rock opera version of Christ's impact on the minds of men.

Les Misérables, Claude-Michel Schönberg, Alain Boublil, and Herbert Kretzmer **(1986)**, 1994

In a musical adaptation of the Victor Hugo novel, tragedy, romance, and poverty trail escaped convict Jean Valjean in the years following the French Revolution.

Man of La Mancha, Mitch Leigh and Joe Darion **(1967)**, 1968

This musical adaptation of *Don Quixote* centers around a mock trial for the defense of Cervantes while imprisoned and held for inquisition.

My Fair Lady, Alan Jay Lerner and Frederick Loewe **(1956)**, 1994

A proper phonetics professor bets he can transform a Cockney flower girl into a society lady.

Oklahoma! Richard Rodgers and Oscar Hammerstein **(1944)**, 1966, 1968, 1971, 1988, 1994

Dance, music, and story are integrated in this look at the settling of the Oklahoma Territory.

Pal Joey, Richard Rodgers and Lorenz Hart **(1940)**, 1988

This musical tells the story of an ambitious schemer.

The Pirates of Penzance, W. S. Gilbert and Arthur Sullivan **(1879)**, 1988, 1994

Must Frederic, a slave of duty, give up Mabel and remain a pirate because of a "most ingenious paradox"?

Quilters, Barbara Damashek and Molly Newman **(1986)**, 1994

Combining music and dance with scenes of dramatic intensity, this play is an eloquent tribute to the courage and spirit of pioneer women.

Rent, Jonathan Larson **(1996)**, 1999

This award-winning musical depicts life, death, passion, and loyalty among AIDS-stricken artists.

Sweeney Todd: The Demon Barber of Fleet Street, Stephen Sondheim **(1985)**, 1988

The demon barber of Fleet Street seeks a grisly revenge.

The Threepenny Opera, Kurt Weill **(1929)**, 1988

Crime pays for Mack the Knife in this musical.

West Side Story, Leonard Bernstein, Arthur Laurents, and Stephen Sondheim **(1950),** 1988, 1994, 1999

> The Jets and Sharks battle it out in song and dance as Tony and Maria fall in love in this musical based on Shakespeare's *Romeo and Juliet.*

Books about the Theater

50 Great Scenes for Student Actors, Lewy Olfson (ed.) **(1970),** 1982

> A collection of scenes for two; ideal for those looking for audition material.

Act One: An Autobiography, Moss Hart **(1955),** 1961, 1963, 1965, 1966, 1968, 1971, 1988, 1991

> The author's life up to his first successful play gives the reader many funny and touching moments in the world of the theater.

An Actor Prepares, Konstantin Stanislavsky **(1936),** 1982, 1988, 1991

> Disliking the classical methods of acting, this Russian actor and producer spends his life developing a system in which realism based on inner truth of a character is essential.

Actors Talk about Acting, Lewis Funke and John E. Booth **(1961),** 1966, 1968

> Fourteen of America's and Britain's most distinguished actors discuss their profession.

Advice to the Players, Robert Lewis **(1980),** 1982

> Lewis covers everything from relaxation and energizing to transformation into a complete character.

American Musical Comedy: From Adonis to Dreamgirls, Gerald Bordman **(1982),** 1988, 1991

> Musical comedy in the United States began in the nineteenth century and continues to evolve as a reflection of musical tastes.

Angry Theatre: New British Drama, John Russell Taylor **(1962),** 1971

> Young dramatists of the 1950s and 1960s discussed here include John Osborne, Anne Jellicoe, Joan Littlewood, Arnold Wesker, David Rudkin, and Harold Pinter.

Broadway, Day and Night, Kenneth Marsolais, Rodger McFarlane, and Tom Viola (eds.) **(1992),** 1994

> Tony Award winners talk about amusing, affecting, and prophetic moments that shaped their careers.

Broadway Musicals, Martin Gottfried **(1984),** 1982

> An extravaganza of photographs and text demonstrates what makes the show go on.

Building a Character, Konstantin Stanislavsky **(1977),** 1991

Disliking the classical methods of acting, this Russian actor and producer spent his life developing a system in which realism based on inner truth of a character is essential.

The Burns Mantle Best Plays Series, Robert Burns Mantle **(1948),** 1966, 1968, 1994

These annual publications give plot outlines and excerpts from the ten best plays of a given year.

The Complete Phantom of the Opera, George C. Perry **(1987),** 1994

This book outlines the history and provides the complete libretto of the blockbuster musical.

Creating a Role, Konstantin Stanislavsky **(1961),** 1991

Disliking the classical methods of acting, this Russian actor and producer spent his life developing a system in which realism based on innter truth of a character is essential.

The Development of the Theatre: A Study of Theatrical Art from the Beginnings to the Present Day, Allardyce Nicoll **(1966),** 1971

Many illustrations accompany this chronological history of the theater.

Encyclopedia of Acting Techniques, John Perry **(1997),** 2004

The actor's life—see how it's done by the pros in this extravagantly illustrated primer on dramatic performance.

Good Night, Sweet Prince: The Life and Time of John Barrymore, Gene Fowler **(1944),** 1966, 1968

John Barrymore is one of America's greatest and most flamboyant actors.

Great Stars of the American Stage: A Pictorial Record, Daniel Blum **(1952),** 1966, 1968

This book introduces stage stars with biographies and photos.

Great Theatrical Disasters, Gyles Brandreth **(1982),** 1988, 1991

Theatrical calamities include forgotten lines, missed cues, showing up drunk onstage, and collapsing sets falling on leading ladies.

History of the Theatre, Oscar G. Brockett **(1968),** 1994

Through both illustrations and text, Brockett provides a comprehensive examination of theatrical heritage.

A History of the Theatre, Glynne W. Wickham **(1985),** 1988, 1991

The author provides a historical survey of the theater from ancient Oriental, Greek, and Roman times to the twentieth century.

How to Break into the Theatre, Charlotte Harmon **(1961),** 1966

The practicalities of becoming an actor, producer, playwright, director, or costume designer are discussed.

I Wanted to Be an Actress: The Autobiography of Katharine Cornell, Katharine Cornell **(1939)**, 1966

> A great actress writes about her life in and out of the theater.

The Idea of a Theater: A Study of Ten Plays, the Art of Drama in Changing Perspective, Francis Fergusson **(1949)**, 1971

> Ten plays are analyzed to provide a picture of the art of drama.

James Earl Jones: Voices and Silences, James Earl Jones and Penelope Niven **(1993)**, 1994

> From a stuttering child to a consummate actor with a world famous, cultivated voice, Jones chronicles his life and theatrical triumphs.

Laurette, Marguerite Courtney **(1955)**, 1966, 1968

> Laurette Taylor wages a successful battle against alcoholism and returns triumphantly to the stage.

Masters of the Drama, John Gassner **(1940)**, 1971

> Gassner presents the history of drama and describes the people who shaped it.

The Musical Theatre: A Celebration, Alan Jay Lerner **(1986)**, 1988

> An active participant provides a passionate personal history of the musical theater.

The Player: A Profile of an Art, Lillian Ross and Helen Ross **(1962)**, 1966, 1968

> Actors and actresses discuss their lives and careers.

Playwright at Work, John Van Druten **(1953)**, 1966

> There are practical ways to meet the problems encountered in play writing.

Reflections: Essays on Modern Theatre, Martin Esslin **(1969)**, 1971

> The modern theater is described in a series of essays.

Respect for Acting, Uta Hagen, with Haskel Frankel **(1973)**, 1982

> An actress provides a look at the art of acting and helps an aspiring actor master the techniques of the profession.

The Rodgers and Hammerstein Story, Stanley Green **(1963)**, 1966

> Rodgers and Hammerstein collaborate to produce some of America's best-known musicals.

The Same Only Different: Five Generations of a Great Theatre Family, Margaret Webster **(1968)**, 1968

> The history of English and American theater is seen through five generations of a great theatrical family.

Sondheim, Martin Gottfried **(1993)**, 1994

> Steven Sondheim, Broadway's musical and lyrical genius, is studied and analyzed through his works.

Stage Crafts, Chris Hoggett **(1975),** 1982

> The many detailed illustrations show the student of the theater the techniques of designing and building sets, props, costumes, and much more.

Stage Makeup, Richard Corson **(1989),** 1994

> Makeup artistry is more than assembling the right ingredients, as this illustrated, detailed examination proves.

Theater in America: 200 Years of Plays, Players, and Productions, Mary C. Henderson **(1986),** 1988, 1991, 1994

> This comprehensive history of American theater begins with showboats and tent shows and ends with Broadway productions.

The Theater in Spite of Itself, Walter Kerr **(1963),** 1971

> A critic comments on the theater.

The Theater of Mixed Means: An Introduction to Happenings, Kinetic Environments, and Other Mixed-Means Performances, Richard Kostelanetz **(1968),** 1971

> Kostelanetz examines drama as an art form.

The Theatre: Three Thousand Years of Drama, Acting, and Stagecraft, Sheldon Cheney **(1952),** 1971

> The drama of the development of theater unfolds in this historical account.

Theatre Backstage from A to Z, Warren C. Lounsbury and Norman C. Boulanger **(1989),** 1994

> An explanation of all that goes on backstage, from props to lights to sets.

The Theatre of Commitment, and Other Essays on Drama in Our Society, Eric Bentley **(1967),** 1971

> Bentley brings life to a study of theater.

The Theatre of Revolt: An Approach to the Modern Drama, Robert Brustein **(1964),** 1971

> Brustein discusses the modern approach to drama.

The Theatre of the Absurd, Martin Esslin **(1961),** 1971

> A new type of drama is examined.

Theatre World, Daniel Blum **(annual),** 1966, 1968

> This is an annual photographic and statistical record of all plays produced on and off broadway since 1944.

The Third Theatre, Robert Brustein **(1968),** 1968

> The Dean of the Yale School of Drama discusses off-off Broadway, living theater, and other happenings in the theater.

Towards a Poor Theatre, Jerzy Grotowski **(1968),** 1971

> The author presents his methods and training for actors.

Underfoot in Show Business, Helene Hanff **(1962),** 1982

> A witty autobiography describes the funny side of her failures in the world of the theater.

What Is Theater: A Query in Chronicle Form, Eric Bentley **(1956),** 1971

> Bentley attempts to define theater.

William Shakespeare: A Reader's Guide, Alfred Harbage **(1963),** 1971

> Harbage helps the reader understand Shakespeare's works.

The Working Actor: A Guide to the Profession, Katinka Matson **(1976),** 1982

> This guide tells how to choose a school, make the rounds, audition, and choose a manager.

World Theatre in Pictures: From Ancient Times to Modern Broadway, Tom Prideaux **(1953),** 1966, 1968

> Photographs and essays present a portrait of the theater from ancient times to modern Broadway.

Years Ago, Ruth Gordon **(1947),** 1966

> Ruth Gordon is stagestruck in Boston.

The Young Actor's Workbook, Judith Roberts Seto (comp.) **(1979),** 1982

> An anthology of scenes and monologues from contemporary plays is provided to use for analyzing a scene.

Nonfiction

Good books are the warehouses of ideas.

H. G. Wells

These lists are definitely warehouses—warehouses of fact rather than fiction. Everything that man has ever created, studied, invented, or developed is represented here. The ideas and concepts of ancient as well as modern times are represented. Some of the titles are dated, but they remain to serve as a reminder of the evolving nature of people and civilizations. The subjects covered serve as a profile of the changing times we live in; this is especially noticeable in science, technology, and music.

ART, ARCHITECTURE, AND PHOTOGRAPHY

The pictures in this book represent a survey of relationships between couples from the Middle Ages to the present day. They reflect man's constant longing for an emotion that has still lost none of its fascination despite all the theories and the weight of cultural pessimism.

From *Lovers in Art,* by Sabine Adler

ABC of Architecture, James F. O'Gorman **(1998),** 1999

Function, structure, and beauty are the interdependent basics—the ABC—of architecture.

American Art Deco, Alastair Duncan **(1986),** 1991

This profusely illustrated book explores the tradition of art deco in America.

Annotated Art, Robert Cumming **(1995),** 1999

Art masterpieces are made understandable through the exploration of some of the world's greatest paintings.

The Annotated Mona Lisa: A Crash Course in Art History from Prehistoric to Post-Modern, Carol Strickland and John Boswell **(1992),** 1994, 1999

From cave paintings to conceptual art, art history is demystified.

Ansel Adams: An Autobiography, Ansel Adams and Mary Street Alinder **(1985),** 1988

A master of light and images recounts his life and relationships with important photographers of the twentieth century.

Art as Image and Idea, Edmund Burke Feldman **(1967),** 1971

The functions, styles, and structure of art, the interaction of medium and meaning, and last, the problems of art criticism.

Art Attack: A Short Cultural History of the Avant-Garde, Marc Aronson **(1998),** 1999

Discover everything you ever wanted to know about bohemians, hipsters, and the development of the world's most radical art.

Art Deco, Victor Arwas **(1976),** 1994

The style of art deco extends to all the arts—from architecture, painting, and sculpture to crafts and decorations.

Art Deco, Alastair Duncan **(1988),** 1991

The art deco movement of the 1920s and '30s was especially influential in decorative and applied arts.

Art: A History of Painting, Sculpture, and Architecture, Frederick Hartt **(1976),** 1991, 1994

An account of all the artistic endeavors of the Western world reveals the rich heritage left to us.

The Art of Photography, 1839–1989, Mike Weaver **(1989),** 1991

A catalog of an exhibition looks at 150 years of photography.

The Arts of the North American Indian: Native Traditions in Evolution, Edwin L. Wade and Carol Haralson (eds.) **(1986),** 1994

A unique and thorough examination details the rich tradition of American Indian Art.

Brassaï: Letters to My Parents, Brassaï **(1998),** 2004

European photographer Brassaï details his life's experiences in his letters home, describing both his own development as an artist and the fascinating world of Paris from 1920 to 1940.

Break-Up: The Core of Modern Art, Katherine Kuh **(1965),** 1976

Analyzes examples of modern art in terms of the attempt to present life in its structural elements rather than its wholeness.

Brunelleschi's Dome: How a Renaissance Genius Reinvented Architecture, Ross King **(2000),** 2004

In this vivid re-creation of the political and artistic milieu of fifteenth-century Florence, an audacious architect achieves the impossible, and makes possible modern building.

Castle, David Macaulay **(1977),** 1994

Follow the planning and construction of a typical thirteenth-century castle in text and detailed drawings.

The Complete Photography Careers Handbook: Updated and Expanded to Include Electronic Imaging, George Gilbert **(1992),** 1994

Learn about photography as a career.

Exploring Black and White Photography, Arnold Gassan and A. J. Meek **(1993),** 1994

The author instructs the reader on the use of intuition, craft, and analysis in the art of photography.

Exploring World Art, Andrea P. A. Belloli **(1999),** 2004

Take a fresh look at Western European art in a global context and discover the ways in which artists of different times and cultures express universal themes.

Graphic History of Architecture, John Mansbridge **(1967),** 1971

The three-dimensional form and dynamic construction of buildings are shown through plans, elevations, cutaways, and isometric drawings in a way unmatched by words or photographs.

A History of African-American Artists: From 1792 to the Present, Romare Bearden and Harry Henderson **(1993),** 1994

A lavishly illustrated volume traces African American artists from the late eighteenth century to the present.

History of Art, H. W. Janson and Anthony F. Janson **(1986),** 1994

This story of art is an adventure which enlarges our capacity to understand and appreciate individual painters.

History of Modern Art: Painting, Sculpture, Architecture, Photography, H. H. Arnason and Marla F. Prather **(1986),** 1994

By tracing contemporary art and architecture through the mid-1980s, Arnason and Prather uncover the varied stories of our modern artistic roots.

How Buildings Work: The Natural Order of Architecture, Edward Allen **(1980),** 1988, 1991

A look at the inside of all that brick, concrete, steel—and even straw. A concise, understandable description of how buildings function and behave.

How to Look at Sculpture: Text and Photographs, David Finn **(1989)**, 1991, 1994, 1999

>   To understand sculpture, you have to know what to look for.

Images of Nature: The Photographs of Tom Mangelsen, Tom Mangelsen **(1989)**, 1991

>   Photography captures the glory and wonder of the natural world.

Just Looking: Essays on Art, John Updike **(1989)**, 1991

>   Updike gives his personal views of various artists, pieces of art, and diverse artistic items including illustrations of children's books.

Last Traces: The Lost Art of Auschwitz, Joseph P. Czarnecki **(1989)**, 1991

>   A Polish photojournalist discovers fine art in drawings, graffiti, and decorations on the walls of various buildings in the Auschwitz concentration camp.

Learning to Look: A Handbook for the Visual Arts, Joshua C. Taylor **(1957)**, 1971, 1976

>   A clear, concrete explanation of what to look for in art.

Lovers in Art, Sabine Adler **(2002)**, 2004

>   Romance and art are natural companions in this gorgeous book that spans five centuries of Western European art.

Mainstreams of Modern Art, John Canaday **(1959)**, 1971

>   The art editor of the *New York Times* examines art from David to Picasso, discussing classicism, romanticism, and realism.

Michelangelo, Howard Hibbard **(1975)**, 1976, 1988

>   Michelangelo lives and works in the fourteenth century as a sculptor, painter, architect, and poet.

Modern Classicism, Robert A. M. Stern **(1988)**, 1991, 1994

>   This description of the modern classical architecture movement uses carefully selected photographs as well as text for better understanding.

More Joy of Photography, Eastman Kodak Company (eds.) **(1988)**, 1991

>   The 35mm camera user will find the techniques and examples of photographs helpful.

Odyssey: The Art of Photography at *National Geographic*, Jane Livingston, with Frances Fralin and Declan Haun **(1988)**, 1991

>   *National Geographic* pioneers documentary photography and showcases its work in this book.

On the Art of Fixing a Shadow: One Hundred and Fifty Years of Photography, Sarah Greenough **(1989)**, 1991

>   This catalog of an exhibition commemorates photography's sesquicentennial with 450 photographs arranged chronologically and prefaced by essays on photographic periods.

Painting and Sculpture in Europe, 1880–1940, George Heard Hamilton **(1978)**, 1988

>   The author surveys modern art in Europe.

Passages in Modern Sculpture, Rosalind E. Krauss **(1981),** 1988

Ideas that formed twentieth-century sculpture are examined.

The Photographer's Handbook, John Hedgecoe **(1992),** 1994

For beginners as well as experienced photographers, this volume explores the full spectrum of photography.

Photography: An Illustrated History, Martin W. Sandler **(2002),** 2004

Everything you want to know about photography and the people behind the cameras is beautifully presented in a book for readers and browsers of all ages.

Plain Painters: Making Sense of American Folk Art, John Michael Vlach **(1988),** 1991

Folk art and artists influence all aspects of American art.

The Power of Photography: How Photographs Changed Our Lives, Vicki Goldberg **(1991),** 1994, 1999

Photographers and photographs evolve, rather than spring forth fully formed.

Shoot! Everything You Ever Wanted to Know about 35mm Photography, Liz Harvey (ed.) **(1993),** 1994

A clear description of 35mm photography develops understanding.

Shooting under Fire: The World of the War Photographer, Peter Howe **(2002),** 2004

War photographers seek out the most horrifying and dangerous places in the world to practice their craft. What compels them to do it?

Space, Time and Architecture: The Growth of a New Tradition, S. Giedion **(1967),** 1971

A fundamental text illuminates the interrelation of materials, techniques, and human needs in terms of architectural design and city planning.

The Story of Art, E. H. Gombrich **(1995),** 1999

Everything from cave paintings to the experimental art of today is covered, in words and pictures, in this sixteenth edition of one of the most famous and popular art books ever published.

The Sweet Flypaper of Life, Roy DeCarava and Langston Hughes **(1955),** 1988, 1991

Outstanding photographs and poetic writing combine in a brilliant photo-essay on Harlem in the 1950s.

Why Buildings Stand Up: The Strength of Architecture, Mario George Salvadori **(1980),** 1988, 1991

From the pyramids to the skyscrapers, this history of architecture is a readable explanation of why buildings stand up.

Women Artists: An Illustrated History, Nancy G. Heller **(1987),** 1991, 1994

This chronicle presents five centuries of painting and sculpture by women, most of whom have been neglected in more traditional art histories.

BIOGRAPHY

*I woke up the next morning to the voices of my
brothers and father whispering to each other about
what went on in the night.*

*"Pa," Meng said in a frightened voice, "a man
told me the noise last night was Khmer Rouge
soldiers opening fire on all the people who registered
for work. They killed every one of them." Their words
push at my temples, making my head throb with fear.*

From *First They Killed My Father,*
by Loung Ung

Abraham Lincoln, Benjamin P. Thomas **(1952),** 1961, 1963, 1965

The author paints a realistic and sympathetic portrait.

Abraham Lincoln: The Prairie Years and the War Years, Carl Sandburg **(1954),**
1968, 1971, 1976, 1982, 1988

Sandburg describes Lincoln's life from his birth in the log cabin on Nolin
Creek to his burial at Springfield.

Act One: An Autobiography, Moss Hart **(1955),** 1961, 1963, 1965, 1966, 1968, 1971,
1988, 1991

The author's life up to his first successful play gives the reader many funny
and touching moments in the world of the theater.

All Creatures Great and Small, James Herriot **(1972),** 1982, 1988

A rookie veterinarian reconciles the theories learned in school with his "real
life" experiences in rural England.

Always Running: La Vida Loca; Gang Days in L.A., Luis J. Rodriguez **(1993),** 1994,
1999

Rodriguez tells the story of his life in a Los Angeles gang and his later experiences as a Chicano activist.

Always the Young Strangers, Carl Sandburg **(1953),** 1968, 1971

Sandburg has drawn a sensitive sketch of his early life, especially the problems and thoughts of his teen years.

An American Childhood, Annie Dillard **(1987),** 1991

A writer tells how her life and writings were influenced by childhood experiences in Pittsburgh during the 1950s.

An American Doctor's Odyssey: Adventures in Forty-five Countries, Victor Heiser
(1936), 1961, 1963, 1965, 1968

Adventures of an American doctor who traveled the world to blot out disease.

American Girl: Scenes from a Small-Town Childhood, Mary Cantwell **(1992),** 1994

A successful columnist reminisces about her growing up in a small town in New England.

Angela's Ashes: A Memoir, Frank McCourt **(1996),** 1999

Illness, hunger, alcoholism, and death plague McCourt's childhood in Ireland, but somehow he survives with his spirit intact.

Anne Frank Remembered: The Story of the Woman Who Helped to Hide the Frank Family, Miep Gies and Alison Leslie Gold **(1987),** 1991, 1994

At great risk to their own lives, the Gies family hides the family of Anne Frank in their attic in Amsterdam, Holland, during World War II.

Anne Frank: The Diary of a Young Girl, Anne Frank **(1952),** 1961, 1963, 1965, 1968, 1971, 1982, 1988, 1999

Through the diary she kept while in hiding, thirteen-year-old Anne Frank puts a human face on the Holocaust experience.

Ariel: The Life of Shelley, André Maurois **(1924),** 1961, 1963, 1965, 1968, 1971

A notable biography of one of England's greatest lyric poets.

At School in the Promised Land; or The Story of a Little Immigrant, Mary Antin **(1916),** 1961, 1963, 1965, 1968

A young Russian immigrant relives her experiences during her first days in America.

Atoms in the Family: My Life with Enrico Fermi, Laura Fermi **(1954),** 1961, 1963, 1965, 1968, 1971

The story of Enrico Fermi, one of the leading physicists in the development of the atomic bomb.

Autobiography, Benjamin Franklin **(1791),** 1961, 1963, 1965, 1968, 1971

Franklin's witty self-portrait traces his development in work, religion, literature, and public service.

The Autobiography of Alice B. Toklas, Gertrude Stein **(1933),** 1982, 1988

World War I Paris as seen by Gertrude Stein, the friend of Picasso, Mattisse, Hemingway, and other famous artists of the times.

The Autobiography of Benvenuto Cellini, Benvenuto Cellini. John Addington Symonds (trans.) **(1910),** 1961, 1963, 1965, 1968, 1971

Italian Renaissance art, sculpture, princes, dukes, and popes are brilliantly presented.

The Autobiography of Lincoln Steffens, Lincoln Steffens **(1931),** 1961, 1963, 1965, 1968, 1971

The associations of a fearless journalist with presidents, kings, city bosses, and dictators.

The Autobiography of Malcolm X, Malcolm X (as told to Alex Haley) **(1965)**, 1971, 1976, 1982, 1988, 1994, 1999

A great and controversial Black Muslim figure relates his transformation from street hustler to religious and national leader.

The Autobiography of Mark Twain, Mark Twain. Ed. Charles Neider **(1959)**, 1961, 1963, 1965, 1968, 1971

The life of one of America's most famous humorists.

The Autobiography of William Allen White, William Allen White **(1946)**, 1961

America in its greatest throes of growth and change is vigorously described by a great journalist.

Barefoot Heart: Stories of a Migrant Child, Elva Treviño Hart **(1999)**, 2004

This honest and moving memoir follows a migrant child and her family as they travel from their home in New Mexico to the farm fields of Minnesota and Wisconsin in search of work.

Baruch: My Own Story, Bernard M. Baruch **(1957)**, 1961, 1963, 1965, 1968

Portrait of an extraordinary man who has never held public office but has been a pillar of strength to four presidents.

Ben-Gurion: A Biography, Robert St. John **(1959)**, 1961, 1963, 1965, 1968, 1971

An absorbing profile of a nation builder who dedicated his life to the service of Israel.

Biko, Donald Woods **(1978)**, 1988

Woods, editor of the leading antiapartheid newspaper in South Africa, smuggled out the contents of this book about the life, imprisonment, and unsatisfactory inquest into the death of Biko, the charismatic South African leader.

Bismarck: The Man and the Statesman, A. J. P. Taylor **(1955)**, 1961, 1963, 1965, 1968, 1971

A fascinating portrait of a statesman who united the German people by "blood and iron," not by speeches.

Black Boy: A Record of Childhood and Youth, Richard Wright **(1945)**, 1976, 1982, 1988, 1991, 1994, 1999

Wright recalls his pre-World War II youth when racial and personal obstacles seemed insurmountable.

Black Elk Speaks: Being the Life Story of a Holy Man of the Oglala Sioux, John G. Neihardt **(1961)**, 1982, 1988

A Native American medicine man who survived Custer tells of his visions and the great tribal dances he carried out as a result of these visions.

Blackberry Winter: My Earlier Years, Margaret Mead **(1972)**, 1976, 1982, 1988

A famous anthropologist relates the events in her life before World War II that affected her as a woman and an anthropologist.

Born on the Fourth of July, Ron Kovic **(1976),** 1991, 1994

> An all-American boy joins the Marines, goes to Vietnam, is gravely wounded, and becomes an antiwar activist.

Breaking with Moscow, Arkady N. Shevchenko **(1985),** 1988

> A former Russian spy uncovers layers of Soviet secrets as he describes increasing doubts about his native country and his defection to the United States.

Bridge to the Sun, Gwen Terasaki **(1957),** 1961, 1963, 1965

> An American married to a Japanese diplomat leads a satisfying life until Pearl Harbor brings tragedy, hardship, and heartbreak.

Bright Eyes: The Story of Susette La Flesche, an Omaha Indian, Dorothy Clarke Wilson **(1974),** 1976

> A brilliant, educated, and concerned nineteenth-century Indian woman fights against racism, indifference, and atrocities committed by whites.

Bronx Primitive: Portraits in a Childhood, Kate Simon **(1982),** 1994

> Marked by an unbridgeable generation gap and lack of communication, Simon's difficult Bronx childhood creates great motivation for her writing career.

The Cage, Ruth Minsky Sender **(1986),** 1991

> A teenager comes of age in a Polish ghetto, suffers in a concentration camp, and survives the Holocaust.

The Camera Never Blinks: Adventures of a TV Journalist, Dan Rather with Mickey Herskowitz **(1977),** 1982

> A controversial autobiography by one of the best-known and most respected TV newscasters. Rather's adventures range from his college days in Texas to Vietnam, and from his coverage of the Kennedy assassination to *60 Minutes*.

Capote: A Biography, Gerald Clarke **(1988),** 1994

> Author Truman Capote lived an unorthodox life, as revealed in this candid story.

Charles Dickens: His Tragedy and Triumph, Edgar Johnson **(1952),** 1982

> Dickens emerges from an impoverished and painful childhood to become an immensely popular novelist and then a social reformer.

Chinese Cinderella: The True Story of an Unwanted Daughter, Adeline Yen Mah **(1999),** 2004

> Wu Mei, also called Adeline, is the Fifth Younger Sister of her family, and the one who bears the blame for all their bad fortune. In her inspirational tale of survival in 1940s China, she triumphs against all odds.

A Choice of Weapons, Gordon Parks **(1966),** 1971

> The autobiography of an African American writer-photographer who displays humor, hope, and courage.

Christopher Columbus, Mariner, Samuel Eliot Morison **(1955),** 1961, 1963, 1965, 1968, 1971, 1982

> Columbus's life and voyages are vividly re-created in this lively narrative.

Clarence Darrow for the Defense, Irving Stone **(1941),** 1961, 1963, 1965, 1968, 1971, 1976

> This famous lawyer fought not only for mercy and justice but also for social reform.

The Color of Water: A Black Man's Tribute to His White Mother, James McBride **(1996),** 1999

> McBride blends his story with that of his mother, who battled poverty and racism to raise twelve children.

Coming of Age in Mississippi, Anne Moody **(1968),** 1971, 1994, 1999

> One of the first brave young African American students to participate in a lunch counter sit-in, Moody becomes a heroine of the civil rights movement.

A Conspiracy So Immense: The World of Joe McCarthy, David M. Oshinsky **(1983),** 1988

> Historical background information is given about the "red scare" as well as Wisconsin Senator Joe McCarthy, who personified the anti-Communist movement of the 1950s.

The Court Years, 1939–1975: The Autobiography of William O. Douglas, William O. Douglas **(1980),** 1988

> In this second and final volume, Douglas presents an insider's viewpoint on the workings of the U.S. Supreme Court, describing the interaction between justices and providing information about major decisions.

Dance to the Piper: Memoirs of the Ballet, Agnes de Mille **(1951),** 1994

> De Mille gives her insider's view as one of America's greatest dance choreographers.

Dark Quartet: The Story of the Brontës, Lynne Reid Banks **(1976),** 1982

> The brilliant but tortured lives of the three Brontë sisters and their troubled brother are as dramatic as *Jane Eyre* or *Wuthering Heights.*

Darkness over the Valley, Wendelgard von Staden **(1981),** 1991

> A teenage German girl aids and befriends concentration camp inmates who work on her family's estate.

Daylight Must Come: The Story of a Courageous Woman Doctor in the Congo, Alan Burgess **(1974),** 1976

> The moving story of Dr. Helen Rosevear, a doctor and Protestant missionary who strives against tremendous odds and hardships in the Congo from 1950 through 1973.

Days of Grace: A Memoir, Arthur Ashe and Arnold Rampersad **(1993),** 1994

> A highly respected tennis star and citizen of the world dies of AIDS.

Dear America: Letters Home from Vietnam, Bernard Edelman (ed.) **(1985),** 1999

> Letters from those who made it back and from those who did not return provide a glimpse into the lives of the men and women who served during the Vietnam War.

Death Be Not Proud: A Memoir, John Gunther **(1949),** 1982, 1988

> A father writes lovingly of his bright and promising seventeen-year-old son's long, courageous struggle with a brain tumor.

The Diary of Samuel Pepys, Samuel Pepys **(1825),** 1961, 1963, 1965, 1968, 1971, 1976

> The day-to-day life of a man active in the affairs of London in the 1600s.

Dorothy Thompson: A Legend in Her Time, Marion K. Sanders **(1973),** 1976

> A fascinating American woman journalist who laughed at Hitler, married Sinclair Lewis, and became a well-known radio commentator.

The Double Helix: A Personal Account of the Discovery of the Structure of DNA, James D. Watson **(1968),** 1971, 1976, 1982, 1988, 1999

> The author re-creates the excitement of participating in a momentous discovery and demonstrates to the nonscientist how the scientific method works.

Dr. Schweitzer of Lambaréné, Norman Cousins **(1960),** 1968

> Well-written description of the doctor's personality, character, and work.

E. B. White: Some Writer! Beverly Gherman **(1992),** 1994

> The noted author of *Charlotte's Web*, White is a reserved and witty man who is puzzled by his own success.

The Education of Henry Adams, Henry Adams **(1907),** 1961, 1963, 1965, 1968

> Important events and great men are met in Adams's travels in America, England, and France in the latter part of the 1800s.

Einstein: A Centenary Volume, A. P. French (ed.) **(1979),** 1988

> Essays and letters about Einstein's life, thoughts, and theories help ordinary people understand the genius of this acclaimed nuclear physicist.

Einstein: The Life and Times, Ronald W. Clark **(1971),** 1976

> The life and career of a great scientist viewed against the intellectual, political, and scientific background of his age.

Eleanor and Franklin: The Story of Their Relationship, Based on Eleanor Roosevelt's Private Papers, Joseph P. Lash **(1971),** 1976, 1982, 1988

> A candid and compassionate portrait of a complex relationship that focuses on Eleanor Roosevelt's private role as wife and mother and her public role as First Lady.

Eleanor of Aquitaine and the Four Kings, Amy Ruth Kelly **(1950),** 1961, 1963, 1965, 1968, 1971

> Political and religious wars and the disastrous Second Crusade are the background of this biography of an extraordinary queen.

Eleanor Roosevelt: First Lady of American Liberalism, Lois Scharf **(1987),** 1991

> A shy, homely young woman emerges from a privileged, strict Victorian childhood to become an admired and influential woman of the world.

Eleanor Roosevelt: Vol. 1 1884–1933, Blanche Wiesen Cook **(1992),** 1994, 1999

> Born into a privileged world, Eleanor Roosevelt became a champion of the underprivileged and a fighter for human rights.

Elizabeth the Great, Elizabeth Jenkins **(1958),** 1961, 1963, 1965, 1968, 1971, 1976

> A personal history of England's most fascinating queen.

Emma Goldman: An Intimate Life, Alice Wexler **(1984),** 1988

> This personal and public account of an immigrant anarchist and labor agitator who lived in America in the first half of the twentieth century.

Eric, Doris Lund **(1974),** 1976

> A mother's poignant account of her teenage son who refuses to give up when he has been struck by leukemia.

Ernest Hemingway: A Life Story, Carlos Baker **(1969),** 1971

> "The small boy who shouted 'Fraid o' nothing' becomes the man who discovered that there was plenty to fear."

Escalante: The Best Teacher in America, Jay Mathews **(1988),** 1991

> A dedicated teacher, subject of the movie *Stand and Deliver*, firmly believes anyone can learn calculus.

FDR: A Biography, Ted Morgan **(1985),** 1988

> In this probing psychological study of FDR's life, the biographer analyzes the forces that shaped an ordinary public servant into a world leader.

Fifth Chinese Daughter, Jade Snow Wong **(1950),** 1961, 1963, 1965, 1968

> Life in San Francisco's Chinatown and the adjustment a young girl must make between Chinese customs and the modern American way of life.

Florence Nightingale, 1820–1910, Cecil Woodham-Smith **(1951),** 1961

> After seeing the horrors of the wounded in the Crimean War, Florence Nightingale dedicates her life to worldwide reform of nursing work.

Flush: A Biography, Virginia Woolf **(1933),** 1968

An unusual biography of Elizabeth Barrett Browning's cocker spaniel and his interpretation of her life and romance.

Frank Lloyd Wright: An Interpretive Biography, Robert C. Twombly **(1973),** 1976

A balanced, integrated examination of Frank Lloyd Wright's life and his contribution to architecture and thought.

Freud, the Man and the Cause, Ronald W. Clark **(1980),** 1988

While not definitive, this personal biography offers insight into details of Freud's life that influenced the great thinker's psychoanalytic theories.

Geoffrey Chaucer of England, Marchette Gaylord Chute **(1946),** 1971

A "thrusting, excitable, anxious century" was "blessed by a writer who knew a good joke when he saw one."

George Washington, Man and Monument, Marcus Cunliffe **(1958),** 1963, 1965, 1968

Fact and myth are separated in an interpretation of Washington which covers all aspects of his life.

Georgia O'Keeffe, Georgia O'Keeffe **(1976),** 1982, 1988

Artist O'Keeffe relates how she dares to live life exactly as she sees it.

Georgia O'Keeffe: A Life, Roxana Robinson **(1989),** 1991

A woman artist achieves success and recognition for her work.

Go East, Young Man: The Early Years; The Autobiography of William O. Douglas, William O. Douglas **(1974),** 1976, 1982, 1988

The autobiography of a Supreme Court justice who demonstrates his fighting spirit by overcoming poverty and polio to lead the fight for environmental concerns.

Golda: Golda Meir; The Romantic Years, Ralph G. Martin **(1988),** 1991

From her early days as a Russian emigrant, Meir journeys through life as an American citizen to become Prime Minister of Israel.

Golda: The Life of Israel's Prime Minister, Peggy Mann **(1971),** 1976

The amazing story of a woman who was born in Russia, grew up in Milwaukee, went to Palestine at 23, and ultimately became Israel's prime minister.

Growing Up, Russell Baker **(1982),** 1991, 1994, 1999

A columnist with a sense of humor takes a gentle look at his childhood in Baltimore during the Depression.

Growing Up Female in America—Ten Lives, Eve Merriam **(1971),** 1976

A look at the lives of ten women of different socio-ecomonic backgrounds who were in the forefront of the women's movement.

Hannibal: Challenging Rome's Supremacy, Sir Gavin de Beer **(1969),** 1971

This enigmatic military genius plays a crucial role in history.

Hannibal: One Man against Rome, Harold Lamb **(1958),** 1968

A comparison of the great Carthaginian leader and the Roman generals who opposed him in his incredible journey across the Alps and his persistent raids in Italy.

The Haunted Palace: A Life of Edgar Allan Poe, Frances Winwar **(1959),** 1968, 1971

The psychological portrait of the brilliant but controversial poet Edgar Allan Poe.

Having Our Say: The Delany Sisters' First 100 Years, Sarah Delany and A. Elizabeth Delany with Amy Hill Hearth **(1993),** 1994

Two daughters of former slaves tell their stories of fighting racial and gender prejudice during the twentieth century.

Henry David Thoreau, Joseph Wood Krutch **(1948),** 1961, 1963, 1965, 1968

The New England Yankee sharply criticizes society and becomes one of America's classic writers.

Here I Stand: A Life of Martin Luther, Roland H. Bainton **(1950),** 1961, 1963, 1965, 1971, 1976

Martin Luther changes the way the Western world looks at religion.

Hitler: A Study in Tyranny, Alan Bullock **(1952),** 1976

This chronicle of Hitler's career includes the rise of Nazism and Germany's role in World War II.

Ho, David Halberstam **(1971),** 1976

A short, brilliant portrait of Ho Chi Minh, who twice leads his nation into a successful battle against the West.

Home before Morning: The Story of an Army Nurse in Vietnam, Lynda Van Devanter and Christopher Morgan **(1983),** 1991

A nurse serves her time in Vietnam and finds the horror and unpopularity of the war follow her home.

Home to the Wilderness, Sally Carrighar **(1973),** 1976, 1982

Hated by her own mother, Sally Carrighar ultimately finds peace and happiness as a naturalist living alone in the wilderness.

Honor Bound: A Gay American Fights for the Right to Serve His Country, Joseph Steffan **(1992),** 1994

Steffan, a high-ranking, well-liked cadet at Annapolis, is forced to resign just six weeks before graduation when he reveals he is gay.

House of Houses, Pat Mora **(1997),** 1999

With magic and imagination, author Pat Mora weaves the voices of her ancestors into her own personal account of growing up in a Mexican-American family in El Paso, Texas.

Hunger of Memory: The Education of Richard Rodriguez; An Autobiography, Richard Rodriguez **(1982),** 1999

> Rodriguez's journey through the educational system leads to his belief that family, culture, and language must be left behind to succeed in mainstream America.

I Know Why the Caged Bird Sings, Maya Angelou **(1970),** 1982, 1988, 1994, 1999

> An African American writer, poet, and actress traces her coming of age.

I, Rigoberta Menchú: An Indian Woman in Guatemala, Rigoberta Menchú **(1984),** 1994

> Born in Guatemala into abject poverty marked by violence and lack of education, this Nobel Peace Prize winner has become one of the world's foremost fighters for human rights.

In Her Own Right: The Life of Elizabeth Cady Stanton, Elisabeth Griffith **(1984),** 1988

> The public and private life of a nineteenth-century leader of the women's suffrage movement is portrayed.

Jennie: The Life of Lady Randolph Churchill. Vol. I: The Romantic Years, 1854–1895, Ralph G. Martin **(1969),** 1971

> How a girl from Brooklyn, who became the wife of Randolph Churchill and mother of Sir Winston Churchill, exerts extraordinary influence on the rulers of Europe.

John Adams, David McCullough **(2001),** 2004

> He was a man of his times who transcended his times, and one of the least understood of the Founding Fathers.

John F. Kennedy, Judie Mills **(1988),** 1991

> Overshadowed by his older brother and plagued by ill health, JFK became our youngest president and the symbol of a generation.

John Muir and His Legacy: The American Conservation Movement, Stephen R. Fox **(1981),** 1988

> This study of the "Father of the American Conservation Movement" interprets Muir's life and discusses wildlife preservation.

Kaffir Boy: The True Story of a Black Youth's Coming of Age in Apartheid South Africa; An Autobiography, Mark Mathabane **(1986),** 1991, 1994, 1999

> Growing up under the brutalities of apartheid South Africa, Mathabane describes the growing unrest in his country and his eventual escape through his ties to the tennis community.

Karl Marx: His Life and Thought, David McLellan **(1975),** 1976, 1982

> The private as well as political life and thoughts of Karl Marx explain much of his great influence on the world.

The Ladies of Seneca Falls: The Birth of the Woman's Rights Movement, Miriam Gurko **(1974),** 1982

> Elizabeth Cady Stanton, Susan B. Anthony, Lucy Stone, and others wage a long and stubborn campaign for equal rights.

Lakota Woman, Mary Crow Dog and Richard Erdoes **(1990),** 1994

> A Lakota woman stands with two thousand other Native Americans at the site of the Wounded Knee, South Dakota, massacre, demonstrating for Native American rights.

The Last Algonquin, Theodore L Kazimiroff **(1982),** 1991

> Orphaned at thirteen, Joe Two Trees, an Algonquin Indian, chooses to live out his life alone rather than live in the white man's world.

The Last Lion: Winston Spencer Churchill, William Manchester **(1983),** 1988

> Beginning with his childhood, this popular biography includes Churchill's experiences during World War I, in Parliament, as Chancellor of the Exchequer, and as a scapegoat of the Gallipoli fiasco.

Let the Trumpet Sound: A Life of Martin Luther King, Jr., Stephen B. Oates **(1982),** 1988

> Biography of the man whose nonviolent protests against racial discrimination began the civil rights movement, helping to strike down two centuries of segregation and voter discrimination.

The Liars' Club: A Memoir, Mary Karr **(1995),** 1999

> Growing up in "a family of liars and drunks" is never easy, and yet, despite alcoholism, rape, and other dark secrets, the author makes childhood in an East Texas refinery town sound as funny as it was painful.

Life and Death in Shanghai, Nien Cheng **(1987),** 1991

> Nien Cheng tells the story of seven harrowing years in solitary confinement during China's Cultural Revolution.

The Life and Death of Mary Wollstonecraft, Claire Tomalin **(1974),** 1976

> By not following the rules of eighteenth-century society, Mary was a forerunner of the women's rights movement.

The Life of Samuel Johnson, James Boswell **(1791),** 1961, 1963, 1965, 1968, 1971

> The personality and character of Johnson and the members of his circle.

Lindbergh, A. Scott Berg **(1998),** 2004

> Daring, mysterious, and one of the twentieth century's first superstars—who was the man behind the myth and how did his historic flight across the Atlantic remake the world?

Lives, Plutarch **(c. A.D. 120),** 1961, 1963, 1965, 1968, 1971

> Biographies in which the author parallels the lives of eminent Greeks with those of eminent Romans.

Loss of Eden: A Biography of Charles and Anne Morrow Lindbergh, Joyce Milton **(1993),** 1994

The Lindberghs seem to have everything—fame, intelligence, beauty, and money—until tragedy forces them into isolation.

Louis Armstrong: An American Success Story, James Lincoln Collier **(1985),** 1994

Born in poverty in New Orleans, "Satchmo" trains himself to become a great jazz trumpet player.

Madame Curie: A Biography, Eve Curie **(1937),** 1961, 1963, 1965, 1968, 1971, 1976, 1991, 1994, 1999

In sharing personal papers and her own memories, a daughter pays tribute to her unique and generous mother, a scientific genius.

Madame Sarah, Cornelia Otis Skinner **(1967),** 1971

How a waif from the streets of Paris becomes one of the world's greatest actresses.

Maggie's American Dream: The Life and Times of a Black Family, James P. Comer **(1988),** 1991

An African American family achieves the American dream as they move from the segregated rural South to the North.

Malcolm X: The Man and His Times, John Henrik Clarke (ed.) **(1969),** 1971

A good follow-up to his classic autobiography, this collection contains some of Malcolm X's own speeches as well as essays by people who either knew him personally or felt his impact deeply.

Manchild in the Promised Land, Claude Brown **(1965),** 1971, 1976, 1982

Brown grows up in Harlem at its ugliest, where street gangs and drugs destroy lives.

Martin Luther King, Jr.: To the Mountaintop, William Roger Witherspoon **(1985),** 1991

A great civil rights leader struggles to the top of the mountain and sees some of his "dream" realized before he is assassinated.

Mary, Queen of Scots, Antonia Fraser **(1969),** 1971

She was queen of Scotland by birth, queen of France by marriage, and almost queen of England.

Mary Shelley: Romance and Reality, Emily W. Sunstein **(1989),** 1991

At nineteen, wild, rebellious, and immensely gifted, Mary Shelley creates Frankenstein.

Me Me Me Me Me: Not a Novel, M. E. Kerr **(1983),** 1994

This chronicle of the author's adolescent years includes boyfriends, parent problems, and boarding school.

Men of Mathematics, E. T. Bell **(1937),** 1961, 1963, 1965, 1968, 1994

> The lives and achievements of world renowned mathematicians are told with wit and good humor.

Merton: A Biography, Monica Furlong **(1980),** 1988

> The conflict of his vows as a Trappist monk and what constituted a genuinely religious life is the central theme of this biography.

Microbe Hunters, Paul de Kruif **(1926),** 1968, 1971

> Thirteen scientists from Leeuwenhoek to Ehrlich fight disease by discovering and controlling malignant microbes.

The Most Dangerous Man in America: Scenes from the Life of Benjamin Franklin, Catherine Drinker Bowen **(1974),** 1976

> Important moments illuminate the life of Benjamin Franklin.

Mother Jones: The Most Dangerous Woman in America, Linda Atkinson **(1978),** 1982

> Some called her dangerous, others patriotic, but all would agree that she was unique—a tough union organizer who was still active and outspoken at age ninety.

Moving Violations: War Zones, Wheelchairs, and Declarations of Independence; A Memoir, John Hockenberry **(1995),** 1999

> Journalist Hockenberry is fearless and funny as he relates the personal and professional experiences he encounters from his wheelchair.

Mussolini: A Biography, Denis Mack Smith **(1982),** 1988

> This study sheds light on the twentieth-century Italian dictator.

My Brother, Jamaica Kincaid **(1997),** 1999

> The author returns to the Caribbean island of her birth to help care for her younger brother who is dying of AIDS.

My Forbidden Face: Growing Up under the Taliban; A Young Woman's Story, Latifa (pseud.) **(2002),** 2004

> Sixteen-year-old Latifa dreamed of becoming a professional journalist until the Taliban's repression of women changed her life.

My Lord, What a Morning: An Autobiography, Marian Anderson **(1956),** 1961, 1963, 1965, 1968

> This great artist shares her success on the concert stage, her feelings about prejudice, and her hopes for the future of African Americans.

My Place, Sally Morgan **(1988),** 1991

> Unraveling the mystery of her Australian heritage, Morgan discovers what it means to be an aborigine.

My Several Worlds: A Personal Record, Pearl S. Buck **(1954),** 1961, 1963, 1965, 1968

The world-famous author of *The Good Earth* tells how she happened to grow up with both Chinese and American culture.

N. C. Wyeth: The Collected Paintings, Illustrations, and Murals, Douglas Allen and Douglas Allen Jr. **(1972),** 1976

The life of an American artist is portrayed in words and reproductions of his works.

Nadja, on My Way, Nadja Salerno-Sonnenberg **(1989),** 1991

A young, classical violinist does it her way.

Naked to Mine Enemies: The Life of Cardinal Wolsey, Charles W. Ferguson **(1958),** 1961, 1963, 1965, 1968, 1971

Defying the Pope in annulling the King's marriage brings tragedy to Henry VIII's minister.

Napoleon: A Great Life in Brief, David Chandler **(1974),** 1976

A thorough reexamination reveals much about Napoleon Bonaparte as a man.

Napoleon I, Albert Léon Guérard **(1956),** 1961, 1963, 1965, 1968, 1971

No one disputes Napoleon's genius on the battlefield.

Narrative of the Life of Frederick Douglass, an American Slave, Written by Himself, Frederick Douglass **(1845),** 1999

Former slave and famed abolitionist Frederick Douglass describes the horrors of his enslavement and eventual escape.

Nicholas and Alexandra, Robert K. Massie **(1967),** 1976, 1994, 1999

At the brink of revolution, the last tsar of Russia and his family become victims of their own mismanagement and personal problems.

Pablo Picasso: The Man and the Image, Richard B. Lyttle **(1989),** 1991

A portrait of Picasso reveals his life as a man and an artist.

Papa Hemingway: A Personal Memoir, A. E. Hotchner **(1966),** 1976

Much of Hemingway's personal life is revealed in his conversations with Hotchner.

Part of My Soul Went with Him, Winnie Mandela **(1984),** 1988

South Africa's first black woman social worker married Nelson Mandela in 1958 and carried on his political struggles since his imprisonment in 1962, even though she was banned by the government.

Paul Revere and the World He Lived In, Esther Forbes **(1942),** 1961, 1963, 1965, 1968, 1971

An American patriot lives during colonial and revolutionary times.

NONFICTION—*Biography* **65**

Paula, Isabel Allende **(1995),** 1999

> At the bedside of her dying daughter, Allende spins tales of childhood, of ancestors, and of becoming a novelist.

The Peabody Sisters of Salem, Louise Hall Tharp **(1950),** 1961, 1963, 1965, 1968, 1971

> The author sketches the Peabody sisters, who did much to develop education in America.

Perón: A Biography, Joseph A. Page **(1983),** 1988

> The private life and public career of the Argentine dictator with a well-known wife named Evita.

Peter the Great, Emperor of All Russia, Ian Grey **(1960),** 1961, 1963, 1965, 1968, 1971

> Peter the Great changes Russia from a medieval to a modern country.

Plain Speaking: An Oral Biography of Harry S. Truman, Merle Miller **(1973),** 1976, 1982, 1988, 1991

> Always frank, Harry Truman talks about his life, the presidency, history, and other political "fellas" in a biography produced from hundreds of taped interviews.

Portrait of Myself, Margaret Bourke-White **(1963),** 1976

> A woman newspaper photographer and foreign correspondent valiantly battles Parkinson's disease.

A Precocious Autobiography, Yevgeny Yevtushenko **(1963),** 1968, 1971

> A Russian poet and author describes Soviet Communist society.

Private Demons: The Life of Shirley Jackson, Judy Oppenheimer **(1988),** 1991

> Shirley Jackson writes strange stories and describes her strange life.

Profiles in Courage, John F. Kennedy **(1956),** 1961, 1963, 1965, 1968, 1971, 1976

> Profiles of eight U.S. congressmen who risk political oblivion because their moral principles are stronger than their ambitions.

Queen of France: A Biography of Marie Antoinette, André Castelot **(1957),** 1961, 1963, 1965, 1968

> Court intrigue, desperate flight, imprisonment, and death are what Marie Antoinette meets after her marriage to the king of France.

Queen Victoria, Lytton Strachey **(1921),** 1961, 1963, 1965, 1968, 1971

> The reader meets the queen, the prince consort, and those living during the famous Victorian era.

Quest: The Life of Elisabeth Kübler-Ross, Derek L. T. Gill **(1980),** 1988

> This Swiss-American physician, psychiatrist, pioneer, humanitarian, scientist, lecturer, and mystic is well known as the author of numerous books on death and dying.

R. v. R.: The Life of Rembrandt van Rijn, Hendrik Willem Van Loon **(1953),** 1961, 1963, 1965, 1968

> A great painter is troubled with tragedy and debts.

Red Scarf Girl: A Memoir of the Cultural Revolution, Ji-Li Jiang **(1997),** 1999

> A young Chinese must make difficult choices when the government urges her to repudiate her ancestors and inform on her own parents.

The Road from Coorain, Jill Ker Conway **(1989),** 1991, 1994

> Australian outbacker Jill Ker Conway fights for an education and, against the odds, becomes the first woman president of Smith College.

The Roosevelt Family of Sagamore Hill, Hermann Hagedorn **(1954),** 1961, 1963, 1965, 1968, 1971

> Theodore Roosevelt called Sagamore Hill home.

Second Wind: The Memoirs of an Opinionated Man, Bill Russell and Taylor Branch **(1979),** 1982

> While reflecting on his transformation from an awkward teenager to a college and pro basketball star, Russell also speaks out on racism, politics, and reading.

The Seven Storey Mountain, Thomas Merton **(1948),** 1961, 1963, 1965, 1968, 1971

> Growing up without a faith, an American poet finds happiness in a Trappist monastery after his conversion to the Church of Rome.

Shakespeare of London, Marchette Gaylord Chute **(1949),** 1961, 1963, 1965, 1968

> William Shakespeare is described against the political and cultural background of his age.

Six Wives: The Queens of Henry VIII, David Starkey **(2003),** 2004

> How one man's matrimonial woes elevated a very disparate group of women to temporary positions of power, changed the way a nation was ruled, and shook the foundations of the Catholic Church.

Soul to Soul: A Black Russian American Family, 1865–1992, Yelena Khanga **(1992),** 1994, 1999

> A young Russian journalist of African American and Jewish heritage analyzes and compares attitudes on race, religion, and sexism in Russia and America.

The Sound of Wings: The Life of Amelia Earhart, Mary S. Lovell **(1989),** 1991, 1994

> A famous woman flier has two loves—her husband, George Putnam, and flying.

Sound-Shadows of the New World, Ved Mehta **(1985),** 1991, 1994, 1999

> Leaving his home, family, and culture behind, a blind Indian boy travels to Arkansas to attend a special school where he is challenged by handicap, loneliness, poor preparation, and culture shock.

Stonewall Jackson: The Man, the Soldier, the Legend, James I. Robertson Jr. **(1997),** 1999

> Both the genius and the failings of this confederate Civil War general are chronicled in this meticulous account.

The Story of My Life, Helen Keller **(1902),** 1961, 1963, 1965, 1968, 1971, 1976, 1982, 1988, 1999

> Overcoming deafness and blindness to become an outstanding citizen, Helen Keller embodies courage, passion, and perseverance.

Such a Vision of the Street: Mother Teresa—The Spirit and the Work, Eileen Egan **(1985),** 1988

> Mother Teresa's life—from her childhood in Albania to her world-famous Nobel Prize–winning activities as a hard-working nun with a divine mission to help the poorest of the poor—is shared with a colleague.

Suleiman the Magnificent: Sultan of the East, Harold Lamb **(1951),** 1961, 1963, 1965

> Suleiman rules in exotic Turkey in the sixteenth century.

"Surely You're Joking, Mr. Feynman!": Adventures of a Curious Character, Richard P. Feynman **(1985),** 1999

> This Nobel Prize–winning physicist was also a bongo drummer, a practical joker, and a loving husband.

Susan B. Anthony: A Biography of a Singular Feminist, Kathleen L. Barry **(1988),** 1991

> A woman masterminds the early women's rights movement in America.

They Called Him Stonewall: A Life of Lt. General T. J. Jackson, C.S.A., Burke Davis **(1954),** 1961, 1963, 1965, 1968

> The life of the Confederate Army's most colorful general is described.

This Boy's Life: A Memoir, Tobias Wolff **(1989),** 1991, 1994, 1999

> In and out of trouble in his youth, this charter member of the "Bad Boy's Club" survives a boyhood that stretches from Florida to the Pacific Northwest.

This I Remember, Eleanor Roosevelt **(1949),** 1961, 1963, 1965, 1968

> Eleanor Roosevelt lives in the White House during the crucial 30s and wartime 40s.

This Life, Sidney Poitier **(1980)**, 1982

> Academy Award–winning actor Sidney Poitier, the son of West Indian parents, takes chances and breaks rules to finally achieve his dramatic destiny.

This Little Light of Mine: The Life of Fannie Lou Hamer, Kay Mills **(1993)**, 1994

> An African American sharecropper's daughter uses her considerable courage and singing talent to become a leader in the civil rights movement.

Thomas Jefferson: An Intimate History, Fawn M. Brodie **(1974)**, 1976

> The public and private life of one of America's founders is described.

Thomas More: A Biography, Richard Marius **(1984)**, 1988

> This authoritative popular biography of a Catholic martyr-saint reveals the contradictions in More's character through the author's awareness of modern psychology.

The Thread That Runs So True, Jesse Stuart **(1949)**, 1961, 1963, 1965, 1968, 1971

> Jesse Stuart loves teaching.

Three: An Unfinished Woman, Pentimento, Scoundrel Time, Lillian Hellman **(1979)**, 1976, 1982, 1988

> Author and playwright Lillian Hellman survives a rebellious childhood in the South, anti-Nazi intrigue, Hollywood romance and glamor, and the effects of blacklisting during the McCarthy era.

Three Who Made a Revolution: A Biographical History, Bertram D. Wolfe **(1948)**, 1976, 1982, 1988

> Brief biographies give insight into the lives and thoughts of Lenin, Stalin, and Trotsky, the leaders of the Russian Revolution.

The Three Worlds of Albert Schweitzer, Robert Payne **(1957)**, 1961, 1963, 1965

> Albert Schweitzer was a brilliant philosopher, musician, physician, missionary, and writer.

Tisha: The Story of a Young Teacher in the Alaska Wilderness, Anne Pardy (As told to Robert Specht) **(1976)**, 1982

> Anne Hobbs, a prim and proper nineteen-year-old, arrives in an Alaskan gold-rush town in 1927 to find prejudice, violence, and love.

To Be Young, Gifted and Black: Lorraine Hansberry in Her Own Words, Lorraine Hansberry **(1969)**, 1971

> A writer presents a portrait of herself and her view of the human spirit.

To Dance, Valery Panov and George Feifer **(1978)**, 1982

> Panov, a Russian Jew, defects to the West when, because of his religion, he is not allowed to dance in Russia.

To Destroy You Is No Loss: The Odyssey of a Cambodian Family, JoAn D. Criddle and Teeda Butt Mam **(1987),** 1994

> After the Communists take over Cambodia in 1975, Teeda's upper-class existence is reduced to surviving impossible conditions.

Tolkien: A Biography, Humphrey Carpenter **(1977),** 1982, 1988

> The life of J. R. R. Tolkien, creator of the mythical world of Middle Earth and its inhabitants, tells of his childhood in South Africa, teaching at Oxford, and fame as the author of *Lord of the Rings.*

The True Adventures of John Steinbeck, Writer: A Biography, Jackson J. Benson **(1984),** 1988

> Benson tells the tale of a Nobel Prize–winning American writer who realistically and romantically captures Depression America in print.

Truman, David G. McCullough **(1992),** 1994, 1999

> This notable president earned America's respect by helping to end World War II and reshape the world for postwar peace.

Undaunted Courage: Meriwether Lewis, Thomas Jefferson, and the Opening of the American West, Stephen E. Ambrose **(1996),** 1999

> Lewis and Clark brave the wilds of North America in this vivid account of exploration and adventure.

Up from Slavery: An Autobiography, Booker T. Washington **(1901),** 1961, 1963, 1965, 1968, 1971

> A former slave is determined to build a great school for African Americans in Alabama.

Walls: Resisting the Third Reich—One Woman's Story, Hiltgunt Zassenhaus **(1974),** 1976

> An anti-Nazi German, Hiltgunt Zassenhaus led three lives in order to aid the Norwegian and Danish prisoners of war during the Hitler years.

What Do You Care What Other People Think? Further Adventures of a Curious Character, Richard P. Feynman **(2001),** 2004

> Quirky, hilarious, and fascinating memoirs from one of the last century's greatest physicists cover everything from his early childhood to his work on the atomic bomb and his investigation into the Challenger explosion.

What Manner of Man: A Biography of Martin Luther King, Jr., Lerone Bennett Jr. **(1964),** 1971

> It was King's achievement to give men hope.

When Heaven and Earth Changed Places: A Vietnamese Woman's Journey from War to Peace, Le Ly Hayslip and Jay Wurts **(1989),** 1991

> Caught in her country's civil war in a family divided, Hayslip survives imprisonment, rape, starvation, and torture.

The Whole World in His Hands: A Pictorial Biography of Paul Robeson, Susan Robeson **(1981)**, 1991

> A granddaughter writes a loving memoir of her brilliant, talented, and controversial grandfather.

William Shakespeare: A Biography, A. L. Rowse **(1971)**, 1971

> This is an elaborate account of Shakespeare in his age.

Windows for the Crown Prince, Elizabeth Vining **(1952)**, 1961, 1963, 1965, 1968

> Gray serves as the first American tutor of the Crown Prince of Japan.

Woman in the Mists: The Story of Dian Fossey and the Mountain Gorillas of Africa, Farley Mowat **(1987)**, 1991, 1994

> Mowat describes the turbulent life and mysterious death of a woman who dedicated her life to the study and survival of endangered mountain gorillas.

The Woman Warrior: Memoirs of a Girlhood among Ghosts, Maxine Hong Kingston **(1976)**, 1982, 1988

> The Chinese American experience is passionately portrayed by a young woman who grows up torn between American life in modern San Francisco and the ancient legends, traditions, and folk beliefs of her Chinese heritage.

Woody Guthrie: A Life, Joe Klein **(1980)**, 1982, 1988

> This authentic American folk hero is haunted by family tragedy, misery, and illness.

Wordstruck: A Memoir, Robert MacNeil **(1989)**, 1991

> TV broadcaster MacNeil writes a love letter about the English language.

Yankee from Olympus: Justice Holmes and His Family, Catherine Drinker Bowen **(1944)**, 1961, 1963, 1965, 1968, 1971

> Bowen tells the story of a famous Supreme Court justice and his family.

Yeager: An Autobiography, Chuck Yeager and Leo Janos **(1985)**, 1988

> Mixing boyish enthusiasm with descriptive detail, Air Force General Chuck Yeager—World War II ace and the first man to break the sound barrier—candidly shares the drama of his life and career.

Zelda: A Biography, Nancy Milford **(1970)**, 1976

> Milford recounts the reckless and painful life of Zelda, from childhood in Montgomery, Alabama, through marriage to F. Scott Fitzgerald, and ending with her many years as a patient in mental institutions.

DANCE

The impulse to move is the raw material that cultures shape into evocative sequences of physical activity that we call dance.

From *Dancing: The Pleasure, Power, and Art of Movement,* by Gerald Jonas

101 Stories of the Great Ballets, George Balanchine and Francis Mason **(1975),** 1982, 1988, 1991, 1994

An excellent guide to the most famous stage productions, including background for the novice.

The Alvin Ailey American Dance Theater, Susan Cook and Joseph H. Mazo **(1978),** 1982

Techniques of ballet, modern, jazz, and ethnic dance are performed by Ailey's company and beautifully portrayed in Cook's black-and-white photography.

America Dances, Agnes de Mille **(1980),** 1982

De Mille has drawn a portrait of American classical, ethnic, and popular dance, as performed on Broadway and in film by the great innovators of dance technique.

American Indian Ballerinas, Lili Cockerille Livingston **(1999),** 2004

Four Native American women from Oklahoma share the struggles and triumphs of their dance careers and personal lives in stories that inspire with courage and beauty.

Ballerina: The Art of Women in Classical Ballet, Mary Clarke and Clement Crisp **(1987),** 1991

The role of ballerinas and their great performances enhance the history of the dance.

Ballet and Modern Dance: A Concise History, Jack Anderson **(1986),** 1994

A chronicle of Western theatrical dance into the twentieth century includes quotations from dancers and choreographers.

Barefoot to Balanchine: How to Watch Dance, Mary Kerner **(1990),** 1994, 1999

Understand dance by reading about its history, choreography, and backstage action.

Black Dance in America: A History through Its People, James Haskins **(1990),** 1991, 1994

Historical accounts and biographies trace the many forms of African American dance beginning with its African origins.

Black Dance in the United States: From 1619 to 1970, Lynne Fauley Emery **(1972),** 1988

Chronicles African American contributions to American dance from the arrival of the first Africans to 1970.

The Book of Tap: Recovering America's Long Lost Dance, Jerry Ames and Jim Siegelman **(1977),** 1982, 1988

A study of tap dancing from its early minstrel and vaudeville days to its golden age in Hollywood, with some thoughts on the future of tap.

The Book of the Dance, Agnes de Mille **(1963),** 1971

This lavishly illustrated story of the dance—social, ritual, theatrical—from earliest times to the present day, traces motivation, dance forms, and their development.

The Complete Guide to Modern Dance, Don McDonagh **(1976),** 1982

A representative anthology of performers and choreographers of the twentieth-century modern dance movement.

The Dance Catalog, Nancy Reynolds (ed.) **(1979),** 1982

A dancer's compendium that includes listings of dance companies, teachers, colleges, and career suggestions.

Dance in America, Robert Coe **(1985),** 1988, 1991

Based on the PBS series, this book traces today's dance back to its roots and then brings the story forward through classical ballet to modern dance.

Dancershoes, Daniel S. Sorine and Stephanie Riva Sorine **(1979),** 1982

Dancers stretch, shellac, spray, soak, cut, crush, polish, paint, hammer, and twist their shoes.

Dancing: The Pleasure, Power, and Art of Movement, Gerald Jonas **(1992),** 1994, 1999

A companion volume to an eight-part television series, this international survey explores dance as social, cultural, and religious expression.

Danseur: The Male in Ballet, Richard Philip and Mary Whitney **(1977),** 1982

Spectacular photography enlivens this celebration of the male dancer and choreographer.

Inside Dance: Essays, Murray Louis **(1980),** 1982

Philosophical, insightful thoughts illuminate the various facets of the dance world—the critics, the travel, and the lifestyle.

Jazz Dance: The Story of American Vernacular Dance, Marshall Stearns and Jean Stearns **(1979),** 1988, 1991

In writing a history of what seemed to be a dying art, the author reawakens an interest in some of the rarely practiced forms of jazz dance, such as the Black Bottom, Lindy Hop, and Buzzard Lope.

Men Dancing: Performers and Performances, Alexander Bland and John Percival **(1984),** 1988, 1991, 1994

> The history of men in dance, highlighting Astaire, Baryshnikov, Merce Cunningham, and many others.

On Wings of Joy: The Story of Ballet from the 16th Century to Today, Trudy Garfunkel **(1994),** 1999, 2004

> Immerse yourself in the world of ballet, from its earliest choreography to the life of a modern ballerina.

On Your Toes: Beginning Ballet, Wendy Neale **(1980),** 1982

> This book offers practical advice for beginning dancers and their parents and explains the preparations necessary for a dance career.

People Who Dance: 22 Dancers Tell Their Own Stories, John Gruen **(1988),** 1991, 1994

> Interviews give insights into the special world of the dancer.

Private View: Inside Baryshnikov's American Ballet Theatre, John Fraser **(1988),** 1991

> During the 1986–87 season, the ABT has castings, rehearsals, and a national tour.

Prodigal Son: Dancing for Balanchine in a World of Pain and Magic, Edward Villella, with Larry Kaplan **(1992),** 1994

> Villella shares his view of ballet as he discloses intimate details of his training, performances, and his relationship with Balanchine.

Push Comes to Shove, Twyla Tharp **(1992),** 1994

> Dancer/choreographer Tharp reveals her dedication to dance, her explorations in movement, and the sources of her creative ideas.

Terpsichore in Sneakers: Post-Modern Dance, Sally Banes **(1980),** 1982

> Banes looks at the predominant personalities of "post-modern" dance and the techniques that emphasize free movement in an inventive, nontraditional way.

Where She Danced: The Birth of American Art-Dance, Elizabeth Kendall **(1979),** 1994, 1999

> The contributions of major innovators and the conditions of their times are the basis for this history of modern American dance.

Winter Season: A Dancer's Journal, Toni Bentley **(1982),** 1988, 1991

> Ballet can be beautiful to watch, but the dancers suffer to present that beauty.

Worlds Apart: The Autobiography of a Dancer from Brooklyn, Robert Maiorano **(1980),** 1982

> A dancer bridges the world of his Brooklyn ghetto existence with the glamour of New York's professional dance world.

FILM AND TELEVISION

*From the movies we learn precisely how to hold
a champagne flute, kiss a mistress, pull a trigger,
turn a phrase . . . [but] the movies spoil us for life;
nothing ever lives up to them.*

Edmund White

"And So It Goes": Adventures in Television, Linda Ellerbee **(1986)**, 1988

Ellerbee details her career in this humorous account of the machinations of the television industry.

The Art of Hanna-Barbera: Fifty Years of Creativity, Ted Sennett **(1989)**, 1991

Cartoon characters including Tom and Jerry, the Flintstones and Yogi Bear demonstrate Hanna-Barbera's contribution to the development of film animation.

The Art of Walt Disney: From Mickey Mouse to the Magic Kingdoms, Christopher Finch **(1973)**, 1991

Mickey Mouse and Donald Duck make Walt Disney known throughout the world.

Chuck Amuck: The Life and Times of an Animated Cartoonist, Chuck Jones **(1989)**, 1994

Jones's autobiography includes intimate pictures, stills, and text from cartoons.

The Citizen Kane Book: Raising Kane, Pauline Kael **(1971)**, 1988

The shooting script by Herman J. Mankiewicz and Orson Welles explains how the movie came to be.

The Cool Fire: How to Make It in Television, Bob Shanks **(1976)**, 1982

A former producer explains the business and technology of television, the history of the networks, and how programs are planned, produced, and presented.

Elements of Film, Lee R. Bobker **(1969)**, 1982

An introduction to the technical aspects of filmmaking, including an analysis of the work of sixteen contemporary filmmakers and a discussion of the importance of film criticism.

Film Maker's Guide to Super 8: The "How-to-Do-It" Book for Beginning and Advanced Film Makers, compiled by the editors of *Super 8 Filmaker* magazine **(1980)**, 1982

A collection of articles on equipment, sound techniques and effects, scriptwriting, filming techniques, animation, editing, making documentaries, and more.

Films of Science Fiction and Fantasy, Baird Searles **(1988),** 1991

Photographs of movie stills and frame enlargements accompany this description of science fiction and fantasy movies.

Getting into Film, Mel London **(1977),** 1982

A career guide covering every aspect of the film industry from production and cinematography to makeup, costumes, and special effects with information on agents, auditions, education, and unions.

The Hollywood History of the World: From *One Million Years B.C.* to *Apocalypse Now*, George MacDonald Fraser **(1988),** 1994

Hollywood lore enlivens this history, which is illustrated with still photographs.

Hollywood: The Pioneers, Kevin Brownlow and John Kobal **(1980),** 1982, 1988, 1991, 1994

A superb history of film and filmmakers from the early days of story-slide shows to the end of the silent picture era, enhanced by unique photographs of actual productions.

Inside Oscar: The Unofficial History of the Academy Awards, Mason Wiley and Damien Bona **(1986),** 1988

An informative and breezy tour through Hollywood, from Oscar's beginning to the 1980s.

Making Movies Work: Thinking Like a Filmmaker, Jon Boorstin **(1995),** 1999

Both novice and expert can enjoy this behind-the-scenes look at the art of filmmaking.

The Movies, Mr. Griffith, and Me, Lillian Gish **(1969),** 1988

The colorful, moving memoir of Lillian Gish describes the silent motion picture industry and her innovative director.

Murrow: His Life and Times, A. M. Sperber **(1986),** 1988

Story of the man who set the style and standards for radio and television journalism.

Our Movie Heritage, Tom McGreevey and Joanne L. Yeck **(1997),** 2004

Everyone loves movies. But film must be preserved or these cinematic treasures will be lost.

Stunt Man: The Autobiography of Yakima Canutt, Yakima Canutt, with Oliver Drake **(1979),** 1982

"Yak" discusses his performance in such films as *Gone with the Wind*, *Stagecoach*, and *Ben Hur*, giving a fascinating account of the industry, stunting, and special effects.

The Technique of Film Animation, John Halas and Roger Manvell **(1959),** 1982

>This is a complete and illustrated guide to film animation techniques for beginning and advanced filmmakers.

Television, Michael Winship **(1988),** 1994

>Television pioneers give their special insights into the history of the medium.

They Sang! They Danced! They Romanced! A Pictorial History of the Movie Musical, John Springer **(1981),** 1994

>Illustrations detail the positive and negative aspects of movie musicals.

Toms, Coons, Mulattoes, Mammies, and Bucks: An Interpretative History of Blacks in American Films, Donald Bogle **(1989),** 1991, 1994

>African Americans contribute to American films from *Uncle Tom's Cabin* in 1903 to *Do the Right Thing* in the 1980s.

Video Visions: A Medium Discovers Itself, Jonathan Price **(1977),** 1982

>Video has the potential for educational and artistic use.

When the Shooting Stops . . . the Cutting Begins: A Film Editor's Story, Ralph Rosenblum and Robert Karen **(1979),** 1982, 1988

>The art and profession of editing are described in this autobiographical account of working experiences with filmmakers Woody Allen, Mel Brooks, documentary great Robert Flaherty, and others.

HISTORY

>*The surface of American society is covered with a layer of democratic paint, but from time to time one can see the old aristocratic colors breaking through.*
>
>From *Democracy in America,*
>by Alexis de Tocqueville

Ain't Gonna Study War No More: The Story of America's Peace Seekers, Milton Meltzer **(1985),** 1988

>A chronicle of resistance to war and violence in America's history, this work tells the story of passionate believers in peace who often forfeit their reputations and livelihoods for those beliefs.

Alistair Cooke's America, Alistair Cooke **(1973),** 1976, 1982

>Based on the popular PBS television series, this lavishly illustrated book presents an Englishman's refreshing view of his adopted country's history.

All the President's Men, Carl Bernstein and Bob Woodward **(1974)**, 1976, 1994

> Following lead after lead, two *Washington Post* reporters lift the veil of secrecy surrounding the Nixon administration's Watergate cover-up.

The American Political Tradition and the Men Who Made It, Richard Hofstadter **(1948)**, 1971

> Incisive essays interpret the historical significance of such figures as Jefferson, Lincoln, Wilson, Hoover, and Franklin Delano Roosevelt.

Anasazi: Ancient People of the Rock, Donald G. Pike and David Muench **(1974)**, 1991

> Archeological evidence and the written records of Spanish explorers reveal the history of an ancient people.

Barbarians at the Gate: The Fall of RJR Nabisco, Bryan Burrough and John Helyar **(1990)**, 1994

> Wall Street's largest takeover reveals greed, deceit, and clever maneuvers.

Battle Cry of Freedom: The Civil War Era, James M. McPherson **(1988)**, 1994

> From the Mexican War to Appomattox, the political, military, and economic aspects of the Civil War are examined.

Before the Mayflower: A History of Black America, Lerone Bennett Jr. **(1962)**, 1976

> From the African past through slavery, wars, and reconstructions—the dramatic story of the African Americans' sojourn in North America.

The Best and the Brightest, David Halberstam **(1972)**, 1994

> Kennedy-Johnson intellectuals orchestrate American foreign policy in Indochina.

Bloods: An Oral History of the Vietnam War, Black veterans and Wallace Terry (ed.) **(1984)**, 1988

> During the Vietnam War, the African American soldiers endured a higher percentage of casualties and returned to a higher percentage of unemployment than any other ethnic group.

A Bright Shining Lie: John Paul Vann and America in Vietnam, Neil Sheehan **(1989)**, 1994, 1999

> A soldier exposes the corruption undermining the American war effort in Vietnam.

Bury My Heart at Wounded Knee: An Indian History of the American West, Dee Brown **(1971)**, 1976, 1982, 1988, 1994, 1999

> There's another side of America's western expansion: the one seen through Native American eyes.

Columbus in the Americas, William Least Heat-Moon **(2003),** 2004

Was he a visionary and daring explorer, or a ruthless conquistador with dreams of riches and glory? Discover the truth behind the myth of a man whose impact still resonates through the continents he stumbled across.

The Constitution: Reflection of a Changing Nation, Margot C. J. Mabie **(1987),** 1991

The Constitution of the United States is a living document that adapts to changes in our history.

Day One: Before Hiroshima and After, Peter Wyden **(1984),** 1988

The race to develop the atomic bomb and the aftermath of its first use are covered in this account of the birth of the atomic age.

Democracy in America, Alexis de Tocqueville **(1835),** 1971, 1976, 1982, 1988

This classic in political literature examines American society from the viewpoint of a leading French magistrate who visited the United States in 1831.

A Distant Mirror: The Calamitous 14th Century, Barbara W. Tuchman **(1978),** 1994, 2004

Tuchman uses the example of a single feudal lord to trace the history of the fourteenth century.

The Dream: Martin Luther King, Jr., and the Speech That Inspired a Nation, Drew D. Hansen **(2003),** 2004

This great humanitarian and leader did indeed have a dream, and it has resonated through the years to expand all of our hopes for a future built on tolerance.

Eight Men Out: The Black Sox and the 1919 World Series, Eliot Asinof **(1963),** 1994, 1999

It's all here: the players, the scandal, the shame, and the damage the 1919 World Series caused for America's national pastime.

The Endurance: Shackleton's Legendary Antarctic Expedition, Caroline Alexander **(1998),** 2004

It's man against nature at the dawn of World War I, as the lure of the last unclaimed land on earth dazzles with its beauty and danger in this adventure of discovery and survival.

Everything We Had: An Oral History of the Vietnam War by Thirty-three American Soldiers Who Fought It, Al Santoli **(1981),** 1982

Veterans of the Vietnam War from all branches of the service recount the impact of the war on their lives.

Eyes on the Prize: America's Civil Rights Years, 1954–1965, Juan Williams **(1987),** 1991, 1994, 1999

From *Brown v. Board of Education* to the Voting Rights Act, Williams outlines the social and political gains of African Americans.

Final Harvest: An American Tragedy, Andrew H. Malcolm **(1986),** 1988

A poverty-stricken, uneducated farmer murders the local bank manager who foreclosed on his 80 acres, making both men victims of the painful changes affecting America's agricultural heartland.

Fire in the Lake: The Vietnamese and the Americans in Vietnam, Frances FitzGerald **(1972),** 1991

A knowledge of the history of Vietnam helps the reader understand the reasons for the Vietnam War.

The First Freedom: The Tumultuous History of Free Speech in America, Nat Hentoff **(1980),** 1982

This historical study of the First Amendment includes important court cases.

First They Killed My Father: A Daughter of Cambodia Remembers, Loung Ung **(2001),** 2004

The perils of life under the brutal Pol Pot regime change a young woman's life forever, as she and her family find themselves fugitives of war, without even their names to remind them of what they lost.

Founding Brothers: The Revolutionary Generation, Joseph J. Ellis **(2000),** 2004

What seems like a foregone conclusion—the founding of the United States—was anything but. Six dramatic vignettes reveal the men behind the events of the most decisive decade in American history.

The Gateway to History, Allan Nevins **(1938),** 1971

Nevin defines the scope and variety of the field of history and outlines views on history's objectives, both as a science and as an art.

Good Neighbors? The United States and Latin America, Ann E. Weiss **(1985),** 1988

The ongoing, complex relationship between the United States and Latin America is presented in an easy-to-read style.

The Guinness Book of Records 1492: The World Five Hundred Years Ago, Deborah Manley (ed.) **(1992),** 1994

Discover the world as it was over 500 years ago.

Hiroshima, John Hersey **(1946),** 1988, 1994, 1999

Six Hiroshima survivors reflect on the aftermath of the first atomic bomb.

Hunter's Stew and Hangtown Fry: What Pioneer America Ate and Why, Lila Perl **(1977),** 1991

The food choices of early pioneers continue to influence what we eat in various parts of the country.

The Imperial Presidency, Arthur M. Schlesinger Jr. **(1973),** 1976, 1982

Power has been used and abused by American presidents.

Indian Givers: How the Indians of the Americas Transformed the World, Jack Weatherford **(1990),** 2004

> Discover how profoundly the native peoples of North and South America influenced what we eat, how we trade, and our system of government.

Into Thin Air: A Personal Account of the Mount Everest Disaster, Jon Krakauer **(1997),** 1999

> His dream expedition to Everest became a nightmare when human error and a sudden storm combined to claim the lives of some of the world's best mountain climbers.

Invisible Men: Life in Baseball's Negro Leagues, Donn Rogosin **(1983),** 1994

> The great Negro League players finally gain recognition for their contributions to baseball.

Jefferson's Children: The Story of One American Family, Shannon Lanier and Jane Feldman **(2000),** 2004

> Thomas Jefferson fathered two families—one black, one white, brought together by his determined young descendant. This is a story about family, a story about identity, a story about secrets revealed, and history made complete.

The Johnstown Flood, David McCullough **(1968),** 1994

> McCullough shares the story behind one of America's most devastating disasters.

Krakatoa: The Day the World Exploded: August 27, 1883, Simon Winchester **(2003),** 2004

> When the earth's most dangerous volcano exploded off the coast of Java, hundred-foot waves flung ships inland, a rain of hot ash made temperatures plummet, the shock wave traveled around the world seven times, and 40,000 people died. The aftermath of this disaster saw the rise of radical Islam, civil unrest, and a legacy of anti-Western militancy that continues today.

La Raza: The Mexican Americans, Stan Steiner **(1970),** 1971, 1976, 1991

> A study of the problems of "The Race," which includes an account of the journey of César Chávez from the boyhood of a migrant farmworker to the role of leader of his people.

Legends, Lies, and Cherished Myths of World History, Richard Shenkman **(1988),** 1994

> Legends, myths, and lies reveal history's errors with humor.

Let Us Now Praise Famous Men, James Agee and Walker Evans **(1960),** 1976, 1982, 1988

> Agee and Evans portray three tenant farmer families at the depths of the Depression in words and photographs that are perhaps closer to art than to commentary.

The Little Ice Age: How Climate Made History, 1300–1850, Brian Fagan **(2002),** 2004

Fagan provides a fascinating look at how climate change influenced the course of the last thousand years of Western history. He highlights climate's profound influence on the Viking discovery of North America, the Industrial and French Revolutions, and the Irish Potato Famine.

The Making of a Counter Culture: Reflections on the Technocratic Society and Its Youthful Opposition, Theodore Roszak **(1969),** 1971, 1976

The influence of such personalities as Herbert Marcuse, Allen Ginsberg, Timothy Leary, and Paul Goodman is examined together with the leading causes of youthful dissent in the sixties.

Miracle at Philadelphia: The Story of the Constitutional Convention, May to September, 1787, Catherine Drinker Bowen **(1986),** 1988

The historic formation of the Constitution is recounted in this day-by-day report of the debates and compromises that took place in Philadelphia.

Modern Times: The World from the Twenties to the Eighties, Paul Johnson **(1983),** 1988

A fascinating presentation of world history and politics is combined with thought-provoking critical interpretation.

My Soul Is Rested: Movement Days in the Deep South Remembered, Howell Raines **(1983),** 1988

The gathering force of the civil rights movement from the Montgomery bus boycott of 1955 to the death of Martin Luther King Jr. in 1968, as told by the men and women who remember the glory and tragedy of those days.

Never to Forget: The Jews of the Holocaust, Milton Meltzer **(1976),** 1982, 1988

This book "is an act of mourning and a call to remember" so that history will not be repeated.

Our House Divided: Seven Japanese American Families in World War II, Tomi Kaizawa Knaefler **(1991),** 1994

The United States is a place of neither shelter nor freedom for Japanese Americans during World War II.

The Rape of Nanking: The Forgotten Holocaust of World War II, Iris Chang **(1997),** 1999

Barely a postscript in official Japanese history, the horrific rape, mutilation, torture, and murder of hundreds of thousands of Chinese citizens took place over the course of just seven weeks.

Rescue: The Story of How Gentiles Saved Jews in the Holocaust, Milton Meltzer **(1988),** 1991, 1994

Many people risked their lives to save others during the Holocaust.

The Right Stuff, Tom Wolfe **(1983),** 1988

> This inside story reveals the glory and exploitation that attended the selection, training, and flight of America's first astronauts.

Sagas of Icelanders: A Selection, Various **(2001),** 2004

> Nordic epics open up a world of wonder and power, a Viking world of heroic adventure and discovery at the turn of the first millennium.

The Search for King Arthur, David Day **(1995),** 1999

> Discover through magnificent illustrations and romantic retellings what is fact and what is legend about this fifth-century hero.

Season Ticket: A Baseball Companion, Roger Angell **(1988),** 1994

> A veteran sports writer profiles the sport's 1983–87 seasons.

Smoke and Ashes: The Story of the Holocaust, Barbara Rogasky **(2002),** 2004

> Some of history's darkest days are examined in this new look at the horror and humanity of the Holocaust and its aftermath.

The Strange Career of Jim Crow, C. Vann Woodward **(1955),** 1976

> The effects of southern segregation laws and of the aftermath of the Civil Rights movement in both North and South are analyzed.

Strange Footprints on the Land: Vikings in America, Constance H. Frick Irwin **(1980),** 1991

> Historians perform unusual detective work to solve the mystery of the Viking influence in pre-Columbia America.

Taking on the Press: Constitutional Rights in Conflict, Melvyn Bernard Zerman **(1986),** 1988

> Freedom of the press is examined through a discussion of landmark cases that cause controversy over whose rights should prevail.

Terror of the Spanish Main: Sir Henry Morgan and His Buccaneers, Albert Marrin **(1999),** 2004

> What lies behind the dark and romantic image of the pirate, and what is the legacy of this brutal and bloody time?

There Is a River: The Black Struggle for Freedom in America, Vincent Harding **(1981),** 1982, 1988

> African Americans from the first captives in Africa to the end of the Civil War rebel against slavery.

Thunder on the Right: The "New Right" and the Politics of Resentment, Alan Crawford **(1980),** 1982

> A conservative explores the dangers of the New Right, its leaders, and its groups.

To Bear Any Burden: The Vietnam War and Its Aftermath in the Words of Americans and Southeast Asians, Al Santoli **(1985)**, 1988

> The Vietnam War's origins and its aftermath come alive through interviews with American civilians and military personnel as well as Southeast Asians.

Triangle: The Fire That Changed America, David Von Drehle **(2003)**, 2004

> Beyond the terror, destruction, and loss of life, this event changed the landscape of our cities and the lives of working people everywhere.

Twelve Years a Slave, Solomon Northup **(1968)**, 1994

> A free man is kidnapped and sold into slavery.

Understanding September 11th: Answering Questions about the Attacks on America, Mitch Frank **(2002)**, 2004

> These events are burned into images we can never forget—but after the pain of September 11 we ask "why" and "what" do we need to learn about the historical, religious, and cultural issues that sparked the attacks.

Unforgettable Fire: Pictures Drawn by Atomic Bomb Survivors, Japanese Broadcasting Corp. **(1981)**, 1982

> Survivors of Hiroshima draw over one hundred pictures.

Vietnam: A History, Stanley Karnow **(1983)**, 1994

> Karnow covers over two centuries of armed conflict in Vietnam.

War Clouds in the West: Indians and Cavalrymen, 1860–1890, Albert Marrin **(1984)**, 1991

> Native Americans fight to survive in the late nineteenth century when increasing numbers of pioneers settle on their land.

War Letters: Extraordinary Correspondence from American Wars, Andrew Carroll **(2001)**, 2004

> The Legacy Project preserves the voices of soldiers and statesmen who lived through violent times that changed the course of nations. Listen to their stories in their words—they will inform and inspire you.

Witch-Hunt: Mysteries of the Salem Witch Trials, Marc Aronson **(2003)**, 2004

> Revisit a time of nightmare, fear, hysteria—beyond The Crucible. Sift through the myths, half-truths, and misinformation to make up your own mind about what really happened in Salem Village and why.

A World History, William H. McNeill **(1967)**, 1971

> McNeill provides a comprehensive history of the world.

The World Must Know: The History of the Holocaust as Told in the United States Holocaust Memorial Museum, U.S. Holocaust Memorial Museum **(1993)**, 1994

> This history covers both the persecuted and the persecutors of the Holocaust.

HUMANITIES

Although I was on the verge of receiving a degree in French literature, what I really wanted to study was philosophy. I was interested in Marx, his predecessors and successors. Whenever I could find the time, I read philosophy on the side. I didn't really know what I was doing, except that it gave me a feeling of security and comfort to read what people had to say about such formidable things as the universe, history, human beings, knowledge. —Angela Davis

From *Falling in Love with Wisdom,*
edited by David D. Karnos
and Robert G. Shoemaker

An American Dilemma: The Negro Problem and Modern Democracy, Gunnar Myrdal **(1944)**, 1971

This classic study of the African Americans in America by a social economist becomes also a critical evaluation of American civilization as a whole.

Among Schoolchildren, Tracy Kidder **(1989)**, 1991

An elementary teacher tells about the children and events during one school year.

Amusing Ourselves to Death: Public Discourse in the Age of Show Business, Neil Postman **(1985)**, 1988

The author believes the act and art of public discourse are being degraded by television, which turns important issues into mass media entertainment.

And the Band Played On: Politics, People, and the AIDS Epidemic, Randy Shilts **(1987)**, 1991

A reporter takes a detailed look at the first five years of the unfolding AIDS epidemic.

Apartheid in Crisis, Mark A. Uhlig (ed.) **(1986)**, 1988

The various South African factions reveal their attitudes and take their stands.

Arctic Dreams: Imagination and Desire in a Northern Landscape, Barry Lopez **(1986)**, 1988

Real life and dreams of the Arctic land, its animals, and its people are celebrated.

The Art of Living: The Classic Manual on Virtue, Happiness, and Effectiveness, Epictetus and Sharon Lebell **(1995)**, 1999

A modern interpretation of the Stoic philosopher answers the timeless questions of how to be a good person and live a good life.

The Ascent of Man, J. Bronowski **(1973),** 1976, 1982, 1988

> A scientist's history of the human mind and the human condition.

Backlash: The Undeclared War against American Women, Susan Faludi **(1991),** 1994, 1999

> This unflinching analysis examines the current status of American women.

Blue Highways: A Journey into America, William Least Heat-Moon **(1982),** 1988

> Traveling miles along the small backroads of the United States allows the author to introduce a series of diverse and unique Americans.

The Body Project: An Intimate History of American Girls, Joan Jacobs Brumberg **(1998),** 1999

> The historical evolution of body perception has turned the value system of American girls inside out.

Borrowing Time: Growing Up with Juvenile Diabetes, Pat Covelli **(1979),** 1982

> A first-person account of taking responsibility for one's own survival.

Bradshaw on the Family: A Revolutionary Way of Self-Discovery, John Bradshaw **(1988),** 1991

> By focusing on family problems such as guilt and co-dependency, Bradshaw helps the reader to grow and change.

The Broken Cord, Michael Dorris **(1989),** 1994, 1999

> The persistent physical and emotional problems of his adopted son baffle the author until he learns the condition has a name: Fetal Alcohol Syndrome.

Changing Bodies, Changing Lives: A Book for Teens on Sex and Relationships, Ruth Bell **(1980),** 1982, 1988

> A direct, thorough, and explicit guide for young adults concerning both physical and emotional aspects of sexuality.

China Men, Maxine Hong Kingston **(1980),** 1991

> A description of the lives of several generations of Chinese males contribute to an understanding of the experiences of Chinese immigrants.

Civil Disobedience, Henry David Thoreau **(1849),** 1976, 1982

> Thoreau discusses the individual's rights in relation to government.

Civilisation: A Personal View, Kenneth Clark **(1970),** 1971, 1999

> Clark explores history through the works, impulses, and beliefs of the great creative individuals of Western civilization.

The Closing of the American Mind: How Higher Education Has Failed Democracy and Impoverished the Souls of Today's Students, Allan Bloom **(1987),** 1991

> The author maintains Western civilization is in crisis because its intellectual tradition has been abandoned.

Common Ground: A Turbulent Decade in the Lives of Three American Familes,
J. Anthony Lukas **(1985),** 1988

> A remarkable, intensive analysis of the lives of three families—one African American, one Irish, and one Yankee—who clash in the violent climate of prejudice and racism that erupted in the 1968 Boston school integration crisis.

Conduct Unbecoming: Gays and Lesbians in the U.S. Military, Vietnam to the Persian Gulf, Randy Shilts **(1993),** 1994

> Shilts discusses the contributions and conflicts of gays and lesbians serving in the American armed forces.

Coping with Date Rape and Acquaintance Rape, Andrea Parrot **(1988),** 1991

> Both men and women can use these suggested techniques for avoiding date and acquaintance rape.

The Corner: A Year in the Life of an Inner-City Neighborhood, David Simon and Edward Burns **(1997),** 1999

> Crack owns this corner and infects the lives of all those within reach.

The Control of Nature, John McPhee **(1989),** 1994

> McPhee turns his attention to Alaska, the last American frontier.

Counting Coup: A True Story of Basketball and Honor on the Little Big Horn,
Larry Colton **(2000),** 2004

> Working through racism, alcoholism, and domestic violence, the players on Hardin High School's girls' basketball team come out winners in life as well as on the court.

A Country Year: Living the Questions, Sue Hubbell **(1986),** 1999

> A former wife and librarian observes her natural surroundings during a year spent as a beekeeper on a beautiful Ozark farm.

Cultural Literacy: What Every American Needs to Know, E. D. Hirsch Jr. **(1987),** 1991

> An educated, "culturally literate" member of contemporary American society must understand certain key terms and concepts from history.

Culture and Commitment: The New Relationships between the Generations in the 1970s, Margaret Mead **(1970),** 1976, 1982

> We need not only to recognize global problems, Mead argues, but also to commit ourselves to solving them.

Cycles of Fire: Stars, Galaxies, and the Wonder of Deep Space, William K. Hartmann **(1987),** 1991

> This book explores the formation of stars, the characteristics of the Milky Way, and the possibilities of other worlds in deep space.

The Dark Side of the Marketplace: The Plight of the American Consumer, Warren Grant Magnuson and Jean Carper **(1968),** 1976

> While Ralph Nader has been the consumer advocate from without, Magnuson has worked within Congress to counter abuses.

The Death and Life of Great American Cities, Jane Jacobs **(1961),** 1976

> A witty and passionate defense of the primary role of people in city planning and urban renewal.

The Decade of Women: A *Ms.* History of the Seventies in Words and Pictures, Suzanne Levine and Harriet Lyons (eds.) **(1980),** 1982

> Discusses various aspects of women's lives in the 1970s through quotations and photographs.

The Desert Smells like Rain: A Naturalist in Papago Indian Country, Gary Paul Nabhan **(1982),** 1994

> Nature plays a vital part in Papago Indian culture.

The Devil in the Shape of a Woman: Witchcraft in Colonial New England, Carol F. Karlsen **(1987),** 1994

> The status of women in Colonial society affects the Salem witch accusations.

Do What You Love, the Money Will Follow: Discovering Your Right Livelihood, Marsha Sinetar **(1989),** 1991

> This New Age self-help manual works with self-esteem and other concepts to develop personal satisfaction in employment and life.

Domestic Revolutions: A Social History of American Family Life, Steven Mintz and Susan Kellogg **(1988),** 1994

> Is the American family changing its structure and purpose?

The Essential Writings of Mahatma Gandhi, Mahatma Gandhi. Ed. Raghavan Iyer **(1991),** 1994

> Gandhi discusses the philosophical underpinnings that guided his nonviolent life.

Falling in Love with Wisdom: American Philosophers Talk about Their Calling, David D. Karnos and Robert G. Shoemaker (eds.) **(1993),** 1999

> Contemporary philosophers share their contemplations and epiphanies.

The Fate of the Earth, Jonathan Schell **(1982),** 1988

> The fear of human extinction by a nuclear holocaust is discussed in this profoundly sobering and frightening book.

Father Greg and the Homeboys: The Extraordinary Journey of Father Greg Boyle and His Work with the Latino Gangs of East L.A., Celeste Fremon **(1995),** 1999

> Conscience, parent, motivator, drill sergeant: Father Greg was all this and more to the gangbangers who called his barrio parish community home.

Favorite Folktales from around the World, Jane Yolen (ed.) **(1986)**, 1991, 1994, 1999

This collection of international folktales provides an understanding of the roots of diverse cultures.

The Feminine Mystique, Betty Friedan **(1963)**, 1976, 1988

Many feel that the first edition of this book precipitated the women's liberation movement by inspiring new appraisals of roles and aspirations.

The Fire Next Time, James Baldwin **(1963)**, 1994

Expatriate Baldwin issues a wake-up call to counteract America's racist attitudes.

A First Dictionary of Cultural Literacy: What Our Children Need to Know, E. D. Hirsch Jr. **(1989)**, 1991

Using a dictionary format, hundreds of "windows" reveal what it means to be a culturally literate educated American citizen.

Friday Night Lights: A Town, a Team, and a Dream, H. G. Bissinger **(2003)**, 2004

In Odessa, Texas, high school football is more than a recreational interest; it is the whole town's passion.

The Friendly Shakespeare: A Thoroughly Painless Guide to the Best of the Bard, Norrie Epstein **(1993)**, 1994

Gain a perspective of Shakespeare's works through these sidelights, interpretations, anecdotes, and historical insights.

Future Shock, Alvin Toffler **(1970)**, 1971, 1976

This book stimulates discussion of the effects of rapidly accelerating change in our society.

Girl, Interrupted, Susanna Kaysen **(1993)**, 1994

Kaysen provides unique insight into mental illness.

Give Me My Father's Body: The Life of Minik, the New York Eskimo, Kenn Harper **(2000)**, 2004

Imagine the horror as Minik visits the Museum of Natural History and learns the true fate of his father. The next time you visit a museum, will you wonder about the exhibits, and the dark price sometimes paid to extend our understanding of our world?

The Glory and the Dream: A Narrative History of America, 1932–1972, William Manchester **(1974)**, 1982

From major calamities to minor trivia, this remarkable exploration celebrates modern America in a spirited, lively narrative.

Goddesses in Everywoman: A New Psychology of Women, Jean Shinoda Bolen **(1984)**, 1991

Women have many roles in contemporary everyday life.

Gods in Everyman: A New Psychology of Men's Lives and Loves, Jean Shinoda Bolen **(1989)**, 1991

Psychological analysis demonstrates that men display certain traits that are similar to the archetypes of Greek gods.

Great Expectations: America and the Baby Boom Generation, Landon Y. Jones **(1980)**, 1982

Being part of the largest generation in American history has its strengths and its problems.

Growing Up Asian American: An Anthology, Maria Hong (ed.) **(1993)**, 1994

Asian American authors are featured in this literary collection focused on growing up.

A History of Art and Music, H. W. Janson, with Dora Jane Janson and Joseph Kerman **(1968)**, 1971

This book offers a panoramic history of art and music in the Western world.

A History of Western Philosophy, Bertrand Russell **(1945)**, 1971

Philosophy emerges as "an integral part of social and political life; not as the isolated speculations of remarkable individuals, but as both an effect and a cause of the character of the various communities in which different systems flourish."

Holy Bible: New Revised Standard Version, (1990), 1991, 1999

Biblical scholars revise text and modernize terms to bring one version of the Bible up-to-date.

Hometown Heroes: Successful Deaf Youth in America, Diane Robinette **(1990)**, 1994

These profiles show handicapped youth succeeding in today's world.

How to Get Started When You Don't Know Where to Begin, Patricia Hoyt **(1980)**, 1982

Issues such as renting an apartment, opening a checking account, doing the laundry, and other practical situations are addressed.

Ideas and Men: The Story of Western Thought, Crane Brinton **(1950)**, 1971

This work presents an analysis of the major ideas and concepts which have helped to shape the course of Western civilization.

The Illustrated World's Religions: A Guide to Our Wisdom Traditions, Huston Smith **(1995)**, 2004

The interconnectivity of the world's great religious movements, with their parallel and disparate beliefs, is lyrically explored.

In Search of Excellence: Lessons from America's Best Run Companies, Thomas J. Peters and Robert H. Waterman Jr. **(1982)**, 1991

Consultants identify 42 companies and tell why they are successful.

In Search of Meaning: Living Religions of the World, Carl Hermann Voss **(1968),** 1971

> The history and origins of the great religions including their spiritual, cultural, and ethical values.

In These Girls, Hope Is a Muscle, Madeleine Blais **(1995),** 1999

> Learn about the year of heart, sweat, and muscle that transformed the Amherst Lady Hurricanes basketball team into state champions.

Insider's Guide to the Colleges, Yale Daily News **(1970),** 1991

> This irreverent manual explores current trends in the changing college scene and supplements standard guides.

Intimate Play: Creating Romance in Everyday Life, William Betcher **(1987),** 1991

> These playful strategies may help you bond with family and friends, spouses or partners.

Joining the Tribe: Growing Up Gay and Lesbian in the '90s, Linnea Due **(1995),** 1999

> Being young and gay in America means surviving cruelty, abuse, and isolation, as these individual stories of courage from teens around the country attest.

The Joy of Sects: A Spirited Guide to the World's Religious Traditions, Peter Occhiogrosso **(1994),** 1999

> This lively, easy to understand guidebook is for everyone from the faithful believer to the curious doubter.

Keepers of the Earth: Native American Stories and Environmental Activities for Children, Michael J. Caduto and Joseph Bruchac **(1988),** 1991

> This manual provides insights into the Native American world through stories, recipes, and outdoor activities.

Living by the Word: Selected Writings, 1973–1987, Alice Walker **(1988),** 1994

> Walker's essays on race, politics, women, and life are collected in this volume.

The Lonely Days Were Sundays: Reflections of a Jewish Southerner, Eli N. Evans **(1993),** 1994

> A Jewish Southerner shares his reflections on his life and society.

Maus: A Survivor's Tale. Volume I: My Father Bleeds History, Art Spiegelman **(1986),** 1994, 1999

> Using comic book format, the author chronicles his father's experience of the Holocaust and its impact on his family.

Maus: A Survivor's Tale. Volume II: And Here My Troubles Began, Art Spiegelman **(1991),** 1994, 1999

> Spiegelman continues his comic book story about his father and the Holocaust.

The Measure of Our Success: A Letter to My Children and Yours, Marian Wright Edelman **(1992)**, 1994, 1999

> A child advocate shares her thoughts on values, raising families, and the future of our country.

Minding the Body, Mending the Mind, Joan Borysenko **(1987)**, 1991

> Harvard Medical School presents an integrated approach to healing based on meditation, diet, anxiety release, exercise, and relaxation.

The Miracle of Language, Richard Lederer **(1991)**, 1994

> Words are often used incorrectly, and the results can be humorous.

The Most Beautiful House in the World, Witold Rybczynski **(1989)**, 1999

> The author's dream of building a boat evolves into the building of a home, a process he uses to explain complex architectural ideas.

Move Your Shadow: South Africa, Black and White, Joseph Lelyveld **(1985)**, 1988, 1991

> From a personal point of view, the author describes the South African conflict.

Mythology, Edith Hamilton **(1942)**, 1971, 1976, 1982, 1988, 1999

> Gods and heroes, their clashes and adventures, come alive in this splendid retelling of the Greek, Roman, and Norse myths.

The New Our Bodies, Ourselves, Boston Women's Health Book Collective **(1992)**, 1994

> This revised edition of the 1973 classic examines the total implications of womanhood, from the physical to the psychological.

The New World of Philosophy, Abraham Kaplan **(1961)**, 1971, 1976

> Kaplan interprets the main movements in modern philosophic thought, including existentialism, Freudian psychology, Communism, Buddhism, Chinese philosophy, and Zen.

One Boy at War: My Life in the AIDS Underground, Paul Sergios **(1993)**, 1994

> Those suffering from AIDS take desperate measures in their efforts to survive.

One Child, Torey L. Hayden **(1980)**, 1982

> A severely abused and emotionally disturbed child gradually realizes her potential with the help of a courageous teacher.

The Other Side of the River: A Story of Two Towns, a Death, and America's Dilemma, Alex Kotlowitz **(1998)**, 1999

> Geographically, only a river separates two closely neighboring towns, but the murder mystery surrounding the death of a young black man exposes a deeply rooted racial divide.

Philosophy: An Introduction, John Herman Randall Jr. and Justus Buchler **(1942),** 1971

> The different branches of philosophy—aesthetics, ethics, epistemology, logic, metaphysics, and axiology—are explained.

The Portable World Bible, Robert O. Ballou (ed.) **(1976),** 1976, 1982, 1988

> This Bible covers the Hindu, Buddhist, Parsi, Judeo-Christian, Moslem, Confucian, and Taoist religious traditions and includes background information on each.

The Power of Myth, Joseph Campbell, with Bill Moyers **(1988),** 1991, 1994

> Themes and symbols present in our daily lives reflect many world religions and mythologies.

Prisoner without a Name, Cell without a Number, Jacobo Timerman **(1981),** 1982

> A master journalist recounts his imprisonment and torture in an Argentine prison and speaks out for human rights.

Race: How Blacks and Whites Think and Feel about the American Obsession, Studs Terkel **(1992),** 1994

> Interviews uncover the full range of America's views on racial issues.

Rachel and Her Children: Homeless Families in America, Jonathan Kozol **(1988),** 1991

> Men, women, and children who are residents of a hotel for the homeless in New York discuss their predicament.

The Road Less Traveled, M. Scott Peck **(1985),** 1991

> An exploration of the nature of love relationships and ways that psychiatry and religion enrich our lives.

A Sand County Almanac, Aldo Leopold **(1949),** 1994

> Leopold shares his present and future visions of a natural world.

Soul on Ice, Eldridge Cleaver **(1968),** 1971, 1994

> Through essays and open letters written while in prison, Eldridge Cleaver expresses the inner feelings and drives of the outraged African American man.

The Souls of Black Folk: Essays and Sketches, W. E. B. DuBois **(1903),** 1994, 1999

> Educator DuBois describes the lives and history of African American farmers, including the career of Booker T. Washington.

The Story of Philosophy: The Lives and Opinions of the Greater Philosophers, Will Durant **(1926),** 1976, 1982, 1988

> Certain personalities dominate the story of philosophy.

Summerhill: A Radical Approach to Child Rearing, Alexander Sutherland Neill **(1960),** 1976

> A famous experimental school where freedom and nonrepression create a different kind of learning environment is described.

The Telling of the World: Native American Stories and Art, W. S. Penn **(1996)**, 1999

Traditional and contemporary legends, stories, and art from many tribes explain our world and its lifeforms.

Terrorism: A Special Kind of Violence, Margaret O. Hyde and Elizabeth H. Forsyth **(1987)**, 1991

The authors explore the origin of terrorism and discuss the political, religious, and psychological implications of this type of violence.

Theory of Literature, René Wellek and Austin Warren **(1949)**, 1971

This theory of criticism examines the nature, functions, form, and contents of literature, rather than the environment that influences its creation.

There Are No Children Here: The Story of Two Boys Growing Up in the Other America, Alex Kotlowitz **(1991)**, 1994

Two young boys struggle to survive in one of Chicago's worst housing projects.

Thinking Out Loud: On the Personal, the Political, the Public, and the Private, Anna Quindlen **(1993)**, 1994

Op-Ed pieces from the *New York Times* underscore Quindlen's thoughts on human rights, abortion, and justice.

The Third Wave, Alvin Toffler **(1980)**, 1982

A futuristic look at what Toffler perceives to be civilization's imminent entrance into a new age of social development.

Thirty Days to a More Powerful Vocabulary, Wilfred John Funk and Norman Lewis **(1988)**, 1991

The English vocabulary of educated people can be mastered with these useful techniques.

A Tribe Apart: A Journey into the Heart of American Adolescence, Patricia Hersch **(1998)**, 1999

An intimate three-year journey through contemporary adolescence with eight "typical" teens reveals a separate culture spawned not from personal choice, but rather from adult alienation and abandonment.

Two Old Women: An Alaska Legend of Betrayal, Courage and Survival, Velma Wallis **(1994)**, 1994

Two old Athabaskan women, abandoned by their tribe, discover the strength to survive.

Understanding Media: The Extensions of Man, Marshall McLuhan **(1964)**, 1976

McLuhan suggests a study of the media as a means for better perception of our environment and our relationship to it.

Voices from the Streets: Young Former Gang Members Tell Their Stories, S. Beth Atkin **(1996),** 1999

Gang members from all races and backgrounds describe why they joined, and why—and how—they left.

The Voices of AIDS: Twelve Unforgettable People Talk about How AIDS Has Changed Their Lives, Michael Thomas Ford **(1995),** 1999

Individuals whose AIDS experiences have been catalysts for making a difference share their poignant and personal stories.

Walden, Henry David Thoreau **(1854),** 1976, 1982

Thoreau celebrates nature and independence.

A Walk across America, Peter Jenkins **(1979),** 1982

A personal account of one man's efforts to understand his own life within the context of life around him, as he takes a walking journey from Connecticut to New Orleans.

War Is a Force That Gives Us Meaning, Chris Hedges **(2002),** 2004

A Pulitzer Prize–winning author presents a passionate, thought-provoking look at wars through the ages, and exposes the myths of the culture of combat.

A Way of Love, a Way of Life: A Young Person's Introduction to What It Means to Be Gay, Frances Hanckel and John Cunningham **(1979),** 1982

This positive guide to what being homosexual means—physically, emotionally, and socially—is presented through photographs, interviews, and personal histories.

What Does It Mean to Be Human? Reverence for Life Reaffirmed by Responses from around the World, Frederick Franck, Janis Roze, and Richard Connolly (eds.) **(2000),** 2004

Thought-provoking essays on one of the most essential questions one can ask.

Who's to Know? Information, the Media, and Public Awareness, Ann E. Weiss **(1990),** 1994

Who decides what's reported on TV and in the papers?

Working: People Talk about What They Do All Day and How They Feel about What They Do, Studs Terkel **(1974),** 1976, 1982

Terkel interviews an industrial spy, a jockey, a nurse, and many others who reveal that the American feeling for work ranges from utter indifference to total commitment.

The Worldly Philosophers: The Lives, Times, and Ideas of the Great Economic Thinkers, Robert L. Heilbroner **(1953),** 1971, 1976, 1982, 1988

The lives and doctrines of David Ricardo, the Utopians, Karl Marx, Thorstein Veblen, and John Maynard Keynes are explored.

Yen! Japan's New Financial Empire and Its Threat to America, Daniel Burstein **(1988),** 1991

An analysis of Japanese corporate politics reveals the influence of Japanese business on the global economy.

MUSIC

And who that wasn't there in the beginning, who didn't experience the joyous creation of (to quote Sly Stone) a whole new thing, can say that this feeling is wrong? But in return, we have gained the most significant and most innovative cultural force since the emergence of rock 'n' roll in the 1950's. Hip hop has quite simply changed the world, and after years of fighting off the stigma that it was surely nothing more than a passing fad, the time has come to take a look back, to examine everything that has brought the music to the extraordinary, hard-fought status it enjoys today. The time has come to recognize.

From *The Vibe History of Hip Hop,*
edited by Alan Light

The Beatles, Hunter Davies **(1968),** 1982

An authorized biography of the Beatles who, as the most influential musicians of the sixties, have left an indelible mark on contemporary music.

The Big Band Years, Bruce Crowther and Mike Pinfold **(1988),** 1991

Jazz greats collaborate to found the big band style of the "swing era" in the 1930s.

The Black Chord, David Corio and Vivien Goldman **(1999),** 2004

The often painful evolution of African American music is explored with a funky text and lively photographs.

Black Music in America: A History through Its People, James Haskins **(1987),** 1991

African American music and musicians had an impact historically on other types of music.

Classical Music, Clive D. Griffin **(1988),** 1991

This comprehensive and entertaining volume includes information on composers and instruments, the influence of society and world events, maps, a dateline and much more.

The Complete Idiot's Guide to Classical Music, Robert Sherman and Philip Seldon **(1997),** 1999

This practical guide will help you understand and enjoy classical music.

Conductors: A New Generation, Philip Hart **(1983),** 1988

The dreams and realities of orchestra conducting as shown through interviews with the new and rising stars of the profession, updated with a revised list of recordings.

The Country Music Book, Michael Mason (ed.) **(1985),** 1988

More than you ever thought you wanted to know: the history, the stars, the business—the works.

Country Music, U.S.A., Bill C. Malone **(1985),** 1994

Malone examines country music, including the evolution of country-pop and early country music TV shows.

Demented: The World of the Opera Diva, Ethan Mordden **(1984),** 1988, 1991

Temperamental opera stars are praised and denounced by an author with a deliciously wicked point of view.

The Glorious Ones: Classical Music's Legendary Performers, Harold C. Schonberg **(1985),** 1988, 1991

This book describes and evaluates the legendary performers in classical music, from the castrati to Pavarotti.

Glory Days: Bruce Springsteen in the 1980s, Dave Marsh **(1987),** 1988

Continuing observations on the life and career of The Boss, Bruce Springsteen.

James Brown: The Godfather of Soul; An Autobiography, James Brown and Bruce Tucker **(1986),** 1988

The "hardest-working man in show business" gives a look at what it takes to be successful, when you're born poor and African American in the richest country in the world.

Jazz, Mervyn Cooke **(1999),** 1999

Cooke provides a comprehensive guide to this uniquely American musical form.

The Joy of Music, Leonard Bernstein **(1959),** 1971, 1994, 1999

Bernstein describes all aspects of classical music.

The Latin Tinge: The Impact of Latin American Music on the United States, John Storm Roberts **(1979),** 1982

From the tango to disco, Latin American music has influenced American music over the past century.

Making It with Music: Kenny Rogers' Guide to the Music Business, Kenny Rogers and Len Epand **(1978)**, 1982

> This first-rate primer provides an understanding of the components of the music business, with Kenny Rogers adding his personal experiences.

Music and Technology, H. P. Newquist **(1989)**, 1994

> Modern artists chronicle the history and the future of music technology.

Musicians in Tune: Seventy-five Contemporary Musicians Discuss the Creative Process, Jenny Boyd **(1992)**, 1994

> An insider to the music scene interviews the biggest stars.

The New Grove Dictionary of Jazz, Barry Kernfeld (ed.) **(1988)**, 1991

> This dictionary provides comprehensive coverage of a distinctly American art form.

Nothing but the Best: The Struggle for Perfection at the Julliard School, Judith Kogan **(1987)**, 1994

> Revealed are the rigors endured by music students before and during acceptance at the Julliard School of Music.

Nowhere to Run: The Story of Soul Music, Gerri Hirshey **(1984)**, 1988

> The most recent and definitive look at soul music.

Off the Record: An Oral History of Popular Music, Joe Smith and Mitchell Fink (eds.) **(1989)**, 1991

> More than 200 music professionals of the past and present represent all types of music, including jazz, folk, country, pop, and heavy metal.

The Orchestra, Michael Hurd **(1980)**, 1982

> The history and development of the orchestra are discussed, and profiles of well-known conductors and coverage of the major orchestras are included.

Pavarotti: My Own Story, Luciano Pavarotti, with William Wright **(1981)**, 1982

> An opera singer rises to superstardom.

Pianist's Progress, Helen Drees Ruttencutter **(1979)**, 1982

> Excellence does not guarantee success at the Juilliard School of Music.

Rock of Ages: The *Rolling Stone* History of Rock and Roll, Ed Ward, Geoffrey Stokes, and Ken Tucker **(1986)**, 1988

> Three rock journalists cover rock and roll from its birth in the 1950s to almost yesterday.

Rock Star Interviews: Conversations with Leading Performers and Songwriters, Petra Zeitz **(1993)**, 1994

> A music journalist presents short biographies and in-depth interviews covering musical careers and the industry.

The *Rolling Stone* Illustrated History of Rock and Roll, Jim Miller **(1980)**, 1982, 1991

Rolling Stone magazine presents the history of rock and roll.

Say It Loud! The Story of Rap Music, K. Maurice Jones **(1994)**, 1999

From a village in west Africa to a street in Brooklyn, to MTV, rappers make the Scene.

Segovia: A Celebration of the Man and His Music, Graham Wade **(1984)**, 1988

Overcoming prejudice against the guitar as a serious instrument, Segovia becomes the founding father of the modern guitar movement.

Singing in the Spirit: African-American Sacred Quartets in New York City, Ray Allen **(1991)**, 1994

Join Allen at a gospel service as he illustrates the close relationship between gospel and popular music.

Star-Making Machinery: Inside the Business of Rock and Roll, Geoffrey Stokes **(1976)**, 1982

The accountants and disc jockeys are as important as the musicians in the popular music industry.

Starting Your Own Band: Rock, Disco, Folk, Jazz, Country and Western, Lani Van Ryzin **(1980)**, 1982

This no-nonsense guide provides basic information for starting, managing, and promoting your own musical group.

Stomping the Blues, Albert Murray **(1976)**, 1999

An afficionado gives the lowdown on what it is and its origins.

Talking Jazz: An Illustrated Oral History, Ben Sidran **(1992)**, 1994

Personal memoirs, biographical sketches, interviews, and archival photographs reveal the history of jazz.

The *Vibe* History of Hip Hop, Alan Light (ed.) **(1999)**, 2004

Vibe magazine looks at the music, dance, and fashion that have evolved into hip-hop culture.

The Virgin Directory of World Music, Philip Sweeney **(1992)**, 1994

World music is growing in popularity and is influencing other modern music genres.

Watermelon Wine: The Spirit of Country Music, Frye Gaillard **(1978)**, 1982

Country music is celebrated with an emphasis on the performers and their music.

What to Listen For in Music, Aaron Copland **(1939)**, 1976, 1982, 1999

The composer provides a basic introduction to the mysteries of musical composition and music appreciation.

Willie and Dwike: An American Profile, William Zinsser **(1984)**, 1988

> The stories of jazz musicians, improvisers, and teachers will excite and inspire new musicians.

SCIENCE AND TECHNOLOGY

The inventions and inventors in this book were picked both because they have contributed to raising human standards of living and because they are interesting good fun, if you like.

Some of them have contributed to making human life longer and healthier—medical devices, water purification, the traffic signal. Some of them helped make life more fun—TV, video games, the outboard engine. Some are ubiquitous—plastics, the computer mouse. Some serve the human desire to wander—the auto assembly line. But they have all combined to make us what we are.

From *Inventing Modern America,*
by David E. Brown

50 Simple Things You Can Do to Save the Earth, Earth Works Group **(1989)**, 1991

> Everyone can help to save the earth if they use these suggestions in their daily lives.

African Exodus: The Origins of Modern Humanity, Christopher Stringer and Robin McKie **(1997)**, 1999

> The authors support the theory of a single origin of modern humanity with paleoanthropological, archaeological, and DNA evidence.

Atom: An Odyssey from the Big Bang to Life on Earth . . . and Beyond, Lawrence M. Krauss **(2001)**, 2004

> Follow a single oxygen atom on a fantastic voyage from the beginning of the universe and far into the future.

Being Born, Sheila Kitzinger **(1986)**, 1991

> Intrauterine photographs explain the wonders of gestation and birth.

Blind Watchers of the Sky: The People and Ideas That Shaped Our View of the Universe, Rocky Kolb **(1996)**, 1999

> Kolb delivers a witty and lively history of astronomy and cosmology.

Bones of Contention: Controversies in the Search for Human Origins, Roger Lewin **(1987)**, 1991

> The description of a series of episodes in paleoanthropology brings to light the ongoing debate about the origin of humans.

A Brief History of Time: From the Big Bang to Black Holes, Stephen W. Hawking **(1988)**, 1991, 1994, 1999

> Cosmology becomes understandable as the author discusses the origin, evolution, and fate of our universe.

Brighter than a Thousand Suns: A Personal History of the Atomic Scientists, Robert Jungk **(1958)**, 1976, 1982

> This vivid account of the development of the atomic bomb achieves continuing relevance by focusing on the moral and psychological problems related to weapons research.

Bully for Brontosaurus: Reflections in Natural History, Stephen Jay Gould **(1991)**, 1994

> Essays offer thoughts on evolution and other scientific principles.

Chaos: Making a New Science, James Gleick **(1987)**, 1994

> Gleick chronicles the development of chaos, the complex new science.

The Cognitive Computer: On Language, Learning, and Artificial Intelligence, Roger C. Schank and Peter G. Childers **(1984)**, 1988

> Artificial intelligence experts put computers into perspective and indicate future uses, especially in education.

The Complete Book of Pregnancy and Childbirth, Sheila Kitzinger **(1984)**, 1991

> Here's everything you need to know about the emotional and physical changes that occur during the first nine months of human life.

Cosmos, Carl Sagan **(1980)**, 1982, 1991

> A universal history of the galaxy presents choices for the future.

Darwin's Century: Evolution and the Men Who Discovered It, Loren C. Eiseley **(1958)**, 1971, 1976, 1982, 1988

> There have been evolutionary theories from the Renaissance to the twentieth century.

The Demon in the Freezer: A True Story, Richard Preston **(2002)**, 2004

> A striking portrait of smallpox makes readers uncomfortably aware that it could rise again as a biological weapon of mass destruction.

Dinner at the New Gene Café: How Genetic Engineering Is Changing What We Eat, How We Live, and the Global Politics of Food, Bill Lambrecht **(2001)**, 2004

> Lambrecht traces the scientific and political controversies surrounding the use of genetically modified organisms and the food we eat.

Don Coyote: The Good Times and the Bad Times of a Much Maligned American Original, Dayton O. Hyde **(1986),** 1991

A rancher defends the place of coyotes in the environmental scheme of things after rescuing and caring for one of the breed.

Dr. Tatiana's Sex Advice to All Creation: The Definitive Guide to the Evolutionary Biology of Sex, Olivia Judson **(2002),** 2004

A "Dear Abby" style science column that answers the what, when, where, why, who, and how of a fascinating variety of sexual activity for all creatures, great and small.

The Dream Is Alive, Barbara Embury **(1990),** 1994

Join Embury on a typical shuttle flight using photographs from a 1984 mission.

El Niño: Unlocking the Secrets of the Master Weather-Maker, J. Madeleine Nash **(2002),** 2004

Hard work and chance lead to the discovery of El Niño and La Niña, powerful climactic systems that we still struggle to understand.

Eureka! Scientific Breakthroughs That Changed the World, Leslie Alan Horvitz **(2002),** 2004

Horvitz explores the dramatic events and thought processes of twelve great minds that lead to profound scientific discoveries. The author examines the impact of these discoveries on the way we live, think, and view the world around us.

Fermat's Enigma: The Epic Quest to Solve the World's Greatest Mathematical Problem, Simon Singh **(1997),** 1999

A Princeton professor pursues a lifelong dream of solving a 350-year-old mathematical puzzle.

The Five Senses, F. Gonzalez-Crussi **(1989),** 1991

Constant repetition on the human senses leads the author into a remembrance of his past.

Gödel, Escher, Bach: An Eternal Golden Braid, Douglas R. Hofstadter **(1979),** 1982

Math, computers, art, music, and puzzles combined in a "fugue on minds and machines."

Gods, Graves, and Scholars: The Story of Archeology, C. W. Ceram **(1951),** 1971, 1976, 1982, 1988

This work reviews archaeological discoveries of the last two centuries—in Pompeii, Troy, Crete, Egypt, Assyria, Babylonia, Sumeria, and the Yucatan—and introduces the people who made them.

The Golden Ratio: The Story of Phi, the World's Most Astonishing Number, Mario Livio **(2002),** 2004

A captivating journey through art and architecture, botany and biology, physics and mathematics, this ratio, 1.6180339887. . . impacts so many facets of our lives that it has fascinated us through the ages.

Gorillas in the Mist, Dian Fossey **(1983),** 1991

Observing and defending the endangered mountain gorilla in Africa became Dian Fossey's life work and her obsession.

Great Projects: The Epic Story of the Building of America, from the Taming of the Mississippi to the Invention of the Internet, James Tobin **(2001),** 2004

Milestones of engineering and vision that connected us and moved a nation forward.

The Greenhouse Effect, Kathlyn Gay **(1986),** 1991

Rising levels of carbon dioxide in the atmosphere are causing changes in the earth's climate.

How the World Was One: Beyond the Global Village, Arthur C. Clarke **(1992),** 1994

International telecommunications are changing the way we view ourselves and our world.

Hydrogen: The Essential Element, John S. Rigden **(2002),** 2004

A fascinating history is revealed in this probe of a scientific giant, the hydrogen atom.

In Code: A Mathematical Journey, Sarah Flannery and David Flannery **(2001),** 2004

One teenager's discoveries in the science of cryptography dramatically impact the modern world.

In Suspect Terrain, John McPhee **(1983),** 1991, 1999

Traveling along I-80 with geologist Anita Harris, McPhee describes the geologic features that reveal the history of the Appalachians.

In the Shadow of Man, Jane Goodall **(1983),** 1991

Goodall describes the chimpanzee group she studied in the Gombe Stream Chimpanzee Reserve in Tanzania.

Innumeracy: Mathematical Illiteracy and Its Consequences, John Allen Paulos **(1988),** 1999

Paulos illustrates the importance of understanding and the consequences of misunderstanding mathematical concepts in everyday life.

Insect Lives: Stories of Mystery and Romance from a Hidden World, Erich Hoyt and Ted Schultz **(1999),** 2004

Hoyt and Schultz compile a diverse collection of brief essays and illustrations that entices readers to explore the fascinating and mysterious world of insects.

Inventing Modern America: From the Microwave to the Mouse, David E. Brown **(2002),** 2004

Whose idea was it? The human stories and faces behind American scientific and technological innovations and achievements.

Invention by Design: How Engineers Get from Thought to Thing, Henry Petroski **(1996),** 1999

Using examples from paper clips to monumental bridges, Petroski shows how engineers work.

The Language of Cities, Fran P. Hosken **(1968),** 1971

An architect and city planner shows how cities are places of scale and space, light and shadow, color and texture, form and movement.

Last Breath: Cautionary Tales from the Limits of Human Endurance, Peter Stark **(2001),** 2004

Whether the danger is hypothermia, mountain sickness, or cerebral malaria, this blend of adventure and science takes you to the absolute edges of human endurance.

Last Chance to See, Douglas Adams and Mark Carwardine **(1991),** 1994

Adams delivers a humorous, touching view of his travels to find endangered species around the world.

Laying Waste: The Poisoning of America by Toxic Chemicals, Michael H. Brown **(1980),** 1982, 1988

The improper disposal of toxic chemicals in the Love Canal area of Niagara Falls, N.Y., is one of many situations chronicled in this book, which serves as a call to action on a serious environmental problem.

Licit and Illicit Drugs: The Consumers Union Report, Edward M. Brecher **(1972),** 1982

An authoritative reference work about drugs used in the United States.

The Lives of a Cell: Notes of a Biology Watcher, Lewis Thomas **(1974),** 1976, 1982, 1988, 1999

These essays offer an optimistic scientist's view of a wide variety of subjects.

The Living Planet: A Portrait of the Earth, David Attenborough **(1984),** 1994

Various habitats expand the vision of planet Earth.

The Loch Ness Monster: Opposing Viewpoints, Robert D. San Souci **(1989),** 1991

The presentation of diverse viewpoints allows the reader to form independent judgments about "Nessie."

Longitude: The True Story of a Lone Genius Who Solved the Greatest Scientific Problem of His Time, Dava Sobel **(1995),** 2004

The little known story behind the greatest innovation in navigational science: an 18th-century version of the Global Positioning System (GPS).

Lucy: The Beginnings of Human Kind, Donald C. Johanson and Maitland A. Edey **(1980),** 1982, 1988

> An account of the discovery of a 3.5 million-year-old prehuman skeleton and its impact on the study of our ancestors.

Madness: A Brief History, Roy Porter **(2002),** 2004

> What is meant when we say "madness"? Examine the wide range of possibilities this question covers, from witches to electric shock therapy to Prozac.

Mathematics in Western Culture, Morris Kline **(1953),** 1976

> Kline explores the role of mathematics as it relates to other disciplines.

The Medical Detectives, Berton Roueché **(1984),** 1991

> Scientists, doctors, and epidemiologists work to discover the causes of many different diseases.

The Mismeasure of Man, Stephen Jay Gould **(1981),** 1999

> Gould's history of the attempt to quantify intelligence could be called the "misuse of science."

The Modern Mind: An Intellectual History of the 20th Century, Peter Watson **(2001),** 2004

> It was a time of marvelous optimism and belief in the perfectibility of man through science and new ideas. Explore the thoughts of the major players from Freud to Einstein, and places from Kitty Hawk to the distant reaches of the universe.

Mothers of Invention: From the Bra to the Bomb; Forgotten Women and Their Unforgettable Ideas, Ethlie Ann Vare and Greg Ptacek **(1988),** 1994

> Women inventors overcome obstacles.

Next of Kin: What Chimpanzees Have Taught Me about Who We Are, Roger Fouts **(1997),** 1999

> Describing his career of communicating with chimpanzees, Fouts explains evolutionary, genetic, and emotional bonds with our next of kin.

The Next Whole Earth Catalog: Access to Tools, Stewart Brand (ed.) **(1980),** 1982

> Tools aid in the process of education and the shaping of the environment.

The Number Devil: A Mathematical Adventure, Hans Magnus Enzensberger **(1998),** 2004

> A boy dreams a devil who guides him through a colorful, Alice in Wonderland-like world of mathematical concepts.

Number: The Language of Science, Tobias Dantzig **(1954),** 1971

> This classic on the history of numbers, "the world's universal language," explains concepts, ideas, and their implementation.

One Two Three—Infinity: Facts and Speculations of Science, George Gamow **(1961),** 1971

> This collection brings together some of the most interesting facts and theories of modern science.

Operating Manual for Spaceship Earth, R. Buckminster Fuller **(1969),** 1976, 1982

> The inventor of the geodesic dome admonishes us to consider our planet as a complete environment.

The Perfect Storm: A True Story of Men against the Sea, Sebastian Junger **(1997),** 1999

> Haunting premonitions didn't save seven fisherman from the ferocious and deadly power of the sea.

Planet Earth, Jonathan Weiner **(1986),** 1991

> This book summarizes current discoveries and current thinking in the earth sciences.

The Primal Teen: What the New Discoveries about the Teenage Brain Tell Us about Our Kids, Barbara Strauch **(2001),** 2004

> Ever wonder what makes teens tick? A tour of the teenage brain reveals startling new research about this pivotal and exciting time of life.

Promised the Moon: The Untold Story of the First Women in the Space Race, Stephanie Nolen **(2002),** 2004

> The history of women in aviation and as astronauts is revealed in this compelling story.

The Sea around Us, Rachel Carson **(1951),** 1971

> This scientific and poetic account reveals the changes in the sea that began over two billion years ago, as well as explorations and important developments in oceanographic research.

The Secret Family: Twenty-four Hours inside the Mysterious World of Our Minds and Bodies, David Bodanis **(1997),** 1999

> The unseen world around us and within our bodies is shown in vivid detail as we follow a typical family through their day.

The Seven Daughters of Eve: The Science That Reveals Our Genetic Ancestry, Bryan Sykes **(2001),** 2004

> Fascinating mitochondrial DNA evidence supports the idea that almost all modern Europeans are descended from just seven women.

A Short History of Nearly Everything, Bill Bryson **(2003),** 2004

> A renowned travel writer brings complex scientific concepts to life by describing how the universe and life as we know it came to be.

Should Drugs Be Legalized? Susan Neiburg Terkel **(1990),** 1994

> Following an overview of drug use in the United States, Terkel discusses the regulation of illegal drugs.

Silent Spring, Rachel Carson **(1964),** 1971, 1976, 1988, 1994, 1999

This landmark book gave birth to the environmental movement.

The Sportsmedicine Book, Gabe Mirkin and Marshall Hoffman **(1978),** 1982

Sports medicine focuses on physical and psychological effects of physical activity, with emphasis on preventing injury.

Stephen Hawking's Universe, John Boslough **(1984),** 1991

Hawking's theories on the universe in general, and black holes in particular.

Stiff: The Curious Lives of Human Cadavers, Mary Roach **(2003),** 2004

Discover the amazing life-after-death adventures of human bodies in this examination of how medical and research scientists use cadavers to make our lives better.

T. Rex and the Crater of Doom, Walter Alvarez **(1997),** 1999

Geologist Alvarez presents the development of the impact theory of dinosaur extinction as the adventure/mystery it was.

The Two Cultures, C. P. Snow **(1964),** 1971

A scientist who is also a successful novelist discusses the split between art and science.

The Universe in a Nutshell, Stephen Hawking **(2001),** 2004

The physics guru illuminates startling new theories about our world in a lavishly illustrated sequel to *A Brief History of Time*.

Virus Ground Zero: Stalking the Killer Viruses with the Centers for Disease Control, Ed Regis **(1996),** 1999

The history of the CDC is told through the handling of the Ebola outbreak in Zaire.

Water, Ice, and Stone: Science and Memory on the Antarctic Lakes, Bill Green **(1995),** 1999

A chemist investigates Antarctica's ice-covered lakes and discovers beauty and poetry.

The Way Things Work, David Macaulay **(1988),** 1991

By dealing with basic principles, the author relates how approximately 350 machines function.

The What's Happening to My Body? Book for Boys: A Growing Up Guide for Parents and Sons, Lynda Madaras and Dane Saavedra **(1984),** 1991

Here's detailed information about male bodies as they change and mature.

The What's Happening to My Body? Book for Girls: A Growing Up Guide for Parents and Daughters, Lynda Madaras and Area Madaras **(1987),** 1991

Here's detailed information about female bodies as they change and mature.

Where Wizards Stay Up Late: The Origins of the Internet, Katie Hafner and Matthew Lyon **(1996),** 1999

> The origins of the world's first computer network are explained, with tales of the motivations, breakthroughs, and personalities that created it.

The Youngest Science: Notes of a Medicine-Watcher, Lewis Thomas **(1983),** 1994

> A single lifetime serves as the framework for this history of medicine.

SOCIAL SCIENCES

Venola tries to read as much as she can during her free time. She is one of the few students in her AP English class who reads for pleasure, which is one reason she scored better than most of her classmates on her PSAT test.

From *And Still We Rise,*
by Miles Corwin

An American Insurrection: The Battle of Oxford, Mississippi, 1962, William Doyle **(1962),** 2004

> When James Meredith decided to integrate the University of Mississippi, it caused the worst crisis in American history since the Civil War.

And Still We Rise: The Trials and Triumphs of Twelve Gifted Inner-City Students, Miles Corwin **(2000),** 2004

> Twelve seniors from Crenshaw High School's Advanced Placement English class in Los Angeles dream of going to college, but the harsh realities of their lives threaten to derail their plans.

Crossing Over: A Mexican Family on the Migrant Trail, Ruben Martinez **(2001),** 2004

> Martinez explores the powerful forces that drive men, women, and even children to risk their lives crossing the border illegally from Mexico to the United States to find work.

Damned Lies and Statistics: Untangling Numbers from the Media, Politicians, and Activists, Joel Best **(2001),** 2004

> Do you know the difference between "good" and "bad" statistics or how statistics and public policy are connected?

The Dance of Legislation, Eric Redman **(1973),** 1976, 1982

> A Senate aide demystifies the legislative process while conveying its attendant drama, frustration, and comedy.

Fast Food Nation: The Dark Side of the All-American Meal, Eric Schlosser **(2001),** 2004

> The growth of the fast food industry has changed America's eating habits and greatly impacted agriculture, the meatpacking industry, the minimum wage, and other aspects of American life.

Fires in the Mirror: Crown Heights, Brooklyn, and Other Identities, Anna Deavere Smith **(1999),** 2004

> A dramatic look at the Crown Heights riots and race in the United States through the voices of twenty-three fascinating and unique characters, based on interviews with real people.

The Gatekeepers: Inside the Admissions Process of a Premier College, Jacques Steinberg **(2002),** 2004

> Getting in—who and what drives the college admissions cycle? Find out in a behind the scenes look at Wesleyan University through the eyes of an admissions officer seeking members for the class of 2004.

Geeks: How Two Lost Boys Rode the Internet Out of Idaho, Jon Katz **(2001),** 2004

> Eric and Jesse, poor students and online geeks, find their obsession with computers and technology is their ticket to college and success.

Gideon's Trumpet, Anthony Lewis **(1964),** 1994

> One determined convict changes the American legal system.

Guns, Germs, and Steel: The Fates of Human Societies, Jared Diamond **(1997),** 1999, 2004

> Why do some societies become rich and powerful while others remain poor and powerless? Diamond contends that three elements, guns, germs and steel, determined the course of history.

Light at the Edge of the World: A Journey through the Realm of Vanishing Cultures, Wade Davis **(2001),** 2004

> Through photographs and eloquent text, the author unveils the diversity and unique quality of human culture around the world.

Man and His Symbols, Carl G. Jung **(1964),** 1991, 1994

> A psychiatrist introduces the concept of the collective unconscious.

Media Sexploitation, Wilson Bryan Key **(1977),** 1991

> A look at the complex world of advertising reveals the way consumers are led to make purchases based on imagery.

Megatrends: Ten New Directions Transforming Our Lives, John Naisbitt **(1983),** 1988

> Naisbitt investigates the societal changes of the 1980s.

The Middle of Everywhere: The World's Refugees Come to Our Town, Mary Pipher **(2002),** 2004

> An exploration of the difficulties and struggles of refugees settled by the United States government in Lincoln, Nebraska, as they try to adjust and build a life in America.

Millennium: Tribal Wisdom and the Modern World, David Maybury-Lewis **(1992),** 1994

> Maybury-Lewis profiles members of several tribal cultures.

Naked Economics: Undressing the Dismal Science, Charles Wheelan **(2002),** 2004

> Without using charts, graphs, or jargon, Wheelan makes economics understandable, even interesting, as he demystifies basic concepts and applies them to everyday life.

The New Industrial State, John Kenneth Galbraith **(1967),** 1971

> Galbraith urges that we drastically reexamine our concepts of the market place, the state, public versus private, and the impact of large corporations on our times.

Newjack: Guarding Sing Sing, Ted Conover **(2000),** 2004

> Gripping and sometimes humorous insider's look at Sing Sing prison, through the eyes of a writer who worked for a year as a corrections officer.

Nickel and Dimed: On (Not) Getting By in America, Barbara Ehrenreich **(2001),** 2004

> Can you really survive on minimum wage? To find out, the author left her middle-class life for a year to see what life is really like for America's working poor.

No Matter How Loud I Shout: A Year in the Life of Juvenile Court, Edward Humes **(1996),** 1999

> Humes paints a tragic and heartbreaking portrait of the chaos characterizing America's juvenile justice system where, as one inmate writes, "my screams have no voice, no matter how loud I shout."

Occupational Outlook Handbook, U.S. Bureau of Labor Statistics **(annual),** 1991

> This handbook lists qualifications, potential earnings, working conditions, employment trends and job opportunities for many careers.

On Aggression, Konrad Lorenz **(1966),** 1971, 1976, 1982, 1988

> A thought-provoking analysis of the fighting instinct in beast and man which is directed against members of the same species.

On Violence, Hannah Arendt **(1970),** 1971, 1976, 1991

> The author explores the reasons why violence is so prevalent in modern society.

The Other America: Poverty in the United States, Michael Harrington **(1962),** 1971

> This book shocked America into realizing the extent to which its affluence is creating poverty.

Other Lives, Other Selves: A Jungian Psychotherapist Discovers Past Lives, Roger J. Woolger **(1987)**, 1991

Case studies of reincarnation illuminate theories and strategies.

Patterns of Culture, Ruth Benedict **(1934)**, 1976, 1982

For a quarter of a century, this book has provided an introduction to the understanding of anthropology.

The Pelican History of Psychology, Robert Thomson **(1968)**, 1971

Psychology had its beginnings in philosophy and evolved through the achievements of Freud, Jung, and others.

Persepolis, Marjane Satrapi **(2002)**, 2004

Growing up in Iran wasn't all that bad, or all that different, except that Marjane wanted to be a prophet when she grew up. Dramatic black-and-white illustrations tell her story.

The Person: His and Her Development throughout the Life Cycle, Theodore Lidz **(1968)**, 1971

This treatment of personality development moves through fifteen stages from prebirth to death.

Reviving Ophelia: Saving the Selves of Adolescent Girls, Mary Pipher **(1994)**, 1999

Pipher looks at societal "girl poisoning" and the emotional and psychological havoc it wreaks on the lives of young women.

Riding the Bus with My Sister: A True Life Journey, Rachel Simon **(2002)**, 2004

Rachel Simon's sister, who has mental retardation, spends her days riding buses in the Pennsylvania city where she lives. When Rachel begins to accompany her sister on the bus, she learns a lot about her sister and her disability, and about her own limitations.

Savage Inequalities: Children in America's Schools, Jonathan Kozol **(1991)**, 1994, 1999

Kozol's stinging indictment of America's public school system advocates an equal distribution of per pupil funding to right the gross inequities in our current system.

Small Victories: The Real World of a Teacher, Her Students, and Their High School, Samuel G. Freedman **(1990)**, 1994, 1999

How does this overcrowded, underfunded inner city school send 92 percent of its graduates to college?

Speak Truth to Power: Human Rights Defenders Who Are Changing Our World, Kerry Kennedy Cuomo **(2000)**, 2004

A collection of biographical sketches and haunting photographs of ordinary people from thirty-five countries who are leading the fight to ensure basic human rights for everyone.

Sugar's Life in the Hood: The Story of a Former Welfare Mother, Sugar Turner and Tracy Bachrach Ehlers **(2003)**, 2004

> An anthropologist who befriends a welfare mother learns about her world and the strategies she uses to get off welfare and into college.

Today's Isms: Communism, Fascism, Capitalism, Socialism, William Ebenstein and Edwin Fogelman **(1985)**, 1971, 1976, 1982, 1988

> The authors provide an approach to various social systems and analyze the psychological appeal of each.

The True Believer: Thoughts on the Nature of Mass Movements, Eric Hoffer **(1951)**, 1976

> Hoffer analyzes fanaticism, nationalism, and other "isms" in terms of the psychology of mass movements.

True Notebooks, Mark Salzman **(2003)**, 2004

> When Salzman agreed to teach a writing class at Central Juvenile Hall in Los Angeles, he had no idea how moved he would be by the lives and the eloquence of his students, all high-risk violent offenders.

Tuesdays with Morrie: An Old Man, a Young Man, and Life's Greatest Lesson, Mitch Albom **(1997)**, 2004

> Mitch Albom's Tuesday night visits with his dying sociology professor, Morrie, offer valuable lessons about the art of living and dying with dignity.

Violence! Our Fastest-Growing Public Health Problem, John Langone **(1984)**, 1988

> The violence in our homes, streets, prisons, and sports arenas is examined to provide insight into the underlying causes and possible solutions to this serious social problem.

We the People: An Atlas of America's Ethnic Diversity, James Paul Allen and Eugene James Turner **(1988)**, 1991

> Maps show the ethnic makeup of the American population.

What Is Sociology? An Introduction to the Discipline and Profession, Alex Inkeles **(1964)**, 1971

> Inkeles reviews the issues facing sociology, the many varying methods, interpretations, and conceptions of man and social processes.

Why Terrorism Works: Understanding the Threat, Responding to the Challenge, Alan M. Dershowitz **(2002)**, 2004

> Focusing on the idea that terrorism is caused largely by the actions of Western governments, Dershowitz suggests steps to reduce the frequency and severity of these attacks.

OTHER NONFICTION

"So Scott, what's your next project going to be now that you've finished ZOT."

"Well, it's a bit hard to describe, Matt. It's sort of a comic book about comics."

"You mean like a history?"

"Not exactly, no, although there is some history in it . . . it's more an examination of the art-form of comics, what it's capable of, how it works." . . .

"Oh. Aren't you kind of young to be doing that sort of thing?"

From *Understanding Comics,*
by Scott McCloud

The Art of the Puppet, Bil Baird **(1965),** 1982

A classic description of the art of puppetry as performed by a famed puppeteer.

The Big Book of Magic, Patrick Page **(1976),** 1982

A treasury of tricks for aspiring magicians using cards, coins, rope, paper, rabbits, and . . . presto!

Bird by Bird: Some Instructions on Writing and Life, Anne Lamott **(1995),** 2004

Advice to the fledgling writer: "Just take it bird by bird." A gentle, anecdotal guide for beginning authors.

The Blackstone Book of Magic and Illusion, Harry Blackstone Jr. **(1985),** 1988, 1994, 1999, 2004

A well-known magician introduces readers to the history, principles, and effects of one of the oldest entertainment arts.

Broadway and Hollywood: Costumes Designed by Irene Sharaff, Irene Sharaff **(1976),** 1988

Costume designer for Hollywood and Broadway, Sharaff contrasts stage and screen design and compares the fashion and entertainment worlds.

Clowns, John H. Towsen **(1976),** 1982

A loving look at the clown throughout history and the world, with descriptions of popular clown acts.

Comedy Greats: A Celebration of Comic Genius Past and Present, Barry Took **(1989),** 1991

The author looks at various geniuses of comedy.

Completely Mad: A History of the Comic Book and Magazine, Maria Reidelbach **(1991),** 1994

> Biographical sketches of contributors dominate this illustrated behind-the-scenes look at *Mad* magazine.

Getting It Down: How to Put Your Ideas on Paper, Judi Kesselman-Turkel and Franklynn Peterson **(1983),** 1991

> This manual can help organize your ideas into a well-planned, clearly written presentation.

How to Read Literature like a Professor: A Lively and Entertaining Guide to Reading between the Lines, Thomas C. Foster **(2003),** 2004

> Every author leaves clues to lead readers deeper into the inner meanings of their writings. Learn how to follow literary bread crumbs in any story.

Making Art Safely: Alternative Methods and Materials in Drawing, Painting, Printmaking, Graphic Design, and Photography, Merle Spandorfer **(1993),** 1994

> Potentially dangerous chemicals and other physical hazards threaten the artist, and Spandorfer reveals alternative materials and methods for safer art.

Mime: A Playbook of Silent Fantasy, Kay Hamblin **(1978),** 1982

> Learn to communicate without words and discover the joy of expressing your ideas with your entire self.

Passing the Hat: Street Performers in America, Patricia J. Campbell **(1981),** 1982

> Campbell interviews performers whose stage is the street and whose audience is the passerby.

Performance: Live Art 1909 to the Present, RoseLee Goldberg **(1979),** 1988

> Live art evolves from the turn-of-the-century futurist to punk rock.

Performing Arts: An Illustrated Guide, Michael Billington **(1980),** 1982

> Performing arts include opera, plays, concert, dance, pantomime, circus, musicals, magic, puppets, jazz, and much more.

Ringmaster! My Year on the Road with "The Greatest Show on Earth," Kristopher Antekeier and Greg Aunapu **(1989),** 1991

> A twenty-seven-year-old aspiring song-and-dance man gives a candid account of the year he worked as ringmaster for Ringling Brothers, Barnum, and Bailey Circus.

Staying Power: Performing Artists Talk about Their Lives, Peter Barton **(1980),** 1982

> Young musicians, actors, and dancers share their experiences, good or bad, in attaining their personal and professional goals.

Treasures of the American Arts and Crafts Movement, 1890–1920, Tod M. Volpe and Beth Cathers **(1988),** 1991

> Designers, architects, and firms work in ceramics, metals, lighting, and other artifacts of the arts-and-crafts movement.

Understanding Comics: The Invisible Art, Scott McCloud **(1993),** 1999

> A comic book asks and answers the question of whether or not comics are a literary form.

The Way to Cook, Julia Child **(1989),** 1991

> An advocate of fine food and good eating presents French and American cooking styles and recipes.

Woe Is I: The Grammarphobe's Guide to Better English in Plain English, Patricia T. O'Conner **(1996),** 2004

> When there's something important to say, how you say it counts. Pronouns, antecedents, and more grammar-ology made fun and painless.

PART TWO

Lists by Year, 2004–1959

2004–1959

2004

History

Sagas of Icelanders: A Selection

Alexander, Caroline — The Endurance: Shackleton's Legendary Antarctic Expedition

Aronson, Marc — Witch-Hunt: Mysteries of the Salem Witch Trials

Berg, A. Scott — Lindbergh

Carroll, Andrew — War Letters: Extraordinary Correspondence from American Wars

Danticat, Edwidge — The Farming of Bones

Ellis, Joseph J. — Founding Brothers: The Revolutionary Generation

Frank, Mitch — Understanding September 11th: Answering Questions about the Attacks on America

Geras, Adèle — Troy

Glancy, Diane — Stone Heart: A Novel of Sacajawea

Hansen, Drew D. — The Dream: Martin Luther King, Jr., and the Speech That Inspired a Nation

Harper, Kenn — Give Me My Father's Body: The Life of Minik, the New York Eskimo

Heat-Moon, William Least — Columbus in the Americas

Lanier, Shannon, and Jane Feldman — Jefferson's Children: The Story of One American Family

Marrin, Albert — Terror of the Spanish Main: Sir Henry Morgan and His Buccaneers

McCullough, David	*John Adams*
Rogasky, Barbara	*Smoke and Ashes: The Story of the Holocaust*
Shapiro, Harvey (ed.)	*Poets of World War II*
Starkey, David	*Six Wives: The Queens of Henry VIII*
Tuchman, Barbara W.	*A Distant Mirror: The Calamitous 14th Century*
Ung, Loung	*First They Killed My Father: A Daughter of Cambodia Remembers*
Von Drehle, David	*Triangle: The Fire That Changed America*
Watson, Peter	*The Modern Mind: An Intellectual History of the 20th Century*
Weatherford, Jack	*Indian Givers: How the Indians of the Americas Transformed the World*
Winchester, Simon	*Krakatoa: The Day the World Exploded—August 27, 1883*

Humanities

Adler, Sabine	*Lovers in Art*
Belloli, Andrea P. A.	*Exploring World Art*
Bissinger, H. G.	*Friday Night Lights: A Town, a Team, and a Dream*
Blackstone, Harry, Jr.	*The Blackstone Book of Magic and Illusion*
Brassaï	*Brassaï: Letters to My Parents*
Card, Orson Scott	*Sarah*
Chevalier, Tracy	*Girl with a Pearl Earring*
Colton, Larry	*Counting Coup: A True Story of Basketball and Honor on the Little Big Horn*
Corio, David, and Vivien Goldman	*The Black Chord*
Crutcher, Chris	*Whale Talk*
Franck, Frederick, Janis Roze, and Richard Connolly (eds.)	*What Does It Mean to Be Human? Reverence for Life Reaffirmed by Responses from around the World*
Garfunkel, Trudy	*On Wings of Joy: The Story of Ballet from the 16th Century to Today*
Goldberg, Myla	*Bee Season*

Greenberg, Jan (ed.)	*Heart to Heart: New Poems Inspired by Twentieth Century American Art*
Hedges, Chris	*War Is a Force That Gives Us Meaning*
Howe, Peter	*Shooting under Fire: The World of the War Photographer*
King, Ross	*Brunelleschi's Dome: How a Renaissance Genius Reinvented Architecture*
Light, Alan (ed.)	*The* Vibe *History of Hip Hop*
Livingston, Lili Cockerille	*American Indian Ballerinas*
McGreevey, Tom, and Joanne L. Yeck	*Our Movie Heritage*
Perry, John	*Encyclopedia of Acting Techniques*
Sandler, Martin W.	*Photography: An Illustrated History*
Smith, Huston	*The Illustrated World's Religions: A Guide to Our Wisdom Traditions*
Vreeland, Susan	*The Passion of Artemisia*

Literature and Language Arts

Abelove, Joan	*Go and Come Back*
Allison, Dorothy	*Bastard Out of Carolina*
Alvarez, Julia	*In the Time of the Butterflies*
Anderson, Laurie Halse	*Speak*
Anderson, M. T.	*Feed*
Bagdasarian, Adam	*Forgotten Fire*
Chambers, Aidan	*Postcards from No Man's Land*
Cisneros, Sandra	*Caramelo*
Foster, Thomas C.	*How to Read Literature like a Professor: A Lively and Entertaining Guide to Reading between the Lines*
Frank, E. R.	*Life Is Funny*
Freymann-Weyr, Garret	*My Heartbeat*
Kaplow, Robert	*Me and Orson Welles*
Kingsolver, Barbara	*The Bean Trees*
Lamott, Anne	*Bird by Bird: Some Instructions on Writing and Life*

Mah, Adeline Yen — *Chinese Cinderella: The True Story of an Unwanted Daughter*

Myers, Walter Dean — *Monster*

Nye, Naomi Shihab — *19 Varieties of Gazelle: Poems of the Middle East*

O'Conner, Patricia T. — *Woe Is I: The Grammarphobe's Guide to Better English in Plain English*

Pullman, Philip — *The Golden Compass*

Reynolds, Sheri — *A Gracious Plenty*

Sapphire — *Push*

Satrapi, Marjane — *Persepolis*

Sebold, Alice — *Lucky*

Shakur, Tupac — *The Rose That Grew from Concrete*

Smith, Anna Deavere — *Fires in the Mirror: Crown Heights, Brooklyn, and Other Identities*

Science and Technology

Bradshaw, Gillian — *The Sand-Reckoner*

Brown, David E. — *Inventing Modern America: From the Microwave to the Mouse*

Bryson, Bill — *A Short History of Nearly Everything*

Enzensberger, Hans Magnus — *The Number Devil: A Mathematical Adventure*

Fagan, Brian — *The Little Ice Age: How Climate Made History, 1300–1850*

Feynman, Richard P. — *What Do You Care What Other People Think? Further Adventures of a Curious Character*

Flannery, Sarah, and David Flannery — *In Code: A Mathematical Journey*

Hawking, Stephen — *The Universe in a Nutshell*

Horvitz, Leslie Alan — *Eureka! Scientific Breakthroughs That Changed the World*

Hoyt, Erich, and Ted Schultz — *Insect Lives: Stories of Mystery and Romance from a Hidden World*

Judson, Olivia — *Dr. Tatiana's Sex Advice to All Creation: The Definitive Guide to the Evolutionary Biology of Sex*

Krauss, Lawrence M. *Atom: An Odyssey from the Big Bang to Life on Earth . . . and Beyond*

Lambrecht, Bill *Dinner at the New Gene Café: How Genetic Engineering Is Changing What We Eat, How We Live, and the Global Politics of Food*

Livio, Mario *The Golden Ratio: The Story of Phi, the World's Most Astonishing Number*

Nash, J. Madeleine *El Niño: Unlocking the Secrets of the Master Weather-Maker*

Nolen, Stephanie *Promised the Moon: The Untold Story of the First Women in the Space Race*

Porter, Roy *Madness: A Brief History*

Preston, Richard *The Demon in the Freezer: A True Story*

Rigden, John S. *Hydrogen: The Essential Element*

Roach, Mary *Stiff: The Curious Lives of Human Cadavers*

Sobel, Dava *Longitude: The True Story of a Lone Genius Who Solved the Greatest Scientific Problem of His Time*

Stark, Peter *Last Breath: Cautionary Tales from the Limits of Human Endurance*

Strauch, Barbara *The Primal Teen: What the New Discoveries about the Teenage Brain Tell Us about Our Kids*

Sykes, Bryan *The Seven Daughters of Eve: The Science That Reveals Our Genetic Ancestry*

Tobin, James *Great Projects: The Epic Story of the Building of America, from the Taming of the Mississippi to the Invention of the Internet*

Social Sciences

Albom, Mitch *Tuesdays with Morrie: An Old Man, A Young Man, and Life's Greatest Lesson*

Best, Joel *Damned Lies and Statistics: Untangling Numbers from the Media, Politicians, and Activists*

Conover, Ted *Newjack: Guarding Sing Sing*

Corwin, Miles *And Still We Rise: The Trials and Triumphs of Twelve Gifted Inner-City Students*

Cuomo, Kerry Kennedy	*Speak Truth to Power: Human Rights Defenders Who Are Changing Our World*
Davis, Wade	*Light at the Edge of the World: A Journey through the Realm of Vanishing Cultures*
Dershowitz, Alan M.	*Why Terrorism Works: Understanding the Threat, Responding to the Challenge*
Diamond, Jared	*Guns, Germs, and Steel: The Fates of Human Societies*
Doyle, William	*An American Insurrection: The Battle of Oxford, Mississippi, 1962*
Ehrenreich, Barbara	*Nickel and Dimed: On (Not) Getting By in America*
Haddon, Mark	*The Curious Incident of the Dog in the Night-Time*
Hart, Elva Treviño	*Barefoot Heart: Stories of a Migrant Child*
Hosseini, Khaled	*The Kite Runner*
Katz, Jon	*Geeks: How Two Lost Boys Rode the Internet Out of Idaho*
Latifa [pseud.]	*My Forbidden Face: Growing Up under the Taliban; A Young Woman's Story*
Martinez, Ruben	*Crossing Over: A Mexican Family on the Migrant Trail*
Pipher, Mary	*The Middle of Everywhere: The World's Refugees Come to Our Town*
Salzman, Mark	*True Notebooks*
Schlosser, Eric	*Fast Food Nation: The Dark Side of the All-American Meal*
Senna, Danzy	*Caucasia*
Simon, Rachel	*Riding the Bus with My Sister: A True Life Journey*
Smith, Zadie	*White Teeth*
Steinberg, Jacques	*The Gatekeepers: Inside the Admissions Process of a Premier College*
Turner, Sugar, and Tracy Bachrach Ehlers	*Sugar's Life in the Hood: The Story of a Former Welfare Mother*
Wheelan, Charles	*Naked Economics: Undressing the Dismal Science*

1999

Biography

Allende, Isabel	*Paula*
Ambrose, Stephen E.	*Undaunted Courage: Meriwether Lewis, Thomas Jefferson, and the Opening of the American West*
Angelou, Maya	*I Know Why the Caged Bird Sings*
Baker, Russell	*Growing Up*
Cook, Blanche Wiesen	*Eleanor Roosevelt: Vol. 1 1884–1933*
Curie, Eve	*Madame Curie: A Biography*
Douglass, Frederick	*Narrative of the Life of Frederick Douglass, an American Slave, Written by Himself*
Edelman, Bernard (ed.)	*Dear America: Letters Home from Vietnam*
Feynman, Richard P.	*"Surely You're Joking, Mr. Feynman!": Adventures of a Curious Character*
Frank, Anne	*Anne Frank: The Diary of a Young Girl*
Hockenberry, John	*Moving Violations: War Zones, Wheelchairs, and Declarations of Independence; A Memoir*
Jiang, Ji-Li	*Red Scarf Girl: A Memoir of the Cultural Revolution*
Karr, Mary	*The Liars' Club: A Memoir*
Keller, Helen	*The Story of My Life*
Khanga, Yelena	*Soul to Soul: A Black Russian American Family, 1865–1992*
Kincaid, Jamaica	*My Brother*
Malcolm X (as told to Alex Haley)	*The Autobiography of Malcolm X*
Massie, Robert K.	*Nicholas and Alexandra*
Mathabane, Mark	*Kaffir Boy: The True Story of a Black Youth's Coming of Age in Apartheid South Africa; An Autobiography*
McBride, James,	*The Color of Water: A Black Man's Tribute to His White Mother*
McCourt, Frank	*Angela's Ashes: A Memoir*
McCullough, David G.	*Truman*
Mehta, Ved	*Sound-Shadows of the New World*

Moody, Anne	*Coming of Age in Mississippi*
Mora, Pat	*House of Houses*
Robertson, James I., Jr.	*Stonewall Jackson: The Man, the Soldier, the Legend*
Rodriguez, Luis J.	*Always Running: La Vida Loca; Gang Days in L.A.*
Rodriguez, Richard	*Hunger of Memory: The Education of Richard Rodriguez: An Autobiography*
Wolff, Tobias	*This Boy's Life: A Memoir*
Wright, Richard	*Black Boy: A Record of Childhood and Youth*

Drama

Albee, Edward	*Three Tall Women*
Beckett, Samuel	*Waiting for Godot: A Tragicomedy in Two Acts*
Bernstein, Leonard, Arthur Laurents, and Stephen Sondheim	*West Side Story*
Christie, Agatha	*The Mousetrap*
Coward, Noël	*Blithe Spirit*
Fugard, Athol	*"Master Harold" . . . and the Boys*
Hansberry, Lorraine	*A Raisin in the Sun*
Hellman, Lillian	*The Little Foxes*
Ibsen, Henrik	*A Doll's House*
Ionesco, Eugène	*Rhinoceros*
Kushner, Tony	*Angels in America: A Gay Fantasia on National Themes. Part 1: Millennium Approaches; Part 2: Perestroika*
Larson, Jonathan	*Rent*
Miller, Arthur	*Death of a Salesman*
O'Neill, Eugene	*Long Day's Journey into Night*
Sartre, Jean-Paul	*No Exit*
Shakespeare, William	*King Lear*
Shaw, George Bernard	*Pygmalion*
Stoppard, Tom	*Rosencrantz and Guildenstern Are Dead*
Uhry, Alfred	*Driving Miss Daisy*

Vogel, Paula	*How I Learned to Drive*
Wilde, Oscar	*The Importance of Being Earnest*
Wilder, Thornton	*Our Town*
Williams, Tennessee	*The Glass Menagerie*
Wilson, August	*Fences*

Fiction

Agee, James	*A Death in the Family*
Allison, Dorothy	*Bastard Out of Carolina*
Alvarez, Julia	*In the Time of the Butterflies*
Anaya, Rudolfo A.	*Bless Me, Ultima*
Atwood, Margaret	*The Handmaid's Tale*
Butler, Octavia E.	*Parable of the Sower*
Card, Orson Scott	*Ender's Game*
Chopin, Kate	*The Awakening*
Cisneros, Sandra	*The House on Mango Street*
Dostoyevsky, Fyodor	*Crime and Punishment*
Ellison, Ralph	*Invisible Man*
Emecheta, Buchi	*The Bride Price*
Faulkner, William	*The Bear*
Frazier, Charles	*Cold Mountain*
Gaines, Ernest J.	*A Lesson before Dying*
Gardner, John	*Grendel*
Gibbons, Kaye	*Ellen Foster*
Heller, Joseph	*Catch-22*
Hemingway, Ernest	*A Farewell to Arms*
Hesse, Hermann	*Siddhartha*
Huxley, Aldous	*Brave New World*
Keneally, Thomas	*Schindler's List*
King, Laurie R.	*The Beekeeper's Apprentice; or, On the Segregation of the Queen*
Kosinski, Jerzy N.	*The Painted Bird*
Le Guin, Ursula K.	*The Left Hand of Darkness*
Lee, Harper	*To Kill a Mockingbird*
Malamud, Bernard	*The Fixer*
Markandaya, Kamala	*Nectar in a Sieve*

Mason, Bobbie Ann	*In Country*
McCullers, Carson	*The Member of the Wedding*
McKinley, Robin	*Beauty: A Retelling of the Story of Beauty and the Beast*
Mori, Kyoko	*Shizuko's Daughter*
Morrison, Toni	*Beloved*
O'Brien, Tim	*The Things They Carried: A Work of Fiction*
O'Connor, Flannery	*Everything That Rises Must Converge*
Potok, Chaim	*The Chosen*
Power, Susan	*The Grass Dancer*
Shaara, Michael	*The Killer Angels*
Steinbeck, John	*The Grapes of Wrath*
Uchida, Yoshiko	*Picture Bride*
Watson, Larry	*Montana 1948*
Wright, Richard	*Native Son*
Yolen, Jane	*Briar Rose*

Nonfiction

	Holy Bible: New Revised Standard Version
Alvarez, Walter	*T. Rex and the Crater of Doom*
Aronson, Marc	*Art Attack: A Short Cultural History of the Avant-Garde*
Asinof, Eliot	*Eight Men Out: The Black Sox and the 1919 World Series*
Atkin, S. Beth	*Voices from the Streets: Young Former Gang Members Tell Their Stories*
Bernstein, Leonard	*The Joy of Music*
Blackstone, Harry, Jr.	*The Blackstone Book of Magic and Illusion*
Blais, Madeleine	*In These Girls, Hope Is a Muscle*
Bodanis, David	*The Secret Family: Twenty-four Hours inside the Mysterious World of Our Minds and Bodies*
Boorstin, Jon	*Making Movies Work: Thinking Like a Filmmaker*
Brown, Dee	*Bury My Heart at Wounded Knee: An Indian History of the American West*
Brumberg, Joan Jacobs	*The Body Project: An Intimate History of American Girls*
Carson, Rachel	*Silent Spring*
Chang, Iris	*The Rape of Nanking: The Forgotten Holocaust of World War II*

Clark, Kenneth	*Civilisation: A Personal View*
Cooke, Mervyn	*Jazz*
Copland, Aaron	*What to Listen for in Music*
Cumming, Robert	*Annotated Art*
Day, David	*The Search for King Arthur*
Diamond, Jared	*Guns, Germs, and Steel: The Fates of Human Societies*
Dorris, Michael	*The Broken Cord*
DuBois, W. E. B.	*The Souls of Black Folk: Essays and Sketches*
Due, Linnea	*Joining the Tribe: Growing Up Gay and Lesbian in the '90s*
Edelman, Marian Wright	*The Measure of Our Success: A Letter to My Children and Yours*
Epictetus, and Sharon Lebell	*The Art of Living: The Classic Manual on Virtue, Happiness, and Effectiveness*
Faludi, Susan	*Backlash: The Undeclared War against American Women*
Finn, David	*How to Look at Sculpture: Text and Photographs*
Ford, Michael Thomas	*The Voices of AIDS: Twelve Unforgettable People Talk about How AIDS Has Changed Their Lives*
Fouts, Roger	*Next of Kin: What Chimpanzees Have Taught Me about Who We Are*
Freedman, Samuel G.	*Small Victories: The Real World of a Teacher, Her Students, and Their High School*
Fremon, Celeste	*Father Greg and The Homeboys: The Extraordinary Journey of Father Greg Boyle and His Work with the Latino Gangs of East L.A.*
Garfunkel, Trudy	*On Wings of Joy: The Story of Ballet from the 16th Century to Today*
Goldberg, Vicki	*The Power of Photography: How Photographs Changed Our Lives*
Gombrich, E. H.	*The Story of Art*
Gould, Stephen Jay	*The Mismeasure of Man*
Green, Bill	*Water, Ice, and Stone: Science and Memory on the Antarctic Lakes*
Hafner, Katie, and Matthew Lyon	*Where Wizards Stay Up Late: The Origins of the Internet*
Hamilton, Edith	*Mythology*
Hawking, Stephen W.	*A Brief History of Time: From the Big Bang to Black Holes*

Hersch, Patricia	*A Tribe Apart: A Journey into the Heart of American Adolescence*
Hersey, John	*Hiroshima*
Hubbell, Sue	*A Country Year: Living the Questions*
Humes, Edward	*No Matter How Loud I Shout: A Year in the Life of Juvenile Court*
Jonas, Gerald	*Dancing: The Pleasure, Power, and Art of Movement*
Jones, K. Maurice	*Say It Loud! The Story of Rap Music*
Junger, Sebastian	*The Perfect Storm: A True Story of Men against the Sea*
Karnos, David D., and Robert G. Shoemaker (eds.)	*Falling in Love with Wisdom: American Philosophers Talk about Their Calling*
Kendall, Elizabeth	*Where She Danced: The Birth of American Art-Dance*
Kerner, Mary	*Barefoot to Balanchine: How to Watch Dance*
Kolb, Rocky	*Blind Watchers of the Sky: The People and Ideas That Shaped Our View of the Universe*
Kotlowitz, Alex	*The Other Side of the River: A Story of Two Towns, a Death, and America's Dilemma*
Kozol, Jonathan	*Savage Inequalities: Children in America's Schools*
Krakauer, Jon	*Into Thin Air: A Personal Account of the Mount Everest Disaster*
McCloud, Scott	*Understanding Comics: The Invisible Art*
McPhee, John	*In Suspect Terrain*
Murray, Albert	*Stomping the Blues*
Occhiogrosso, Peter	*The Joy of Sects: A Spirited Guide to the World's Religious Traditions*
O'Gorman, James F.	*ABC of Architecture*
Paulos, John Allen	*Innumeracy: Mathematical Illiteracy and Its Consequences*
Penn, W. S.	*The Telling of the World: Native American Stories and Art*
Petroski, Henry	*Invention by Design: How Engineers Get from Thought to Thing*
Pipher, Mary	*Reviving Ophelia: Saving the Selves of Adolescent Girls*
Regis, Ed	*Virus Ground Zero: Stalking the Killer Viruses with the Centers for Disease Control*
Rybczynski, Witold	*The Most Beautiful House in the World*

Sheehan, Neil	*A Bright Shining Lie: John Paul Vann and America in Vietnam*
Sherman, Robert, and Philip Seldon	*The Complete Idiot's Guide to Classical Music*
Simon, David, and Edward Burns	*The Corner: A Year in the Life of an Inner-City Neighborhood*
Singh, Simon	*Fermat's Enigma: The Epic Quest to Solve the World's Greatest Mathematical Problem*
Sobel, Dava	*Longitude: The True Story of a Lone Genius Who Solved the Greatest Scientific Problem of His Time*
Spiegelman, Art	*Maus: A Survivor's Tale. Volume I: My Father Bleeds History*
	Maus: A Survivor's Tale. Volume II: And Here My Troubles Began
Strickland, Carol, and John Boswell	*The Annotated Mona Lisa: A Crash Course in Art History from Prehistoric to Post-Modern*
Stringer, Christopher, and Robin McKie	*African Exodus: The Origins of Modern Humanity*
Thomas, Lewis	*The Lives of a Cell: Notes of a Biology Watcher*
Watson, James D.	*The Double Helix: A Personal Account of the Discovery of the Structure of DNA*
Williams, Juan	*Eyes on the Prize: America's Civil Rights Years, 1954–1965*
Yolen, Jane (ed.)	*Favorite Folktales from around the World*

Poetry

Blum, Joshua, Bob Holman, and Mark Pellington (eds.)	*The United States of Poetry*
Carlson, Lori M. (ed.)	*Cool Salsa: Bilingual Poems on Growing Up Latino in the United States*
Ciardi, John	*How Does a Poem Mean?*
Dickinson, Emily	*Poems (Everyman's Library Pocket Poets)*
Dunning, Stephen, Edward Lueders, and Hugh Smith (eds.)	*Reflections on a Gift of Watermelon Pickle . . . and Other Modern Verse*
Giddings, Robert (ed.)	*The War Poets*
Gillan, Maria Mazziotti, and Jennifer Gillan (eds.)	*Unsettling America: An Anthology of Contemporary Multicultural Poetry*

Gordon, Ruth (ed.)	*Pierced by a Ray of Sun: Poems about the Times We Feel Alone*
Heaney, Seamus, and Ted Hughes (eds.)	*The Rattle Bag*
Homer	*The Odyssey of Homer: A Modern Translation*
Miller, E. Ethelbert (ed.)	*In Search of Color Everywhere: A Collection of African-American Poetry*
Niatum, Duane (ed.)	*Harper's Anthology of 20th Century Native American Poetry*
Nye, Naomi Shihab (sel.)	*The Tree Is Older Than You Are: A Bilingual Gathering of Poems and Stories from Mexico, with Paintings by Mexican Artists*
Nye, Naomi Shihab, and Paul B. Janeczko (eds.)	*I Feel a Little Jumpy around You: A Book of Her Poems and His Poems Collected in Pairs*
Oliver, Mary	*New and Selected Poems*
Philip, Neil (ed.)	*Singing America*
Rosenberg, Liz (ed.)	*Earth-Shattering Poems*
Rubin, Robert Alden (ed.)	*Poetry Out Loud*
Smith, Philip (ed.)	*100 Best-Loved Poems*
Stallworthy, Jon (ed.)	*A Book of Love Poetry*

1994

Architecture

Macaulay, David	*Castle*
Stern, Robert A. M.	*Modern Classicism*

Art and Sculpture

Arnason, H. H., and Marla F. Prather	*History of Modern Art: Painting, Sculpture, Architecture, Photography*
Arwas, Victor	*Art Deco*
Bearden, Romare, and Harry Henderson	*A History of African-American Artists: From 1792 to the Present*
Finn, David	*How to Look at Sculpture: Text and Photographs*
Hartt, Frederick	*Art: A History of Painting, Sculpture, and Architecture*
Heller, Nancy G.	*Women Artists: An Illustrated History*

Janson, H. W., and Anthony F. Janson	*History of Art*
Strickland, Carol, and John Boswell	*The Annotated Mona Lisa: A Crash Course in Art History from Prehistoric to Post-Modern*
Wade, Edwin L., and Carol Haralson (eds.)	*The Arts of the North American Indian: Native Traditions in Evolution*

Biography

Angelou, Maya	*I Know Why the Caged Bird Sings*
Ashe, Arthur, and Arnold Rampersad	*Days of Grace: A Memoir*
Baker, Russell	*Growing Up*
Cantwell, Mary	*American Girl: Scenes from a Small-Town Childhood*
Clarke, Gerald	*Capote: A Biography*
Collier, James Lincoln	*Louis Armstrong: An American Success Story*
Conway, Jill Ker	*The Road from Coorain*
Cook, Blanche Wiesen	*Eleanor Roosevelt: Vol. 1 1884–1933*
Criddle, JoAn D., and Teeda Butt Mam	*To Destroy You Is No Loss: The Odyssey of a Cambodian Family*
Crow Dog, Mary, and Richard Erdoes	*Lakota Woman*
Curie, Eve	*Madame Curie: A Biography*
de Mille, Agnes	*Dance to the Piper: Memoirs of the Ballet*
Delany, Sarah, and A. Elizabeth Delany, with Amy Hill Hearth	*Having Our Say: The Delany Sisters' First 100 Years*
Gherman, Beverly	*E. B. White: Some Writer!*
Gies, Miep, and Alison Leslie Gold	*Anne Frank Remembered: The Story of the Woman Who Helped to Hide the Frank Family*
Kerr, M. E.	*Me Me Me Me Me: Not a Novel*
Khanga, Yelena	*Soul to Soul: A Black Russian American Family, 1865–1992*
Kovic, Ron	*Born on the Fourth of July*
Lovell, Mary S.	*The Sound of Wings: The Life of Amelia Earhart*
Malcolm X (as told to Alex Haley)	*The Autobiography of Malcolm X*
Massie, Robert K.	*Nicholas and Alexandra*

Mathabane, Mark	*Kaffir Boy: The True Story of a Black Youth's Coming of Age in Apartheid South Africa; An Autobiography*
McCullough, David G.	*Truman*
Mehta, Ved	*Sound-Shadows of the New World*
Menchú, Rigoberta	*I, Rigoberta Menchú: An Indian Woman in Guatemala*
Mills, Kay	*This Little Light of Mine: The Life of Fannie Lou Hamer*
Milton, Joyce	*Loss of Eden: A Biography of Charles and Anne Morrow Lindbergh*
Moody, Anne	*Coming of Age in Mississippi*
Mowat, Farley	*Woman in the Mists: The Story of Dian Fossey and the Mountain Gorillas of Africa*
Simon, Kate	*Bronx Primitive: Portraits in a Childhood*
Steffan, Joseph	*Honor Bound: A Gay American Fights for the Right to Serve His Country*
Wolff, Tobias	*This Boy's Life: A Memoir*
Wright, Richard	*Black Boy: A Record of Childhood and Youth*

Dance

Anderson, Jack	*Ballet and Modern Dance: A Concise History*
Balanchine, George, and Francis Mason	*101 Stories of the Great Ballets*
Bland, Alexander, and John Percival	*Men Dancing: Performers and Performances*
Gruen, John	*People Who Dance: 22 Dancers Tell Their Own Stories*
Haskins, James	*Black Dance in America: A History through Its People*
Jonas, Gerald	*Dancing: The Pleasure, Power, and Art of Movement*
Kendall, Elizabeth	*Where She Danced: The Birth of American Art-Dance*
Kerner, Mary	*Barefoot to Balanchine: How to Watch Dance*
Tharp, Twyla	*Push Comes to Shove*
Villella, Edward, with Larry Kaplan	*Prodigal Son: Dancing for Balanchine in a World of Pain and Magic*

Fiction

Achebe, Chinua	*Things Fall Apart*
Alvarez, Julia	*How the Garcia Girls Lost Their Accents*
Austen, Jane	*Pride and Prejudice*
Avi	*Nothing but the Truth*
Bradbury, Ray	*Fahrenheit 451*
Brontë, Charlotte	*Jane Eyre*
Camus, Albert	*The Stranger*
Cormier, Robert	*The Chocolate War*
Dickens, Charles	*Great Expectations*
Dorris, Michael	*A Yellow Raft in Blue Water*
Esquivel, Laura	*Like Water for Chocolate: A Novel in Monthly Installments with Recipes, Romance and Home Remedies*
Faulkner, William	*The Portable Faulkner*
Fitzgerald, F. Scott	*The Great Gatsby*
Gaines, Ernest J.	*The Autobiography of Miss Jane Pittman*
	A Gathering of Old Men
Golding, William	*Lord of the Flies*
Hemingway, Ernest	*The Old Man and the Sea*
Hesse, Hermann	*Siddhartha*
Kingsolver, Barbara	*Animal Dreams*
Lee, Gus	*China Boy*
Lee, Harper	*To Kill a Mockingbird*
McCullers, Carson	*The Member of the Wedding*
McKinley, Robin	*Beauty: A Retelling of the Story of Beauty and the Beast*
Morrison, Toni	*The Bluest Eye*
Mowry, Jess	*Way Past Cool: A Novel*
Orwell, George	*Animal Farm*
Paton, Alan	*Cry, the Beloved Country: A Story of Comfort in Desolation*
Poe, Edgar Allan	*Selected Tales of Edgar Allan Poe*
Potok, Chaim	*The Chosen*
Remarque, Erich Maria	*All Quiet on the Western Front*
Salinger, J. D.	*The Catcher in the Rye*
Shaara, Michael	*The Killer Angels*

Smiley, Jane	*Ordinary Love and Good Will: Two Novellas*
Solzhenitsyn, Aleksandr I.	*One Day in the Life of Ivan Denisovich*
Steinbeck, John	*Of Mice and Men*
Tan, Amy	*The Joy Luck Club*
Tolkien, J. R. R.	*The Lord of the Rings*
Twain, Mark	*The Adventures of Huckleberry Finn*
Uchida, Yoshiko	*Picture Bride*
Vonnegut, Kurt	*Slaughterhouse-Five; or, The Children's Crusade*
Walker, Alice	*The Color Purple*

Film

Bogle, Donald	*Toms, Coons, Mulattoes, Mammies, and Bucks: An Interpretative History of Blacks in American Films*
Brownlow, Kevin, and John Kobal	*Hollywood: The Pioneers*
Fraser, George MacDonald	*The Hollywood History of the World: From* One Million Years B.C. *to* Apocalypse Now
Jones, Chuck	*Chuck Amuck: The Life and Times of an Animated Cartoonist*
Springer, John	*They Sang! They Danced! They Romanced! A Pictorial History of the Movie Musical*

Music

Allen, Ray	*Singing in the Spirit: African-American Sacred Quartets in New York City*
Bernstein, Leonard	*The Joy of Music*
Boyd, Jenny	*Musicians in Tune: Seventy-five Contemporary Musicians Discuss the Creative Process*
Kogan, Judith	*Nothing but the Best: The Struggle for Perfection at the Julliard School*
Malone, Bill C.	*Country Music, U.S.A.*
Newquist, H. P.	*Music and Technology*
Sidran, Ben	*Talking Jazz: An Illustrated Oral History*
Sweeney, Philip	*The Virgin Directory of World Music*
Zeitz, Petra	*Rock Star Interviews: Conversations with Leading Performers and Songwriters*

Nonfiction

Adams, Douglas, and Mark Carwardine	*Last Chance to See*
Angell, Roger	*Season Ticket: A Baseball Companion*
Asinof, Eliot	*Eight Men Out: The Black Sox and the 1919 World Series*
Attenborough, David	*The Living Planet: A Portrait of the Earth*
Baldwin, James	*The Fire Next Time*
Bell, E. T.	*Men of Mathematics*
Bernstein, Carl, and Bob Woodward	*All the President's Men*
Boston Women's Health Book Collective	*The New Our Bodies, Ourselves*
Brown, Dee	*Bury My Heart at Wounded Knee: An Indian History of the American West*
Burrough, Bryan, and John Helyar	*Barbarians at the Gate: The Fall of RJR Nabisco*
Campbell, Joseph, with Bill Moyers	*The Power of Myth*
Carson, Rachel	*Silent Spring*
Clarke, Arthur C.	*How the World Was One: Beyond the Global Village*
Cleaver, Eldridge	*Soul on Ice*
Dorris, Michael	*The Broken Cord*
DuBois, W. E. B.	*The Souls of Black Folk: Essays and Sketches*
Edelman, Marian Wright	*The Measure of Our Success: A Letter to My Children and Yours*
Embury, Barbara	*The Dream Is Alive*
Epstein, Norrie	*The Friendly Shakespeare: A Thoroughly Painless Guide to the Best of the Bard*
Evans, Eli N.	*The Lonely Days Were Sundays: Reflections of a Jewish Southerner*
Faludi, Susan	*Backlash: The Undeclared War against American Women*
Freedman, Samuel G.	*Small Victories: The Real World of a Teacher, Her Students, and Their High School*
Gandhi, Mahatma	*The Essential Writings of Mahatma Gandhi*
Gleick, James	*Chaos: Making a New Science*
Gould, Stephen Jay	*Bully for Brontosaurus: Reflections in Natural History*

Halberstam, David	*The Best and the Brightest*
Hawking, Stephen W.	*A Brief History of Time: From the Big Bang to Black Holes*
Hersey, John	*Hiroshima*
Hong, Maria (ed.)	*Growing Up Asian American: An Anthology*
Jung, Carl G.	*Man and His Symbols*
Karlsen, Carol F.	*The Devil in the Shape of a Woman: Witchcraft in Colonial New England*
Karnow, Stanley	*Vietnam: A History*
Kaysen, Susanna	*Girl, Interrupted*
Knaefler, Tomi Kaizawa	*Our House Divided: Seven Japanese American Families in World War II*
Kotlowitz, Alex	*There Are No Children Here: The Story of Two Boys Growing Up in the Other America*
Kozol, Jonathan	*Savage Inequalities: Children in America's Schools*
Lederer, Richard	*The Miracle of Language*
Leopold, Aldo	*A Sand County Almanac*
Lewis, Anthony	*Gideon's Trumpet*
Manley, Deborah (ed.)	*The Guinness Book of Records 1492: The World Five Hundred Years Ago*
Maybury-Lewis, David	*Millennium: Tribal Wisdom and the Modern World*
McCullough, David	*The Johnstown Flood*
McPhee, John	*The Control of Nature*
McPherson, James M.	*Battle Cry of Freedom: The Civil War Era*
Meltzer, Milton	*Rescue: The Story of How Gentiles Saved Jews in the Holocaust*
Mintz, Steven, and Susan Kellogg	*Domestic Revolutions: A Social History of American Family Life*
Nabhan, Gary Paul	*The Desert Smells like Rain: A Naturalist in Papago Indian Country*
Northup, Solomon	*Twelve Years a Slave*
Quindlen, Anna	*Thinking Out Loud: On the Personal, the Political, the Public, and the Private*
Robinette, Diane	*Hometown Heroes: Successful Deaf Youth in America*
Rodriguez, Luis J.	*Always Running: La Vida Loca; Gang Days in L.A.*
Rogosin, Donn	*Invisible Men: Life in Baseball's Negro Leagues*
Sergios, Paul	*One Boy at War: My Life in the AIDS Underground*

Sheehan, Neil	*A Bright Shining Lie: John Paul Vann and America in Vietnam*
Shenkman, Richard	*Legends, Lies, and Cherished Myths of World History*
Shilts, Randy	*Conduct Unbecoming: Gays and Lesbians in the U.S. Military, Vietnam to the Persian Gulf*
Spiegelman, Art	*Maus: A Survivor's Tale. Volume I: My Father Bleeds History*
	Maus: A Survivor's Tale. Volume II: And Here My Troubles Began
Terkel, Studs	*Race: How Blacks and Whites Think and Feel about the American Obsession*
Terkel, Susan Neiburg	*Should Drugs Be Legalized?*
Thomas, Lewis	*The Youngest Science: Notes of a Medicine-Watcher*
Tuchman, Barbara W.	*A Distant Mirror: The Calamitous 14th Century*
U.S. Holocaust Memorial Museum	*The World Must Know: The History of the Holocaust as Told in the United States Holocaust Memorial Museum*
Vare, Ethlie Ann and Greg Ptacek	*Mothers of Invention: From the Bra to the Bomb; Forgotten Women and Their Unforgettable Ideas*
Walker, Alice	*Living by the Word: Selected Writings, 1973–1987*
Wallis, Velma	*Two Old Women: An Alaska Legend of Betrayal, Courage and Survival*
Weiss, Ann E.	*Who's to Know? Information, the Media, and Public Awareness*
Williams, Juan	*Eyes on the Prize: America's Civil Rights Years, 1954–1965*
Yolen, Jane (ed.)	*Favorite Folktales from around the World*

Photography

Gassan, Arnold, and A. J. Meek	*Exploring Black and White Photography*
Gilbert, George	*The Complete Photography Careers Handbook: Updated and Expanded to Include Electronic Imaging*
Goldberg, Vicki	The *Power of Photography: How Photographs Changed Our Lives*
Harvey, Liz (ed.)	*Shoot! Everything You Ever Wanted to Know about 35mm Photography*
Hedgecoe, John	*The Photographer's Handbook*

Poetry

Heaney, Seamus, and Ted Hughes (eds.)	*The Rattle Bag*
Koch, Kenneth, and Kate Farrell	*Sleeping on the Wing: An Anthology of Modern Poetry, with Essays on Reading and Writing*
Luce, William	*The Belle of Amherst*
McClatchy, J. D. (ed.)	*The Vintage Book of Contemporary American Poetry*
Pack, Robert, and Jay Parini (eds.)	*Poems for a Small Planet: Contemporary American Nature Poetry*
Soto, Gary	*A Fire in My Hands: A Book of Poems*

Related Arts

Blackstone, Harry, Jr.	*The Blackstone Book of Magic and Illusion*
Reidelbach, Maria	*Completely Mad: A History of the Comic Book and Magazine*
Spandorfer, Merle	*Making Art Safely: Alternative Methods and Materials in Drawing, Painting, Printmaking, Graphic Design, and Photography*
Winship, Michael	*Television*

Theater

BOOKS ABOUT THE THEATER

Brockett, Oscar G.	*History of the Theatre*
Burns Mantle, Robert	The Burns Mantle Best Plays Series
Corson, Richard	*Stage Makeup*
Gottfried, Martin	*Sondheim*
Henderson, Mary C.	*Theater in America: 200 Years of Plays, Players, and Productions*
Jones, James Earl, and Penelope Niven	*James Earl Jones: Voices and Silences*
Lounsbury, Warren C., and Norman C. Boulanger	*Theatre Backstage from A to Z*
Marsolais, Kenneth, Rodger McFarlane, and Tom Viola (eds.)	*Broadway, Day and Night*
Perry, George C.	*The Complete Phantom of the Opera*

MUSICALS

Bernstein, Leonard,
Arthur Laurents, and
Stephen Sondheim

West Side Story

Gilbert, W. S., and
Arthur Sullivan

The Pirates of Penzance

Herman, Jerry, and
Michael Stewart

Hello, Dolly!

Jones, Tom, and
Harvey Schmidt

The Fantasticks

Lerner, Alan Jay, and
Frederick Loewe

My Fair Lady

Lloyd Webber, Andrew

Cats

Rodgers, Richard, and
Oscar Hammerstein

Oklahoma!

Schönberg, Claude-Michel,
Alain Boublil, and
Herbert Kretzmer

Les Misérables

Sondheim, Stephen, and
James Lapine

Into the Woods

PLAYS

Aristophanes

Lysistrata

Brecht, Bertolt

*Mother Courage and Her Children: A Chronicle of
the Thirty Years' War*

Christie, Agatha

The Mousetrap

Cooper, Susan, and
Hume Cronyn

Foxfire

Coward, Noël

Blithe Spirit

Davis, Ossie

Purlie Victorious: A Commemorative

Damashek, Barbara, and
Molly Newman

Quilters

Fierstein, Harvey

Torch Song Trilogy: Three Plays

Fugard, Athol

"Master Harold" . . . and the Boys

Fuller, Charles

A Soldier's Play

Gardner, Herb

I'm Not Rappaport

Griffin, Tom

The Boys Next Door: A Play in Two Acts

Hecht, Ben, and Charles MacArthur	*The Front Page*
Hellman, Lillian	*The Children's Hour*
Henley, Beth	*Crimes of the Heart*
Hwang, David Henry	*M. Butterfly*
Ibsen, Henrik	*A Doll's House*
Ionesco, Eugène	*Rhinoceros*
John, Errol	*Moon on a Rainbow Shawl: A Play in Three Acts*
Kushner, Tony	*Angels in America: A Gay Fantasia on National Themes. Part 1: Millennium Approaches; Part 2: Perestroika*
Lawrence, Jerome, and Robert E. Lee	*Inherit the Wind*
Medoff, Mark	*Children of a Lesser God*
Miller, Arthur	*Playing for Time: A Screenplay*
Molière	*The Miser*
O'Neill, Eugene	*Ah, Wilderness!*
Pinter, Harold	*Betrayal*
Shakespeare, William	*Romeo and Juliet*
Shange, Ntozake	*For Colored Girls Who Have Considered Suicide / When the Rainbow Is Enuf*
Shaw, George Bernard	*Pygmalion*
Shepard, Sam	*Buried Child and Seduced and Suicide in B-flat*
Shue, Larry	*The Foreigner*
Simon, Neil	*Lost in Yonkers*
Stoppard, Tom	*Rosencrantz and Guildenstern Are Dead*
Walcott, Derek	*Dream on Monkey Mountain, and Other Plays*
Wasserstein, Wendy	*The Heidi Chronicles*
Wilde, Oscar	*The Importance of Being Earnest*
Wilder, Thornton	*The Matchmaker*
Williams, Tennessee	*The Glass Menagerie*
Wilson, August	*Fences* *The Piano Lesson*

1991

Architecture

Allen, Edward	*How Buildings Work: The Natural Order of Architecture*
Salvadori, Mario George	*Why Buildings Stand Up: The Strength of Architecture*
Stern, Robert A. M.	*Modern Classicism*

Art and Sculpture

Czarnecki, Joseph P.	*Last Traces: The Lost Art of Auschwitz*
Duncan, Alastair	*American Art Deco*
	Art Deco
Finn, David	*How to Look at Sculpture: Text and Photographs*
Hartt, Frederick	*Art: A History of Painting, Sculpture, and Architecture*
Heller, Nancy G.	*Women Artists: An Illustrated History*
Updike, John	*Just Looking: Essays on Art*
Vlach, John Michael	*Plain Painters: Making Sense of American Folk Art*

Biography

Baker, Russell	*Growing Up*
Barry, Kathleen L.	*Susan B. Anthony: A Biography of a Singular Feminist*
Cheng, Nien	*Life and Death in Shanghai*
Comer, James P.	*Maggie's American Dream: The Life and Times of a Black Family*
Conway, Jill Ker	*The Road from Coorain*
Curie, Eve	*Madame Curie: A Biography*
Dillard, Annie	*An American Childhood*
Gies, Miep, and Alison Leslie Gold	*Anne Frank Remembered: The Story of the Woman Who Helped to Hide the Frank Family*
Hayslip, Le Ly, and Jay Wurts	*When Heaven and Earth Changed Places: A Vietnamese Woman's Journey from War to Peace*
Kazimiroff, Theodore L.	*The Last Algonquin*
Kovic, Ron	*Born on the Fourth of July*
Lovell, Mary S.	*The Sound of Wings: The Life of Amelia Earhart*
Lyttle, Richard B.	*Pablo Picasso: The Man and the Image*
MacNeil, Robert	*Wordstruck: A Memoir*

Martin, Ralph G.	*Golda: Golda Meir; The Romantic Years*
Mathabane, Mark	*Kaffir Boy: The True Story of a Black Youth's Coming of Age in Apartheid South Africa; An Autobiography*
Mathews, Jay	*Escalante: The Best Teacher in America*
Mehta, Ved	*Sound-Shadows of the New World*
Miller, Merle	*Plain Speaking: An Oral Biography of Harry S. Truman*
Mills, Judie	*John F. Kennedy*
Morgan, Sally	*My Place*
Mowat, Farley	*Woman in the Mists: The Story of Dian Fossey and the Mountain Gorillas of Africa*
Oppenheimer, Judy	*Private Demons: The Life of Shirley Jackson*
Robeson, Susan	*The Whole World in His Hands: A Pictorial Biography of Paul Robeson*
Robinson, Roxana	*Georgia O'Keeffe: A Life*
Salerno-Sonnenberg, Nadja	*Nadja, on My Way*
Scharf, Lois	*Eleanor Roosevelt: First Lady of American Liberalism*
Sender, Ruth Minsky	*The Cage*
Staden, Wendelgard von	*Darkness over the Valley*
Sunstein, Emily W.	*Mary Shelley: Romance and Reality*
Van Devanter, Lynda, and Christopher Morgan	*Home before Morning: The Story of an Army Nurse in Vietnam*
Witherspoon, William Roger	*Martin Luther King, Jr.: To the Mountaintop*
Wolff, Tobias	*This Boy's Life: A Memoir*
Wright, Richard	*Black Boy: A Record of Childhood and Youth*

Books on Theater

Bordman, Gerald	*American Musical Comedy: From Adonis to Dreamgirls*
Brandreth, Gyles	*Great Theatrical Disasters*
Hart, Moss	*Act One: An Autobiography*
Henderson, Mary C.	*Theater in America: 200 Years of Plays, Players, and Productions*
Lawrence, Robert G.	*Restoration Plays*
Stanislavsky, Konstantin	*An Actor Prepares* *Building a Character* *Creating a Role*
Wickham, Glynne W.	*A History of the Theatre*

Dance

Balanchine, George, and Francis Mason	*101 Stories of the Great Ballets*
Bentley, Toni	*Winter Season: A Dancer's Journal*
Bland, Alexander, and John Percival	*Men Dancing: Performers and Performances*
Clarke, Mary, and Clement Crisp	*Ballerina: The Art of Women in Classical Ballet*
Coe, Robert	*Dance in America*
Fraser, John	*Private View: Inside Baryshnikov's American Ballet Theatre*
Gruen, John	*People Who Dance: 22 Dancers Tell Their Own Stories*
Haskins, James	*Black Dance in America: A History through Its People*
Stearns, Marshall, and Jean Stearns	*Jazz Dance: The Story of American Vernacular Dance*

Fiction

Achebe, Chinua	*Things Fall Apart*
Anaya, Rudolfo A.	*Bless Me, Ultima*
Austen, Jane	*Pride and Prejudice*
Bradbury, Ray	*Fahrenheit 451*
Brontë, Charlotte	*Jane Eyre*
Camus, Albert	*The Stranger*
Doctorow, E. L.	*Ragtime*
Dorris, Michael	*A Yellow Raft in Blue Water*
Doyle, Arthur Conan	*Sherlock Holmes: Selected Stories*
Faulkner, William	*The Portable Faulkner*
Fitzgerald, F. Scott	*The Great Gatsby*
Flaubert, Gustave	*Madame Bovary*
Gaines, Ernest J.	*A Gathering of Old Men*
Golding, William	*Lord of the Flies*
Greenberg, Joanne	*Of Such Small Differences*
Hemingway, Ernest	*A Farewell to Arms*
Hesse, Hermann	*Siddhartha*
Joyce, James	*A Portrait of the Artist as a Young Man*

Keneally, Thomas	*The Chant of Jimmie Blacksmith*
Lee, Harper	*To Kill a Mockingbird*
London, Jack	*The Call of the Wild*
Malamud, Bernard	*The Fixer*
Mason, Bobbie Ann	*In Country*
McCullers, Carson	*The Member of the Wedding*
Morrison, Toni	*Beloved*
O'Connor, Flannery	*Everything That Rises Must Converge*
Paton, Alan	*Cry, the Beloved Country: A Story of Comfort in Desolation*
Potok, Chaim	*The Chosen*
Renault, Mary	*The King Must Die*
Salinger, J. D.	*The Catcher in the Rye*
Solzhenitsyn, Aleksandr I.	*One Day in the Life of Ivan Denisovich*
Steinbeck, John	*East of Eden*
Tan, Amy	*The Joy Luck Club*
Tevis, Walter S.	*The Queen's Gambit*
Tolkien, J. R. R.	*The Lord of the Rings*
Twain, Mark	*The Adventures of Huckleberry Finn*
Tyler, Anne	*The Accidental Tourist*
Vidal, Gore	*Lincoln: A Novel*
White, T. H.	*The Once and Future King*

Film

Bogle, Donald	*Toms, Coons, Mulattoes, Mammies, and Bucks: An Interpretative History of Blacks in American Films*
Brownlow, Kevin, and John Kobal	*Hollywood: The Pioneers*
Finch, Christopher	*The Art of Walt Disney: From Mickey Mouse to the Magic Kingdoms*
Searles, Baird	*Films of Science Fiction and Fantasy*
Sennett, Ted	*The Art of Hanna-Barbera: Fifty Years of Creativity*

Music

Crowther, Bruce, and Mike Pinfold	*The Big Band Years*
Griffin, Clive D.	*Classical Music*

Haskins, James	*Black Music in America: A History through Its People*
Kernfeld, Barry (ed.)	*The New Grove Dictionary of Jazz*
Miller, Jim	*The* Rolling Stone *Illustrated History of Rock and Roll*
Mordden, Ethan	*Demented: The World of the Opera Diva*
Schonberg, Harold C.	*The Glorious Ones: Classical Music's Legendary Performers*
Smith, Joe, and Mitchell Fink (eds.)	*Off the Record: An Oral History of Popular Music*

Nonfiction

	Holy Bible: New Revised Standard Version '
Allen, James Paul, and Eugene James Turner	*We the People: An Atlas of America's Ethnic Diversity*
Arendt, Hannah	*On Violence*
Betcher, William	*Intimate Play: Creating Romance in Everyday Life*
Bloom, Allan	*The Closing of the American Mind: How Higher Education Has Failed Democracy and Impoverished the Souls of Today's Students*
Bolen, Jean Shinoda	*Goddesses in Everywoman: A New Psychology of Women*
	Gods in Everyman: A New Psychology of Men's Lives and Loves
Borysenko, Joan	*Minding the Body, Mending the Mind*
Boslough, John	*Stephen Hawking's Universe*
Bradshaw, John	*Bradshaw on the Family: A Revolutionary Way of Self-Discovery*
Burstein, Daniel	*Yen! Japan's New Financial Empire and Its Threat to America*
Caduto, Michael J., and Joseph Bruchac	*Keepers of the Earth: Native American Stories and Environmental Activities for Children*
Campbell, Joseph, with Bill Moyers	*The Power of Myth*
Child, Julia	*The Way to Cook*
Earth Works Group	*50 Simple Things You Can Do to Save the Earth*
FitzGerald, Frances	*Fire in the Lake: The Vietnamese and the Americans in Vietnam*
Fossey, Dian	*Gorillas in the Mist*

Funk, Wilfred John, and Norman Lewis	*Thirty Days to a More Powerful Vocabulary*
Gay, Kathlyn	*The Greenhouse Effect*
Gonzalez-Crussi, F.	*The Five Senses*
Goodall, Jane	*In the Shadow of Man*
Hartmann, William K.	*Cycles of Fire: Stars, Galaxies, and the Wonder of Deep Space*
Hawking, Stephen W.	*A Brief History of Time: From the Big Bang to Black Holes*
Hirsch E. D., Jr.	*Cultural Literacy: What Every American Needs to Know*
	A First Dictionary of Cultural Literacy: What Our Children Need to Know
Hyde, Dayton O.	*Don Coyote: The Good Times and the Bad Times of a Much Maligned American Original*
Hyde, Margaret O. and Elizabeth H. Forsyth	*Terrorism: A Special Kind of Violence*
Irwin, Constance H. Frick	*Strange Footprints on the Land: Vikings in America*
Jung, Carl G.	*Man and His Symbols*
Kesselman-Turkel, Judi, and Franklynn Peterson	*Getting It Down: How to Put Your Ideas on Paper*
Key, Wilson Bryan	*Media Sexploitation*
Kidder, Tracy	*Among Schoolchildren*
Kingston, Maxine Hong	*China Men*
Kitzinger, Sheila	*Being Born*
	The Complete Book of Pregnancy and Childbirth
Kozol, Jonathan	*Rachel and Her Children: Homeless Families in America*
Lelyveld, Joseph	*Move Your Shadow: South Africa, Black and White*
Lewin, Roger	*Bones of Contention: Controversies in the Search for Human Origins*
Mabie, Margot C. J.	*The Constitution: Reflection of a Changing Nation*
Macaulay, David	*The Way Things Work*
Madaras, Lynda, and Area Madaras	*The What's Happening to My Body? Book for Girls: A Growing Up Guide for Parents and Daughters*
Madaras, Lynda, and Dane Saavedra	*The What's Happening to My Body? Book for Boys: A Growing Up Guide for Parents and Sons*
Marrin, Albert	*War Clouds in the West: Indians and Cavalrymen, 1860–1890*
McPhee, John	*In Suspect Terrain*

Meltzer, Milton	*Rescue: The Story of How Gentiles Saved Jews in the Holocaust*
Parrot, Andrea	*Coping with Date Rape and Acquaintance Rape*
Peck, M. Scott	*The Road Less Traveled*
Perl, Lila	*Hunter's Stew and Hangtown Fry: What Pioneer America Ate and Why*
Peters, Thomas J., and Robert H. Waterman Jr.	*In Search of Excellence: Lessons from America's Best Run Companies*
Pike, Donald G., and David Muench	*Anasazi: Ancient People of the Rock*
Roueché, Berton	*The Medical Detectives*
Sagan, Carl	*Cosmos*
San Souci, Robert D.	*The Loch Ness Monster: Opposing Viewpoints*
Shilts, Randy	*And the Band Played On: Politics, People, and the AIDS Epidemic*
Sinetar, Marsha	*Do What You Love, the Money Will Follow: Discovering Your Right Livelihood*
Steiner, Stan	*La Raza: The Mexican Americans*
U.S. Bureau of Labor Statistics	*Occupational Outlook Handbook*
Weiner, Jonathan	*Planet Earth*
Williams, Juan	*Eyes on the Prize: America's Civil Rights Years, 1954–1965*
Woolger, Roger J.	*Other Lives, Other Selves: A Jungian Psychotherapist Discovers Past Lives*
Yale Daily News	*Insider's Guide to the Colleges*
Yolen, Jane (ed.)	*Favorite Folktales from around the World*

Photography

Eastman Kodak Company (ed.)	*More Joy of Photography*
Greenough, Sarah	*On the Art of Fixing a Shadow: One Hundred and Fifty Years of Photography*
Livingston, Jane, with Frances Fralin and Declan Haun	*Odyssey: The Art of Photography at* National Geographic
Mangelsen, Tom	*Images of Nature: The Photographs of Tom Mangelsen*
Weaver, Mike	*The Art of Photography, 1839–1989*

Plays

Aeschylus	*Agamemnon*
Anouilh, Jean	*Antigone*
	The Lark
Aristophanes	*Lysistrata*
Baldwin, James	*The Amen Corner: A Play*
Beckett, Samuel	*Waiting for Godot: A Tragicomedy in Two Acts*
Brecht, Bertolt	*Mother Courage and Her Children: A Chronicle of the Thirty Year's War*
Chekhov, Anton	*The Cherry Orchard: A Comedy in Four Acts*
Coward, Noël	*Blithe Spirit*
Fugard, Athol	*"Master Harold" . . . and the Boys*
García Lorca, Federico	*Blood Wedding*
Giraudoux, Jean	*The Madwoman of Chaillot*
Hansberry, Lorraine	*A Raisin in the Sun*
Hellman, Lillian	*The Children's Hour*
Henley, Beth	*Crimes of the Heart*
Ibsen, Henrik	*A Doll's House*
Ionesco, Eugène	*Rhinoceros*
Jones, Tom, and Harvey Schmidt	*The Fantasticks*
Kaufman, George S., and Moss Hart	*You Can't Take It with You*
Lloyd Webber, Andrew	*Cats*
MacLeish, Archibald	*J. B.*
Medoff, Mark	*Children of a Lesser God*
Miller, Arthur	*The Crucible*
Molière	*The Misanthrope*
O'Neill, Eugene	*Long Day's Journey into Night*
Pinter, Harold	*The Birthday Party*
Pirandello, Luigi	*Six Characters in Search of an Author*
Pomerance, Bernard	*The Elephant Man*
Rostand, Edmond	*Cyrano de Bergerac*
Sartre, Jean-Paul	*No Exit*
Shaffer, Peter	*Equus*
Shakespeare, William	*King Lear*
Shaw, George Bernard	*Pygmalion*
	Saint Joan

Shepard, Sam	*The Tooth of Crime; Geography of a Horse Dreamer: Two Plays*
Sheridan, Richard Brinsley	*The School for Scandal*
Simon, Neil	*The Odd Couple*
Sophocles	*Oedipus the King*
Stoppard, Tom	*Rosencrantz and Guildenstern Are Dead*
Strindberg, August	*Miss Julie*
Synge, J. M.	*Riders to the Sea*
Vega, Lope de	*The Sheep Well*
Wilde, Oscar	*The Importance of Being Earnest*
Wilder, Thornton	*The Matchmaker*
Williams, Tennessee	*The Glass Menagerie*
Zindel, Paul	*The Effect of Gamma Rays on Man-in-the-Moon Marigolds: A Drama in Two Acts*

Poetry

Christopher, Nicholas (ed.)	*Under 35: The New Generation of American Poets*
DeCarava, Roy, and Langston Hughes	*The Sweet Flypaper of Life*
Doreski, Carol Kiler and William Doreski	*How to Read and Interpret Poetry*
Hall, Donald, and David Lehman (eds.)	*The Best American Poetry*
Janeczko, Paul B. (sel.)	*Going Over to Your Place: Poems for Each Other*

Related Arts

Antekeier, Kristopher, and Greg Aunapu	*Ringmaster! My Year on the Road with "The Greatest Show on Earth"*
Took, Barry	*Comedy Greats: A Celebration of Comic Genius Past and Present*
Volpe, Tod M., and Beth Cathers	*Treasures of the American Arts and Crafts Movement, 1890–1920*

1988

Art, Architecture, and Photography

Adams, Ansel, and Mary Street Alinder	*Ansel Adams: An Autobiography*

Allen, Edward	*How Buildings Work: The Natural Order of Architecture*
DeCarava, Roy, and Langston Hughes	*The Sweet Flypaper of Life*
Hamilton, George Heard	*Painting and Sculpture in Europe, 1880–1940*
Hibbard, Howard	*Michelangelo*
Krauss, Rosalind E.	*Passages in Modern Sculpture*
Salvadori, Mario George	*Why Buildings Stand Up: The Strength of Architecture*

Biography

Angelou, Maya	*I Know Why the Caged Bird Sings*
Benson, Jackson J.	*The True Adventures of John Steinbeck, Writer: A Biography*
Carpenter, Humphrey	*Tolkien: A Biography*
Clark, Ronald W.	*Freud: The Man and the Cause*
Douglas, William O.	*The Court Years, 1939–1975: The Autobiography of William O. Douglas*
	Go East, Young Man: The Early Years; The Autobiography of William O. Douglas
Egan, Eileen	*Such a Vision of the Street: Mother Teresa—The Spirit and the Work*
Fox, Stephen R.	*John Muir and His Legacy: The American Conservation Movement*
Frank, Anne	*Anne Frank: The Diary of a Young Girl*
French, A. P. (ed.)	*Einstein: A Centenary Volume*
Furlong, Monica	*Merton: A Biography*
Gill, Derek L. T.	*Quest: The Life of Elisabeth Kübler-Ross*
Griffith, Elisabeth	*In Her Own Right: The Life of Elizabeth Cady Stanton*
Gunther, John	*Death Be Not Proud: A Memoir*
Hellman, Lillian	*Three: An Unfinished Woman, Pentimento, Scoundrel Time*
Herriot, James	*All Creatures Great and Small*
Keller, Helen	*The Story of My Life*
Kingston, Maxine Hong	*The Woman Warrior: Memoirs of a Girlhood among Ghosts*
Klein, Joe	*Woody Guthrie: A Life*

Lash, Joseph P.	*Eleanor and Franklin: The Story of Their Relationship, Based on Eleanor Roosevelt's Private Papers*
Malcolm X (as told to Alex Haley)	*The Autobiography of Malcolm X*
Manchester, William	*The Last Lion: Winston Spencer Churchill*
Mandela, Winnie	*Part of My Soul Went with Him*
Marius, Richard	*Thomas More: A Biography*
Mead, Margaret	*Blackberry Winter: My Earlier Years*
Miller, Merle	*Plain Speaking: An Oral Biography of Harry S. Truman*
Morgan, Ted	*FDR: A Biography*
Neihardt, John G.	*Black Elk Speaks: Being the Life Story of a Holy Man of the Oglala Sioux*
Oates, Stephen B.	*Let the Trumpet Sound: A Life of Martin Luther King, Jr.*
O'Keeffe, Georgia	*Georgia O'Keeffe*
Oshinsky, David M.	*A Conspiracy So Immense: The World of Joe McCarthy*
Page, Joseph A.	*Perón: A Biography*
Sandburg, Carl	*Abraham Lincoln: The Prairie Years and the War Years*
Shevchenko, Arkady N.	*Breaking with Moscow*
Smith, Denis Mack	*Mussolini: A Biography*
Stein, Gertrude	*The Autobiography of Alice B. Toklas*
Wexler, Alice	*Emma Goldman: An Intimate Life*
Wolfe, Bertram D.	*Three Who Made a Revolution: A Biographical History*
Woods, Donald	*Biko*
Wright, Richard	*Black Boy: A Record of Childhood and Youth*
Yeager, Chuck, and Leo Janos	*Yeager: An Autobiography*

Dance

Ames, Jerry, and Jim Siegelman	*The Book of Tap: Recovering America's Long Lost Dance*
Balanchine, George, and Francis Mason	*101 Stories of the Great Ballets*
Bentley, Toni	*Winter Season: A Dancer's Journal*
Bland, Alexander, and John Percival	*Men Dancing: Performers and Performances*

Coe, Robert	*Dance in America*
Emery, Lynne Fauley	*Black Dance in the United States: From 1619 to 1970*
Stearns, Marshall, and Jean Stearns	*Jazz Dance: The Story of American Vernacular Dance*

Drama

BOOKS ABOUT THE THEATER

Bordman, Gerald	*American Musical Comedy: From Adonis to Dreamgirls*
Brandreth, Gyles	*Great Theatrical Disasters*
Hart, Moss	*Act One: An Autobiography*
Henderson, Mary C.	*Theater in America: 200 Years of Plays, Players, and Productions*
Lerner, Alan Jay	*The Musical Theatre: A Celebration*
Shewey, Don, and Susan Shacter	*Caught in the Act*
Stanislavsky, Konstantin	*An Actor Prepares*
	Building a Character
Wickham, Glynne W.	*A History of the Theatre*

PLAYS

Albee, Edward	*The Zoo Story: A Play*
Aristophanes	*Lysistrata*
Bernstein, Leonard, Arthur Laurents, and Stephen Sondheim	*West Side Story*
Chekhov, Anton	*The Cherry Orchard: A Comedy in Four Acts*
Coward, Noël	*Blithe Spirit*
Eliot, T. S.	*Murder in the Cathedral*
Gilbert, W. S., and Arthur Sullivan	*The Pirates of Penzance*
Hellman, Lillian	*The Children's Hour*
Ibsen, Henrik	*A Doll's House*
Kander, John	*Cabaret*
Kaufman, George S., and Moss Hart	*You Can't Take It with You*
MacDermot, Galt	*Hair*

Medoff, Mark	*Children of a Lesser God*
Miller, Arthur	*The Price*
Molière	*Le Bourgeois Gentilhomme*
Ndlovu, Duma (ed.)	*Woza Afrika! An Anthology of South African Plays*
O'Neill, Eugene	*Long Day's Journey into Night*
Pirandello, Luigi	*Six Characters in Search of an Author*
Rodgers, Richard, and Lorenz Hart	*Pal Joey*
Rodgers, Richard, and Oscar Hammerstein	*Oklahoma!*
Rostand, Edmond	*Cyrano de Bergerac*
Sartre, Jean-Paul	*No Exit*
Shakespeare, William	*The Tempest* *Twelfth Night*
Shaw, George Bernard	*Arms and the Man* *Pygmalion*
Sheridan, Richard Brinsley	*The School for Scandal*
Simon, Neil	*Brighton Beach Memoirs*
Sondheim, Stephen	*Sweeney Todd: The Demon Barber of Fleet Street*
Sophocles	*Oedipus the King*
Waley, Arthur	*The Noh Drama: Ten Plays from the Japanese 14th and 15th Centuries*
Weill, Kurt	*The Threepenny Opera*
Wilde, Oscar	*The Importance of Being Earnest*
Wilder, Thornton	*Our Town*
Williams, Tennessee	*A Streetcar Named Desire*

Fiction

Austen, Jane	*Pride and Prejudice*
Baldwin, James	*Go Tell It on the Mountain*
Bradbury, Ray	*Fahrenheit 451*
Brin, David	*The Postman*
Brontë, Charlotte	*Jane Eyre*
Cather, Willa	*My Ántonia*
Cormier, Robert	*The Chocolate War*
Crane, Stephen	*The Red Badge of Courage*
Dickens, Charles	*A Tale of Two Cities*
Dostoyevsky, Fyodor	*Crime and Punishment*

Doyle, Arthur Conan	*Sherlock Holmes: Selected Stories*
Emecheta, Buchi	*The Bride Price*
Faulkner, William	*The Reivers: A Reminiscence*
Finney, Jack	*Time and Again*
Fitzgerald, F. Scott	*The Great Gatsby*
Gaines, Ernest J.	*The Autobiography of Miss Jane Pittman*
Gardner, John	*Grendel*
Golding, William	*Lord of the Flies*
Guest, Judith	*Ordinary People*
Hawthorne, Nathaniel	*The Scarlet Letter*
Heller, Joseph	*Catch-22*
Hesse, Hermann	*Siddhartha*
Huxley, Aldous	*Brave New World*
Keneally, Thomas	*Schindler's List*
Le Guin, Ursula K.	*The Left Hand of Darkness*
Lee, Harper	*To Kill a Mockingbird*
Lord, Bette B.	*Spring Moon: A Novel of China*
Malamud, Bernard	*The Fixer*
Markandaya, Kamala	*Nectar in a Sieve*
McCullers, Carson	*The Heart Is a Lonely Hunter*
McKinley, Robin	*Beauty: A Retelling of the Story of Beauty and the Beast*
Mishima, Yukio	*The Sound of Waves*
O'Brien, Tim	*Going after Cacciato*
Orwell, George	*Animal Farm*
Paton, Alan	*Cry, the Beloved Country: A Story of Comfort in Desolation*
Poe, Edgar Allan	*Tales of Terror: Ten Short Stories*
Potok, Chaim	*The Chosen*
Remarque, Erich Maria	*All Quiet on the Western Front*
Salinger, J. D.	*The Catcher in the Rye*
Shange, Ntozake	*Betsey Brown*
Sinclair, Upton	*The Jungle*
Singer, Isaac Bashevis	*The Collected Stories of Isaac Bashevis Singer*
Solzhenitsyn, Aleksandr I.	*One Day in the Life of Ivan Denisovich*
Steinbeck, John	*The Grapes of Wrath*
Stoker, Bram	*Dracula*

Thomas, Dylan	*Portrait of the Artist as a Young Dog*
Tolkien, J. R. R.	*The Lord of the Rings*
Twain, Mark	*The Adventures of Huckleberry Finn*
Vonnegut, Kurt	*Slaughterhouse-Five; or, The Children's Crusade*
Welch, James	*Fools Crow*
Willard, Nancy	*Things Invisible to See*
Wright, Richard	*Native Son*

Film and Television

Brownlow, Kevin, and John Kobal	*Hollywood: The Pioneers*
Ellerbee, Linda	*"And So It Goes": Adventures in Television*
Gish, Lillian	*The Movies, Mr. Griffith, and Me*
Kael, Pauline	*The Citizen Kane Book: Raising Kane*
Rosenblum, Ralph, and Robert Karen	*When the Shooting Stops . . . the Cutting Begins: A Film Editor's Story*
Sperber, A. M.	*Murrow: His Life and Times*
Wiley, Mason, and Damien Bona	*Inside Oscar: The Unofficial History of the Academy Awards*

Nonfiction

Agee, James, and Walker Evans	*Let Us Now Praise Famous Men*
Ballou, Robert O. (ed.)	*The Portable World Bible*
Bell, Ruth	*Changing Bodies, Changing Lives: A Book for Teens on Sex and Relationships*
Black veterans and Wallace Terry (ed.)	*Bloods: An Oral History of the Vietnam War*
Bowen, Catherine Drinker	*Miracle at Philadelphia: The Story of the Constitutional Convention, May to September, 1787*
Bronowski, J.	*The Ascent of Man*
Brown, Dee	*Bury My Heart at Wounded Knee: An Indian History of the American West*
Brown, Michael H.	*Laying Waste: The Poisoning of America by Toxic Chemicals*
Carson, Rachel	*Silent Spring*
Ceram, C. W.	*Gods, Graves, and Scholars: The Story of Archeology*

Durant, Will	*The Story of Philosophy: The Lives and Opinions of the Greater Philosophers*
Ebenstein, William, and Edwin Fogelman	*Today's Isms: Communism, Fascism, Capitalism, Socialism*
Eiseley, Loren C.	*Darwin's Century: Evolution and the Men Who Discovered It*
Friedan, Betty	*The Feminine Mystique*
Hamilton, Edith	*Mythology*
Harding, Vincent	*There Is a River: The Black Struggle for Freedom in America*
Heat-Moon, William Least	*Blue Highways: A Journey into America*
Heilbroner, Robert L.	*The Worldly Philosophers: The Lives, Times, and Ideas of the Great Economic Thinkers*
Hersey, John	*Hiroshima*
Johanson, Donald C., and Maitland A. Edey	*Lucy: The Beginnings of Human Kind*
Johnson, Paul	*Modern Times: The World from the Twenties to the Eighties*
Langone, John	*Violence! Our Fastest-Growing Public Health Problem*
Lelyveld, Joseph	*Move Your Shadow: South Africa, Black and White*
Lopez, Barry	*Arctic Dreams: Imagination and Desire in a Northern Landscape*
Lorenz, Konrad	*On Aggression*
Lukas, J. Anthony	*Common Ground: A Turbulent Decade in the Lives of Three American Familes*
Malcolm, Andrew H.	*Final Harvest: An American Tragedy*
Meltzer, Milton	*Ain't Gonna Study War No More: The Story of America's Peace Seekers*
	Never to Forget: The Jews of the Holocaust
Naisbitt, John	*Megatrends: Ten New Directions Transforming Our Lives*
Postman, Neil	*Amusing Ourselves to Death: Public Discourse in the Age of Show Business*
Raines, Howell	*My Soul Is Rested: Movement Days in the Deep South Remembered*
Santoli, Al	*To Bear Any Burden: The Vietnam War and Its Aftermath in the Words of Americans and Southeast Asians*

Schank, Roger C., and Peter G. Childers	*The Cognitive Computer: On Language, Learning, and Artificial Intelligence*
Schell, Jonathan	*The Fate of the Earth*
Thomas, Lewis	*The Lives of a Cell: Notes of a Biology Watcher*
Tocqueville, Alexis de	*Democracy in America*
Uhlig, Mark A. (ed.)	*Apartheid in Crisis*
Watson, James D.	*The Double Helix: A Personal Account of the Discovery of the Structure of DNA*
Weiss, Ann E.	*Good Neighbors? The United States and Latin America*
Wolfe, Tom	*The Right Stuff*
Wyden, Peter	*Day One: Before Hiroshima and After*
Zerman, Melvyn Bernard	*Taking on the Press: Constitutional Rights in Conflict*

Music

Brown, James, and Bruce Tucker	*James Brown: The Godfather of Soul; An Autobiography*
Hart, Philip	*Conductors: A New Generation*
Hirshey, Gerri	*Nowhere to Run: The Story of Soul Music*
Marsh, Dave	*Glory Days: Bruce Springsteen in the 1980s*
Mason, Michael (ed.)	*The Country Music Book*
Mordden, Ethan	*Demented: The World of the Opera Diva*
Schonberg, Harold C.	*The Glorious Ones: Classical Music's Legendary Performers*
Wade, Graham	*Segovia: A Celebration of the Man and His Music*
Ward, Ed, Geoffrey Stokes, and Ken Tucker	*Rock of Ages: The Rolling Stone History of Rock and Roll*
Zinsser, William	*Willie and Dwike: An American Profile*

Poetry

Amis, Kingsley (ed.)	*The New Oxford Book of Light Verse*
Dickinson, Emily	*Final Harvest: Emily Dickinson's Poems*
Randall, Dudley (ed.)	*The Black Poets*
Rexroth, Kenneth (trans.)	*One Hundred Poems from the Japanese*
Untermeyer, Louis (ed.)	*50 Modern American and British Poets, 1920–1970*
Yevtushenko, Yevgeny	*The Poetry of Yevgeny Yevtushenko*

Related Arts

Blackstone, Harry, Jr.	*The Blackstone Book of Magic and Illusion*
Goldberg, RoseLee	*Performance: Live Art 1909 to the Present*
Sharaff, Irene	*Broadway and Hollywood: Costumes Designed by Irene Sharaff*

1982

Biography

Angelou, Maya	*I Know Why the Caged Bird Sings*
Atkinson, Linda	*Mother Jones: The Most Dangerous Woman in America*
Banks, Lynne Reid	*Dark Quartet: The Story of the Brontës*
Brown, Claude	*Manchild in the Promised Land*
Carpenter, Humphrey	*Tolkien: A Biography*
Carrighar, Sally	*Home to the Wilderness*
Douglas, William O.	*Go East, Young Man: The Early Years; The Autobiography of William O. Douglas*
Frank, Anne	*Anne Frank: The Diary of a Young Girl*
Gunther, John	*Death Be Not Proud: A Memoir*
Gurko, Miriam	*The Ladies of Seneca Falls: The Birth of the Woman's Rights Movement*
Hellman, Lillian	*Three: An Unfinished Woman, Pentimento, Scoundrel Time*
Herriot, James	*All Creatures Great and Small*
Johnson, Edgar	*Charles Dickens: His Tragedy and Triumph*
Keller, Helen	*The Story of My Life*
Kingston, Maxine Hong	*The Woman Warrior: Memoirs of a Girlhood among Ghosts*
Klein, Joe	*Woody Guthrie: A Life*
Lash, Joseph P.	*Eleanor and Franklin: The Story of Their Relationship, Based on Eleanor Roosevelt's Private Papers*
Malcolm X (as told to Alex Haley)	*The Autobiography of Malcolm X*
McLellan, David	*Karl Marx: His Life and Thought*
Mead, Margaret	*Blackberry Winter: My Earlier Years*

Miller, Merle	*Plain Speaking: An Oral Biography of Harry S. Truman*
Morison, Samuel Eliot	*Christopher Columbus, Mariner*
Neihardt, John G.	*Black Elk Speaks: Being the Life Story of a Holy Man of the Oglala Sioux*
O'Keeffe, Georgia	*Georgia O'Keeffe*
Panov, Valery, and George Feifer	*To Dance*
Pardy, Anne (As told to Robert Specht)	*Tisha: The Story of a Young Teacher in the Alaska Wilderness*
Poitier, Sidney	*This Life*
Rather, Dan, with Mickey Herskowitz	*The Camera Never Blinks: Adventures of a TV Journalist*
Russell, Bill, and Taylor Branch	*Second Wind: The Memoirs of an Opinionated Man*
Sandburg, Carl	*Abraham Lincoln: The Prairie Years and the War Years*
Stein, Gertrude	*The Autobiography of Alice B. Toklas*
Wolfe, Bertram D.	*Three Who Made a Revolution: A Biographical History*
Wright, Richard	*Black Boy: A Record of Childhood and Youth*

Dance

Ames, Jerry, and Jim Siegelman	*The Book of Tap: Recovering America's Long Lost Dance*
Balanchine, George, and Francis Mason	*101 Stories of the Great Ballets*
Banes, Sally	*Terpsichore in Sneakers: Post-Modern Dance*
Cook, Susan, and Joseph H. Mazo	*The Alvin Ailey American Dance Theater*
De Mille, Agnes	*America Dances*
Louis, Murray	*Inside Dance: Essays*
Maiorano, Robert	*Worlds Apart: The Autobiography of a Dancer from Brooklyn*
McDonagh, Don	*The Complete Guide to Modern Dance*
Neale, Wendy	*On Your Toes: Beginning Ballet*
Philip, Richard, and Mary Whitney	*Danseur: The Male in Ballet*

Reynolds, Nancy (ed.)   *The Dance Catalog*
Sorine, Daniel S., and   *Dancershoes*
    Stephanie Riva Sorine

Fiction

Austen, Jane   *Pride and Prejudice*
Baldwin, James   *If Beale Street Could Talk*
Borland, Hal   *When the Legends Die*
Bradbury, Ray   *The Martian Chronicles*
Brontë, Charlotte   *Jane Eyre*
Brontë, Emily   *Wuthering Heights*
Camus, Albert   *The Plague*
Cather, Willa   *My Ántonia*
Conrad, Joseph   *Lord Jim*
Crane, Stephen   *The Red Badge of Courage*
Dickens, Charles   *A Tale of Two Cities*
Dostoyevsky, Fyodor   *Crime and Punishment*
Doyle, Arthur Conan   *Sherlock Holmes: Selected Stories*
Du Maurier, Daphne   *Rebecca*
Ellison, Ralph   *Invisible Man*
Faulkner, William   *The Bear*
Finney, Jack   *Time and Again*
Fitzgerald, F. Scott   *The Great Gatsby*
Golding, William   *Lord of the Flies*
Hardy, Thomas   *Far from the Madding Crowd*
Hawthorne, Nathaniel   *The Scarlet Letter*
Heller, Joseph   *Catch-22*
Hemingway, Ernest   *A Farewell to Arms*
Herbert, Frank   *Dune*
Hersey, John   *The Wall*
Hesse, Hermann   *Siddhartha*
Huxley, Aldous   *Brave New World*
Joyce, James   *A Portrait of the Artist as a Young Man*
Kesey, Ken   *One Flew over the Cuckoo's Nest*
Knowles, John   *A Separate Peace*
Le Guin, Ursula K.   *The Left Hand of Darkness*
Lee, Harper   *To Kill a Mockingbird*

Malamud, Bernard	*The Fixer*
McCullers, Carson	*The Heart Is a Lonely Hunter*
O'Brien, Tim	*Going after Cacciato*
Olsen, Tillie	*Tell Me a Riddle*
Orwell, George	*Animal Farm*
Paton, Alan	*Cry, the Beloved Country: A Story of Comfort in Desolation*
Poe, Edgar Allan	*The Fall of the House of Usher, and Other Tales*
Remarque, Erich Maria	*All Quiet on the Western Front*
Salinger, J. D.	*The Catcher in the Rye*
Singer, Isaac Bashevis	*The Slave*
Solzhenitsyn, Aleksandr I.	*One Day in the Life of Ivan Denisovich*
Steinbeck, John	*Of Mice and Men*
Stoker, Bram	*Dracula*
Tolkien, J. R. R.	*The Lord of the Rings*
Tolstoy, Leo	*War and Peace*
Twain, Mark	*The Adventures of Huckleberry Finn*
Vonnegut, Kurt	*Slaughterhouse-Five; or, The Children's Crusade*
Wharton, William	*Birdy*

Film and Television

Bobker, Lee R.	*Elements of Film*
Brownlow, Kevin, and John Kobal	*Hollywood: The Pioneers*
Canutt, Yakima, with Oliver Drake	*Stunt Man: The Autobiography of Yakima Canutt*
Halas, John, and Roger Manvell	*The Technique of Film Animation*
London, Mel	*Getting into Film*
Price, Jonathan	*Video Visions: A Medium Discovers Itself*
Rosenblum, Ralph, and Robert Karen	*When the Shooting Stops . . . the Cutting Begins: A Film Editor's Story*
Shanks, Bob	*The Cool Fire: How to Make It in Television*
Super 8 Filmaker (comp. by eds.)	*Film Maker's Guide to Super 8: The "How-to-Do-It" Book for Beginning and Advanced Film Makers*

Music

Copland, Aaron	*What to Listen for in Music*

Davies, Hunter	*The Beatles*
Gaillard, Frye	*Watermelon Wine: The Spirit of Country Music*
Hurd, Michael	*The Orchestra*
Miller, Jim	*The* Rolling Stone *Illustrated History of Rock and Roll*
Pavarotti, Luciano, with William Wright	*Pavarotti: My Own Story*
Roberts, John Storm	*The Latin Tinge: The Impact of Latin American Music on the United States*
Rogers, Kenny, and Len Epand	*Making It with Music: Kenny Rogers' Guide to the Music Business*
Ruttencutter, Helen Drees	*Pianist's Progress*
Stokes, Geoffrey	*Star-Making Machinery: Inside the Business of Rock and Roll*
Van Ryzin, Lani	*Starting Your Own Band: Rock, Disco, Folk, Jazz, Country and Western*

Nonfiction

Agee, James, and Walker Evans	*Let Us Now Praise Famous Men*
Ballou, Robert O. (ed.)	*The Portable World Bible*
Bell, Ruth	*Changing Bodies, Changing Lives: A Book for Teens on Sex and Relationships*
Benedict, Ruth	*Patterns of Culture*
Brand, Stewart (ed.)	*The Next Whole Earth Catalog: Access to Tools*
Brecher, Edward M.	*Licit and Illicit Drugs: The Consumers Union Report*
Bronowski, J.	*The Ascent of Man*
Brown, Dee	*Bury My Heart at Wounded Knee: An Indian History of the American West*
Brown, Michael H.	*Laying Waste: The Poisoning of America by Toxic Chemicals*
Ceram, C. W.	*Gods, Graves, and Scholars: The Story of Archeology*
Cooke, Alistair	*Alistair Cooke's America*
Covelli, Pat	*Borrowing Time: Growing Up with Juvenile Diabetes*
Crawford, Alan	*Thunder on the Right: The New Right and the Politics of Resentment*
Durant, Will	*The Story of Philosophy: The Lives and Opinions of the Greater Philosophers*

Ebenstein, William, and Edwin Fogelman	*Today's Isms: Communism, Fascism, Capitalism, Socialism*
Eiseley, Loren C.	*Darwin's Century: Evolution and the Men Who Discovered It*
Fuller, R. Buckminster	*Operating Manual for Spaceship Earth*
Hamilton, Edith	*Mythology*
Hanckel, Frances, and John Cunningham	*A Way of Love, a Way of Life: A Young Person's Introduction to What It Means to Be Gay*
Harding, Vincent	*There Is a River: The Black Struggle for Freedom in America*
Hayden, Torey L.	*One Child*
Heilbroner, Robert L.	*The Worldly Philosophers: The Lives, Times, and Ideas of the Great Economic Thinkers*
Hentoff, Nat	*The First Freedom: The Tumultuous History of Free Speech in America*
Hofstadter, Douglas R.	*Gödel, Escher, Bach: An Eternal Golden Braid*
Homer	*The Odyssey of Homer: A Modern Translation*
Hoyt, Patricia	*How to Get Started When You Don't Know Where to Begin*
Japanese Broadcasting Corp.	*Unforgettable Fire: Pictures Drawn by Atomic Bomb Survivors*
Jenkins, Peter	*A Walk across America*
Johanson, Donald C., and Maitland A. Edey	*Lucy: The Beginnings of Human Kind*
Jones, Landon Y.	*Great Expectations: America and the Baby Boom Generation*
Jungk, Robert	*Brighter than a Thousand Suns: A Personal History of the Atomic Scientists*
Larrick, Nancy (sel.)	*Crazy to Be Alive in Such a Strange World: Poems about People*
Levine, Suzanne, and Harriet Lyons (eds.)	*The Decade of Women: A Ms. History of the Seventies in Words and Pictures*
Lorenz, Konrad	*On Aggression*
Manchester, William	*The Glory and the Dream: A Narrative History of America, 1932–1972*
Mead, Margaret	*Culture and Commitment: The New Relationships between the Generations in the 1970s*
Meltzer, Milton	*Never to Forget: The Jews of the Holocaust*
Mirkin, Gabe, and Marshall Hoffman	*The Sportsmedicine Book*

Redman, Eric	*The Dance of Legislation*
Sagan, Carl	*Cosmos*
Santoli, Al	*Everything We Had: An Oral History of the Vietnam War by Thirty-three American Soldiers Who Fought It*
Schlesinger, Arthur M., Jr.	*The Imperial Presidency*
Terkel, Studs	*Working: People Talk about What They Do All Day and How They Feel about What They Do*
Thomas, Lewis	*The Lives of a Cell: Notes of a Biology Watcher*
Thoreau, Henry David	*Civil Disobedience* *Walden*
Timerman, Jacobo	*Prisoner without a Name, Cell without a Number*
Tocqueville, Alexis de	*Democracy in America*
Toffler, Alvin	*The Third Wave*
Watson, James D.	*The Double Helix: A Personal Account of the Discovery of the Structure of DNA*

Related Arts

Baird, Bil	*The Art of the Puppet*
Barton, Peter	*Staying Power: Performing Artists Talk about Their Lives*
Billington, Michael	*Performing Arts: An Illustrated Guide*
Campbell, Patricia J.	*Passing the Hat: Street Performers in America*
Hamblin, Kay	*Mime: A Playbook of Silent Fantasy*
Page, Patrick	*The Big Book of Magic*
Towsen, John H.	*Clowns*

Theater

Gottfried, Martin	*Broadway Musicals*
Hagen, Uta, with Haskel Frankel	*Respect for Acting*
Hanff, Helene	*Underfoot in Show Business*
Hoggett, Chris	*Stage Crafts*
Lewis, Robert	*Advice to the Players*
Matson, Katinka	*The Working Actor: A Guide to the Profession*
Olfson, Lewy (ed.)	*50 Great Scenes for Student Actors*

Seto, Judith Roberts (comp.)   *The Young Actor's Workbook*
Stanislavsky, Konstantin   *An Actor Prepares*
                             Building a Character

1976

Biography

Allen, Douglas and Douglas   *N. C. Wyeth: The Collected Paintings, Illustrations,*
Allen Jr.   *and Murals*
Bainton, Roland H.   *Here I Stand: A Life of Martin Luther*
Bourke-White, Margaret   *Portrait of Myself*
Bowen, Catherine Drinker   *The Most Dangerous Man in America: Scenes from*
                               the Life of Benjamin Franklin
Brodie, Fawn M.   *Thomas Jefferson: An Intimate History*
Brown, Claude   *Manchild in the Promised Land*
Bullock, Alan   *Hitler: A Study in Tyranny*
Burgess, Alan   *Daylight Must Come: The Story of a Courageous*
                               Woman Doctor in the Congo
Carrighar, Sally   *Home to the Wilderness*
Chandler, David   *Napoleon*
Clark, Ronald W.   *Einstein: The Life and Times*
Curie, Eve   *Madame Curie: A Biography*
Douglas, William O.   *Go East, Young Man: The Early Years; The*
                               Autobiography of William O. Douglas
Halberstam, David   *Ho*
Hellman, Lillian   *Three: An Unfinished Woman, Pentimento,*
                               Scoundrel Time
Hibbard, Howard   *Michelangelo*
Hotchner, A. E.   *Papa Hemingway: A Personal Memoir*
Jenkins, Elizabeth   *Elizabeth the Great*
Keller, Helen   *The Story of My Life*
Kennedy, John F.   *Profiles in Courage*
Lash, Joseph P.   *Eleanor and Franklin: The Story of Their*
                               Relationship, Based on Eleanor Roosevelt's
                               Private Papers
Lund, Doris   *Eric*
Malcolm X (as told to   *The Autobiography of Malcolm X*
Alex Haley)

Mann, Peggy	*Golda: The Life of Israel's Prime Minister*
Massie, Robert K.	*Nicholas and Alexandra*
McLellan, David	*Karl Marx: His Life and Thought*
Mead, Margaret	*Blackberry Winter: My Earlier Years*
Merriam, Eve	*Growing Up Female in America—Ten Lives*
Milford, Nancy	*Zelda: A Biography*
Miller, Merle	*Plain Speaking: An Oral Biography of Harry S. Truman*
Pepys, Samuel	*The Diary of Samuel Pepys*
Sandburg, Carl	*Abraham Lincoln: The Prairie Years and the War Years*
Sanders, Marion K.	*Dorothy Thompson: A Legend in Her Time*
Stone, Irving	*Clarence Darrow for the Defense*
Tomalin, Claire	*The Life and Death of Mary Wollstonecraft*
Twombly, Robert C.	*Frank Lloyd Wright: An Interpretive Biography*
Wilson, Dorothy Clarke	*Bright Eyes: The Story of Susette La Flesche, an Omaha Indian*
Wolfe, Bertram D.	*Three Who Made a Revolution: A Biographical History*
Wright, Richard	*Black Boy: A Record of Childhood and Youth*
Zassenhaus, Hiltgunt	*Walls: Resisting the Third Reich—One Woman's Story*

Current

Arendt, Hannah	*On Violence*
Bernstein, Carl, and Bob Woodward	*All the President's Men*
Boston Women's Health Book Collective	*Our Bodies, Ourselves*
Cameron, John	*The Astrologer*
Castaneda, Carlos	*Journey to Ixtlan: The Lessons of Don Juan*
Collins, Michael	*Carrying the Fire: An Astronaut's Journeys*
Commoner, Barry	*The Closing Circle: Confronting the Environmental Crisis*
Cormier, Robert	*The Chocolate War*
Crichton, Michael	*The Terminal Man*
Curtin, Sharon R.	*Nobody Ever Died of Old Age*
Deloria, Vine, Jr.	*Custer Died for Your Sins: An Indian Manifesto*

Fast, Julius — *Body Language*

Friedman, Myra — *Buried Alive: The Biography of Janis Joplin*

Gersh, Marvin J., and Iris F. Litt — *Handbook of Adolescence: A Medical Guide for Parents and Teenagers*

Glasser, Ronald J. — *Ward 402*

Grier, William H., and Price M. Cobbs — *Black Rage*

Habenstreit, Barbara — *"To My Brother Who Did a Crime . . .": Former Prisoners Tell Their Stories in Their Own Words*

Harris, Marilyn — *Hatter Fox*

Harris, Thomas A. — *I'm O.K.—You're O.K.*

Holt, John — *Escape from Childhood: The Needs and Rights of Children*

Howe, Florence, and Ellen Bass (eds.) — *No More Masks! An Anthology of Poems by Women*

Jackson, Donald Dale — *Judges*

Jahn, Mike — *Rock: A Social History of the Music, 1945–1972*

Janeway, Elizabeth — *Between Myth and Morning: Women Awakening*

Kesey, Ken — *One Flew over the Cuckoo's Nest*

Kusche, Larry — *The Bermuda Triangle Mystery: Solved*

Langone, David — *Death Is a Noun: A View of the End of Life*

Loeb, Robert H., Jr., and John P. Maloney — *Your Legal Rights as a Minor*

Maas, Peter — *Serpico*

Mead, Margaret — *Culture and Commitment: The New Relationships between the Generations in the 1970s*

Miller, Merle — *On Being Different: What It Means to Be a Homosexual*

Mostert, Noel — *Supership*

O'Neill, Nena, and George O'Neill — *Open Marriage: A New Life Style for Couples*

Pines, Maya — *The Brain Changers: Scientists and the New Mind Control*

Pirsig, Robert M. — *Zen and the Art of Motorcycle Maintenance: An Inquiry into Values*

Plath, Sylvia — *The Bell Jar*

Read, Piers Paul — *Alive: The Story of the Andes Survivors*

Severn, Bill — *The Right to Privacy*

Steiner, Stan — *La Raza: The Mexican Americans*

Tidyman, Ernest — *Dummy*

Toffler, Alvin (ed.)	*Learning for Tomorrow: The Role of the Future in Education*
Verrett, Jacqueline, and Jean Carper	*Eating May Be Hazardous to Your Health: How Your Government Fails to Protect You from the Dangers in Your Food*
Wigginton, Eliot (ed.)	*The Foxfire Book*
Yette, Samuel F.	*The Choice: The Issue of Black Survival in America*

Fiction

Austen, Jane	*Pride and Prejudice*
Baldwin, James	*Go Tell It on the Mountain*
Camus, Albert	*The Stranger*
Cather, Willa	*My Ántonia*
Cervantes Saavedra, Miguel de	*Don Quixote de la Mancha*
Conrad, Joseph	*Great Short Works of Joseph Conrad*
Crane, Stephen	*The Red Badge of Courage*
Dickens, Charles	*Great Expectations*
Dostoyevsky, Fyodor	*Crime and Punishment*
Ellison, Ralph	*Invisible Man*
Faulkner, William	*The Sound and the Fury*
Fitzgerald, F. Scott	*The Great Gatsby*
Gardner, John	*Grendel*
Golding, William	*Lord of the Flies*
Greenberg, Joanne	*I Never Promised You a Rose Garden*
Hardy, Thomas	*The Return of the Native*
Hawthorne, Nathaniel	*The Scarlet Letter*
Heller, Joseph	*Catch-22*
Hemingway, Ernest	*For Whom the Bell Tolls*
Hesse, Hermann	*Siddhartha*
Huxley, Aldous	*Brave New World*
Joyce, James	*A Portrait of the Artist as a Young Man*
Kafka, Franz	*The Metamorphosis*
Knowles, John	*A Separate Peace*
Kosinski, Jerzy N.	*The Painted Bird*
Lawrence, D. H.	*Sons and Lovers*
Le Guin, Ursula K.	*The Left Hand of Darkness*
Lewis, Sinclair	*Main Street*

Malamud, Bernard   *The Fixer*
Mann, Thomas   *Death in Venice*
Maugham, W. Somerset   *Of Human Bondage*
Melville, Herman   *Moby-Dick*
Paton, Alan   *Cry, the Beloved Country: A Story of Comfort in
                             Desolation*

Poe, Edgar Allan   *The Fall of the House of Usher, and Other Tales*
Remarque, Erich Maria   *All Quiet on the Western Front*
Salinger, J. D.   *The Catcher in the Rye*
Solzhenitsyn, Aleksandr I. *The Gulag Archipelago, 1918–1956: An Experiment
                             in Literary Investigation*
                           One Day in the Life of Ivan Denisovich

Steinbeck, John   *The Grapes of Wrath*
Swift, Jonathan   *Gulliver's Travels*
Tolkien, J. R. R.   *The Lord of the Rings*
Tolstoy, Leo   *War and Peace*
Twain, Mark   *The Adventures of Huckleberry Finn*
Vonnegut, Kurt   *Slaughterhouse-Five; or, The Children's Crusade*
Wolfe, Thomas   *Look Homeward, Angel: A Story of the Buried Life*
Wright, Richard   *Native Son*

Nonfiction

Agee, James, and   *Let Us Now Praise Famous Men*
    Walker Evans

Ballou, Robert O. (ed.)   *The Portable World Bible*
Benedict, Ruth   *Patterns of Culture*
Bennett, Lerone, Jr.   *Before the Mayflower: A History of Black America*
Bronowski, J.   *The Ascent of Man*
Brown, Dee   *Bury My Heart at Wounded Knee: An Indian History
                             of the American West*

Carson, Rachel   *Silent Spring*
Ceram, C. W.   *Gods, Graves, and Scholars: The Story of
                             Archeology*

Ciardi, John   *How Does a Poem Mean?*
Cooke, Alistair   *Alistair Cooke's America*
Copland, Aaron   *What to Listen for in Music*
Durant, Will   *The Story of Philosophy: The Lives and Opinions of
                             the Greater Philosophers*

Ebenstein, William, and Edwin Fogelman	*Today's Isms: Communism, Fascism, Capitalism, Socialism*
Eiseley, Loren C.	*Darwin's Century: Evolution and the Men Who Discovered It*
Friedan, Betty	*The Feminine Mystique*
Fuller, R. Buckminster	*Operating Manual for Spaceship Earth*
Hamilton, Edith	*Mythology*
Heilbroner, Robert L.	*The Worldly Philosophers: The Lives, Times, and Ideas of the Great Economic Thinkers*
Hoffer, Eric	*The True Believer: Thoughts on the Nature of Mass Movements*
Homer	*The Odyssey of Homer: A Modern Translation*
Jacobs, Jane	*The Death and Life of Great American Cities*
Jungk, Robert	*Brighter than a Thousand Suns: A Personal History of the Atomic Scientists*
Kaplan, Abraham	*The New World of Philosophy*
Kline, Morris	*Mathematics in Western Culture*
Kuh, Katherine	*Break-Up: The Core of Modern Art*
Lorenz, Konrad	*On Aggression*
Magnuson, Warren Grant, and Jean Carper	*The Dark Side of the Marketplace: The Plight of the American Consumer*
McLuhan, Marshall	*Understanding Media: The Extensions of Man*
Neill, Alexander Sutherland	*Summerhill: A Radical Approach to Child Rearing*
Redman, Eric	*The Dance of Legislation*
Roszak, Theodore	*The Making of a Counter Culture: Reflections on the Technocratic Society and Its Youthful Opposition*
Schlesinger, Arthur M., Jr.	*The Imperial Presidency*
Taylor, Joshua C.	*Learning to Look: A Handbook for the Visual Arts*
Terkel, Studs	*Working: People Talk about What They Do All Day and How They Feel about What They Do*
Thomas, Lewis	*The Lives of a Cell: Notes of a Biology Watcher*
Thoreau, Henry David	*Civil Disobedience* *Walden*
Tocqueville, Alexis de	*Democracy in America*
Toffler, Alvin	*Future Shock*
Watson, James D.	*The Double Helix: A Personal Account of the Discovery of the Structure of DNA*
Woodward, C. Vann	*The Strange Career of Jim Crow*

Theater

Albee, Edward	*The Zoo Story: A Play*
Anonymous	*Everyman*
Aristophanes	*Lysistrata*
Beckett, Samuel	*Waiting for Godot: A Tragicomedy in Two Acts*
Bolt, Robert	*A Man for All Seasons*
Brecht, Bertolt	*Mother Courage and Her Children: A Chronicle of the Thirty Years' War*
Chekhov, Anton	*The Cherry Orchard: A Comedy in Four Acts*
Congreve, William	*The Way of the World*
Durrenmatt, Friedrich	*The Visit: A Tragi-comedy*
Fry, Christopher	*The Lady's Not for Burning: A Comedy*
García Lorca, Federico	*Blood Wedding*
Genet, Jean	*The Blacks: A Clown Show*
Gibson, William	*The Miracle Worker: A Play for Television*
Giraudoux, Jean	*The Madwoman of Chaillot*
Gorky, Maxim	*The Lower Depths*
Hansberry, Lorraine	*A Raisin in the Sun*
Hellman, Lillian	*The Little Foxes*
Hochhuth, Rolf	*The Deputy*
Ibsen, Henrik	*A Doll's House*
Ionesco, Eugène	*Rhinoceros*
Jonson, Ben	*Volpone*
Lawrence, Jerome, and Robert E. Lee	*Inherit the Wind*
MacLeish, Archibald	*J. B.*
Marlowe, Christopher	*Doctor Faustus*
McCullers, Carson	*The Member of the Wedding*
Miller, Arthur	*Death of a Salesman*
Molière	*The Misanthrope*
O'Casey, Sean	*Juno and the Paycock: A Tragedy in Three Acts*
O'Neill, Eugene	*Long Day's Journey into Night*
Osborne, John	*Look Back in Anger: A Play in Three Acts*
Pinter, Harold	*The Birthday Party*
Pirandello, Luigi	*Six Characters in Search of an Author*
Racine, Jean	*Phaedra*

Rice, Tim, and Andrew Lloyd Webber	*Jesus Christ Superstar: A Rock Opera*
Shakespeare, William	*Macbeth*
	A Midsummer Night's Dream
Shaw, George Bernard	*Saint Joan*
Sheridan, Richard Brinsley	*The School for Scandal*
Sophocles	*Oedipus the King*
Strindberg, August	*Miss Julie*
Synge, J. M.	*The Playboy of the Western World*
Wilde, Oscar	*The Importance of Being Earnest*
Wilder, Thornton	*Our Town*
Williams, Tennessee	*The Glass Menagerie*
Zindel, Paul	*The Effect of Gamma Rays on Man-in-the-Moon Marigolds: A Drama in Two Acts*

1971

Biography

Bainton, Roland H.	*Here I Stand: A Life of Martin Luther*
Baker, Carlos	*Ernest Hemingway: A Life Story*
Bennett, Lerone, Jr.	*What Manner of Man: A Biography of Martin Luther King, Jr.*
Boswell, James	*The Life of Samuel Johnson*
Bowen, Catherine Drinker	*Yankee from Olympus: Justice Holmes and His Family*
Brown, Claude	*Manchild in the Promised Land*
Cellini, Benvenuto	*The Autobiography of Benvenuto Cellini*
Chute, Marchette Gaylord	*Geoffrey Chaucer of England*
Clarke, John Henrik (ed.)	*Malcolm X: The Man and His Times*
Curie, Eve	*Madame Curie: A Biography*
de Beer, Sir Gavin	*Hannibal: Challenging Rome's Supremacy*
de Kruif, Paul	*Microbe Hunters*
Ferguson, Charles W.	*Naked to Mine Enemies: The Life of Cardinal Wolsey*
Fermi, Laura	*Atoms in the Family: My Life with Enrico Fermi*
Forbes, Esther	*Paul Revere and the World He Lived In*
Frank, Anne	*Anne Frank: The Diary of a Young Girl*

Franklin, Benjamin	*Autobiography*
Fraser, Antonia	*Mary, Queen of Scots*
Grey, Ian	*Peter the Great, Emperor of All Russia*
Guérard, Albert Léon	*Napoleon I: A Great Life in Brief*
Hagedorn, Hermann	*The Roosevelt Family of Sagamore Hill*
Hansberry, Lorraine	*To Be Young, Gifted and Black: Lorraine Hansberry in Her Own Words*
Hart, Moss	*Act One: An Autobiography*
Jenkins, Elizabeth	*Elizabeth the Great*
Keller, Helen	*The Story of My Life*
Kelly, Amy Ruth	*Eleanor of Aquitaine and the Four Kings*
Kennedy, John F.	*Profiles in Courage*
Martin, Ralph G.	*Jennie: The Life of Lady Randolph Churchill. Vol. I: The Romantic Years, 1854–1895*
Maurois, André	*Ariel: The Life of Shelley*
Merton, Thomas	*The Seven Storey Mountain*
Moody, Anne	*Coming of Age in Mississippi*
Morison, Samuel Eliot	*Christopher Columbus, Mariner*
Parks, Gordon	*A Choice of Weapons*
Pepys, Samuel	*The Diary of Samuel Pepys*
Plutarch	*Lives*
Rowse, A. L.	*William Shakespeare: A Biography*
Sandburg, Carl	*Abraham Lincoln: The Prairie Years and the War Years*
	Always the Young Strangers
Skinner, Cornelia Otis	*Madame Sarah*
St. John, Robert	*Ben-Gurion: A Biography*
Steffens, Lincoln	*The Autobiography of Lincoln Steffens*
Stone, Irving	*Clarence Darrow for the Defense*
Strachey, Lytton	*Queen Victoria*
Stuart, Jesse	*The Thread That Runs So True*
Taylor, A. J. P.	*Bismarck: The Man and the Statesman*
Tharp, Louise Hall	*The Peabody Sisters of Salem*
Twain, Mark	*The Autobiography of Mark Twain*
Washington, Booker T.	*Up from Slavery: An Autobiography*
Watson, James D.	*The Double Helix: A Personal Account of the Discovery of the Structure of DNA*

Winwar, Frances   The *Haunted Palace: A Life of Edgar Allan Poe*
Yevtushenko, Yevgeny   *A Precocious Autobiography*

Drama

BOOKS ABOUT THE THEATER

Bentley, Eric   *The Theatre of Commitment, and Other Essays on
                            Drama in Our Society*
                           What Is Theater: A Query in Chronicle Form
Brustein, Robert   *The Theatre of Revolt: An Approach to the Modern
                            Drama*
Cheney, Sheldon   *The Theatre: Three Thousand Years of Drama,
                            Acting, and Stagecraft*
Esslin, Martin   *Reflections: Essays on Modern Theatre*
                           The Theatre of the Absurd
Fergusson, Francis   *The Idea of a Theater: A Study of Ten Plays, the Art
                            of Drama in Changing Perspective*
Gassner, John   *Masters of the Drama*
Grotowski, Jerzy   *Towards a Poor Theatre*
Harbage, Alfred   *William Shakespeare: A Reader's Guide*
Kerr, Walter   *The Theater in Spite of Itself*
Kostelanetz, Richard   *The Theater of Mixed Means: An Introduction to
                            Happenings, Kinetic Energy, and Other Mixed-
                            Means Performances*
Nicoll, Allardyce   *The Development of the Theater: A Study of
                            Theatrical Art from the Beginnings to the
                            Present Day*
Taylor, John Russell   *Angry Theatre: New British Drama*

PLAYS

Albee, Edward   *The Zoo Story: A Play*
Anderson, Maxwell   *Winterset: A Play in Three Acts*
Anonymous   *Everyman*
Aristophanes   *Lysistrata*
Beckett, Samuel   *Waiting for Godot: A Tragicomedy in Two Acts*
Behan, Brendan   *The Hostage*
Bolt, Robert   *A Man for All Seasons*
Brecht, Bertolt   *Mother Courage and Her Children: A Chronicle of
                            the Thirty Years' War*

Chekhov, Anton	*The Cherry Orchard: A Comedy in Four Acts*
Congreve, William	*The Way of the World*
Eliot, T. S.	*Murder in the Cathedral*
Gibson, William	*The Miracle Worker: A Play for Television*
Giraudoux, Jean	*The Madwoman of Chaillot*
Goldman, James	*The Lion in Winter*
Hansberry, Lorraine	*A Raisin in the Sun*
Hellman, Lillian	*The Little Foxes*
Hochhuth, Rolf	*The Deputy*
Ibsen, Henrik	*An Enemy of the People: A Play in Five Acts*
Ionesco, Eugène	*Rhinoceros*
Kaufman, George S., and Moss Hart	*You Can't Take It with You*
Lawrence, Jerome, and Robert E. Lee	*Inherit the Wind*
Lewin, John	*House of Atreus: Adapted from the Oresteia*
Lorca, Federico García	*Blood Wedding*
Luke, Peter	*Hadrian VII: A Play*
MacDermot, Galt	*Hair*
MacLeish, Archibald	*J. B.*
Marlowe, Christopher	*Doctor Faustus*
McCullers, Carson	*The Member of the Wedding*
Miller, Arthur	*The Crucible*
Molière	*The Miser*
O'Casey, Sean	*Juno and the Paycock: A Tragedy in Three Acts*
O'Neill, Eugene	*Long Day's Journey into Night*
Osborne, John	*Look Back in Anger: A Play in Three Acts*
Pinter, Harold	*The Birthday Party*
Pirandello, Luigi	*Six Characters in Search of an Author*
Racine, Jean	*Phaedra*
Rattigan, Terence	*The Winslow Boy*
Rodgers, Richard, and Oscar Hammerstein	*Oklahoma!*
Rostand, Edmond	*Cyrano de Bergerac*
Sackler, Howard	*The Great White Hope*
Sartre, Jean-Paul	*No Exit*
Shakespeare, William	*A Midsummer Night's Dream*
	Othello

Shaw, George Bernard	*Saint Joan*
Sheridan, Richard Brinsley	*The School for Scandal*
Simon, Neil	*The Odd Couple*
Sophocles	*Oedipus the King*
Stein, Joseph	*Fiddler on the Roof*
Stoppard, Tom	*Rosencrantz and Guildenstern Are Dead*
Strindberg, August	*The Father*
Synge, J. M.	*The Playboy of the Western World*
Wilde, Oscar	*The Importance of Being Earnest*
Wilder, Thornton	*Our Town*
Williams, Tennessee	*The Glass Menagerie*

Fiction

Agee, James	*A Death in the Family*
Austen, Jane	*Pride and Prejudice*
Bellow, Saul	*The Adventures of Augie March*
Brontë, Charlotte	*Jane Eyre*
Brontë, Emily	*Wuthering Heights*
Buck, Pearl S.	*The Good Earth*
Camus, Albert	*The Plague*
Cather, Willa	*My Ántonia*
Cervantes Saavedra, Miguel de	*Don Quixote de la Mancha*
Collins, Wilkie	*The Moonstone*
Conrad, Joseph	*Lord Jim*
Crane, Stephen	*The Red Badge of Courage*
Dickens, Charles	*Bleak House*
Dostoyevsky, Fyodor	*Crime and Punishment*
Ellison, Ralph	*Invisible Man*
Faulkner, William	*The Sound and the Fury*
Fitzgerald, F. Scott	*The Great Gatsby*
Flaubert, Gustave	*Madame Bovary*
Forster, E. M.	*A Passage to India*
Golding, William	*Lord of the Flies*
Grass, Günter	*The Tin Drum*
Hemingway, Ernest	*For Whom the Bell Tolls*
Hesse, Hermann	*Steppenwolf*

Hugo, Victor	*Les Misérables*
Huxley, Aldous	*Brave New World*
James, Henry	*The Turn of the Screw*
Kafka, Franz	*The Trial*
Kazantzakis, Nikos	*Zorba the Greek*
Keyes, Daniel	*Flowers for Algernon*
Knowles, John	*A Separate Peace*
Lawrence, D. H.	*Sons and Lovers*
Lee, Harper	*To Kill a Mockingbird*
Lewis, Sinclair	*Main Street*
Malamud, Bernard	*The Fixer*
Malraux, André	*Man's Fate*
Mann, Thomas	*The Magic Mountain*
Markandaya, Kamala	*Nectar in a Sieve*
Maugham, W. Somerset	*Of Human Bondage*
Melville, Herman	*Moby-Dick*
Mishima, Yukio	*The Sound of Waves*
Mitchell, Margaret	*Gone with the Wind*
Orwell, George	*1984*
Paton, Alan	*Cry, the Beloved Country: A Story of Comfort in Desolation*
Remarque, Erich Maria	*All Quiet on the Western Front*
Rolvaag, O. E.	*Giants in the Earth*
Saint-Exupéry, Antoine de	*The Little Prince*
Salinger, J. D.	*The Catcher in the Rye*
Solzhenitsyn, Aleksandr I.	*One Day in the Life of Ivan Denisovich*
Steinbeck, John	*The Grapes of Wrath*
Tolkien, J. R. R.	*The Lord of the Rings*
Tolstoy, Leo	*Anna Karenina*
Twain, Mark	*The Adventures of Huckleberry Finn*
Undset, Sigrid	*Kristin Lavransdatter*
Vonnegut, Kurt	*Cat's Cradle*
Wharton, Edith	*Ethan Frome*
Wilde, Oscar	*The Picture of Dorian Gray*
Wilder, Thornton	*The Bridge of San Luis Rey*
Wolfe, Thomas	*Look Homeward, Angel: A Story of the Buried Life*
Wright, Richard	*Native Son*

Nonfiction

Bernstein, Leonard	*The Joy of Music*
Brinton, Crane	*Ideas and Men: The Story of Western Thought*
Canaday, John	*Mainstreams of Modern Art*
Carson, Rachel	*The Sea around Us*
Ceram, C. W.	*Gods, Graves, and Scholars: The Story of Archeology*
Ciardi, John	*How Does a Poem Mean?*
Clark, Kenneth	*Civilisation: A Personal View*
Dantzig, Tobias	*Number: The Language of Science*
De Mille, Agnes	*The Book of the Dance*
Ebenstein, William, and Edwin Fogelman	*Today's Isms: Communism, Fascism, Capitalism, Socialism*
Eiseley, Loren C.	*Darwin's Century: Evolution and the Men Who Discovered It*
Feldman, Edmund Burke	*Art as Image and Idea*
Galbraith, John Kenneth	*The New Industrial State*
Gamow, George	*One Two Three—Infinity: Facts and Speculations of Science*
Giedion, S.	*Space, Time and Architecture: The Growth of a New Tradition*
Hamilton, Edith	*Mythology*
Harrington, Michael	*The Other America: Poverty in the United States*
Heilbroner, Robert L.	*The Worldly Philosophers: The Lives, Times, and Ideas of the Great Economic Thinkers.*
Hofstadter, Richard	*The American Political Tradition and the Men Who Made It*
Hosken, Fran P.	*The Language of Cities*
Inkeles, Alex	*What Is Sociology? An Introduction to the Discipline and Profession*
Janson, H. W., with Dora Jane Janson and Joseph Kerman	*A History of Art and Music*
Kaplan, Abraham	*The New World of Philosophy*
Lidz, Theodore	*The Person: His and Her Development throughout the Life Cycle*
Lorenz, Konrad	*On Aggression*
Mansbridge, John	*Graphic History of Architecture*
McNeill, William H.	*A World History*

Myrdal, Gunnar   *An American Dilemma: The Negro Problem and Modern Democracy*

Nevins, Allan   *The Gateway to History*

Randall, John Herman, Jr., and Justus Buchler   *Philosophy: An Introduction*

Russell, Bertrand   *A History of Western Philosophy*

Snow, C. P.   *The Two Cultures*

Taylor, Joshua C.   *Learning to Look: A Handbook for the Visual Arts*

Thomson, Robert   *The Pelican History of Psychology*

Tocqueville, Alexis de   *Democracy in America*

Voss, Carl Hermann   *In Search of Meaning: Living Religions of the World*

Wellek, René, and Austin Warren   *Theory of Literature*

Now

Arendt, Hannah   *On Violence*

Arnow, Harriette Simpson   *The Weedkiller's Daughter*

Baez, Joan   *Daybreak*

Birmingham, John   *Our Time Is Now: Notes from the High School Underground*

Bloomquist, E. R.   *Marijuana*

Bradford, Richard   *Red Sky at Morning*

Carson, Rachel   *Silent Spring*

Cleaver, Eldridge   *Soul on Ice*

Cohn, Nik   *Rock from the Beginning*

Crichton, Michael   *The Andromeda Strain*

Davies, L. P.   *Psychogeist*

De Bell, Garrett (comp.)   *The Environmental Handbook*

Deloria, Vine, Jr.   *Custer Died for Your Sins: An Indian Manifesto*

Devlin, Bernadette   *The Price of My Soul*

Ehrlich, Paul R.   *The Population Bomb*

Fariña, Richard   *Long Time Coming, and a Long Time Gone*

Gaylin, Willard   *In the Service of Their Country: War Resisters in Prison*

Gerzon, Mark   *The Whole World Is Watching: A Young Man Looks at Youth's Dissent*

Goldstein, Richard   *Poetry of Rock*

Greenberg, Joanne	*I Never Promised You a Rose Garden*
Gregory, Susan	*Hey, White Girl!*
Hansberry, Lorraine	*To Be Young, Gifted and Black: Lorraine Hansberry in Her Own Words*
Hayden, Tom	*Trial*
Head, Ann	*Mr. and Mrs. Bo Jo Jones*
Heller, Joseph	*Catch-22*
Hemphill, Paul	*The Nashville Sound: Bright Lights and Country Music*
Hersh, Seymour M.	*My Lai 4: A Report on the Massacre and Its Aftermath*
Hesse, Hermann	*Siddhartha*
Hopkins, Jerry	*Festival! The Book of American Musical Celebrations*
Hough, John T., Jr.	*A Peck of Salt: A Year in the Ghetto*
Kellogg, Marjorie	*Tell Me That You Love Me, Junie Moon*
Kunen, James S.	*The Strawberry Statement: Notes of a College Revolutionary*
Lederer, William J.	*Our Own Worst Enemy*
Lester, Julius	*Search for the New Land: History as Subjective Experience*
Louria, Donald B.	*The Drug Scene*
Lowenfels, Walter	*The Writing on the Wall: 108 American Poems of Protest*
Malamud, Bernard	*The Fixer*
Malcolm X (as told to Alex Haley)	*The Autobiography of Malcolm X*
Max, Peter	*Peace-Love-Thought-God*
Mead, Margaret	*Culture and Commitment: A Study of the Generation Gap*
Owens, Jesse, and Paul G. Neimark	*Blackthink: My Life As Black Man and White Man*
Postman, Neil, and Charles Weingartner	*The Soft Revolution: A Student Handbook for Turning Schools Around*
Roszak, Theodore	*The Making of a Counter Culture: Reflections on the Technocratic Society and Its Youthful Opposition*
Southard, Helen F.	*Sex before Twenty: New Answers for Youth*
Steiner, Stan	*La Raza: The Mexican Americans*

Swarthout, Glendon	*Bless the Beasts and Children*
Taylor, Gordon Rattray	*The Biological Time Bomb*
Taylor, Harold	*Students without Teachers: The Crisis in the University*
Thompson, Jean [pseud.]	*The House of Tomorrow*
Thompson, Mary Lou (ed.)	*Voices of the New Feminism*
Toffler, Alvin	*Future Shock*
Travers, Milton	*Each Other's Victims*
Westlake, Donald E.	*Up Your Banners: A Novel*
Young, Collier	*The Todd Dossier*
Zwerin, Michael	*The Silent Sound of Needles*

1968

Biography

Adams, Henry	*The Education of Henry Adams*
Anderson, Marian	*My Lord, What a Morning: An Autobiography*
Antin, Mary	*At School in the Promised Land; or, The Story of a Little Immigrant*
Baruch, Bernard M.	*Baruch: My Own Story*
Bell, E. T.	*Men of Mathematics*
Boswell, James	*The Life of Samuel Johnson*
Bowen, Catherine Drinker	*Yankee from Olympus: Justice Holmes and His Family*
Buck, Pearl S.	*My Several Worlds: A Personal Record*
Castelot, André	*Queen of France: A Biography of Marie Antoinette*
Cellini, Benvenuto	*The Autobiography of Benvenuto Cellini*
Chute, Marchette Gaylord	*Shakespeare of London*
Cousins, Norman	*Dr. Schweitzer of Lambaréné*
Cunliffe, Marcus	*George Washington, Man and Monument*
Curie, Eve	*Madame Curie: A Biography*
Davis, Burke	*They Called Him Stonewall: A Life of Lt. General T. J. Jackson, C.S.A.*
de Kruif, Paul	*Microbe Hunters*
Ferguson, Charles W.	*Naked to Mine Enemies: The Life of Cardinal Wolsey*

Fermi, Laura	*Atoms in the Family: My Life with Enrico Fermi*
Forbes, Esther	*Paul Revere and the World He Lived In*
Frank, Anne	*Anne Frank: The Diary of a Young Girl*
Franklin, Benjamin	*Autobiography*
Grey, Ian	*Peter the Great, Emperor of All Russia*
Guérard, Albert Léon	*Napoleon I: A Great Life in Brief*
Hagedorn, Hermann	*The Roosevelt Family of Sagamore Hill*
Hart, Moss	*Act One: An Autobiography*
Heiser, Victor	*An American Doctor's Odyssey: Adventures in Forty-five Countries*
Jenkins, Elizabeth	*Elizabeth the Great*
Keller, Helen	*The Story of My Life*
Kelly, Amy Ruth	*Eleanor of Aquitaine and the Four Kings*
Kennedy, John F.	*Profiles in Courage*
Krutch, Joseph Wood	*Henry David Thoreau*
Lamb, Harold	*Hannibal: One Man against Rome*
Maurois, André	*Ariel: The Life of Shelley*
Merton, Thomas	*The Seven Storey Mountain*
Morison, Samuel Eliot	*Christopher Columbus, Mariner*
Pepys, Samuel	*The Diary of Samuel Pepys*
Plutarch	*Lives*
Roosevelt, Eleanor	*This I Remember*
Sandburg, Carl	*Abraham Lincoln: The Prairie Years and the War Years*
	Always the Young Strangers
St. John, Robert	*Ben-Gurion: A Biography*
Steffens, Lincoln	*The Autobiography of Lincoln Steffens*
Stone, Irving	*Clarence Darrow for the Defense*
Strachey, Lytton	*Queen Victoria*
Stuart, Jesse	*The Thread That Runs So True*
Taylor, A. J. P.	*Bismarck: The Man and the Statesman*
Tharp, Louise Hall	*The Peabody Sisters of Salem*
Twain, Mark	*The Autobiography of Mark Twain*
Van Loon, Hendrik Willem	*R. v. R.: The Life of Rembrandt van Rijn*
Vining, Elizabeth	*Windows for the Crown Prince*
Washington, Booker T.	*Up from Slavery: An Autobiography*
Winwar, Frances	*The Haunted Palace: A Life of Edgar Allan Poe*

Wong, Jade Snow	*Fifth Chinese Daughter*
Woolf, Virginia	*Flush: A Biography*
Yevtushenko, Yevgeny	*A Precocious Autobiography*

Drama

BOOKS ABOUT THE THEATER

Blum, Daniel	*Great Stars of the American Stage: A Pictorial Record* *Theatre World*
Brustein, Robert	*The Third Theatre*
Burns Mantle, Robert	The Burns Mantle Best Plays Series
Courtney, Marguerite	*Laurette*
Fowler, Gene	*Good Night, Sweet Prince: The Life and Time of John Barrymore*
Funke, Lewis, and John E. Booth	*Actors Talk about Acting*
Hart, Moss	*Act One: An Autobiography*
Prideaux, Tom	*World Theatre in Pictures: From Ancient Times to Modern Broadway*
Ross, Lillian, and Helen Ross	*The Player: A Profile of an Art*
Webster, Margaret	*The Same Only Different: Five Generations of a Great Theatre Family*

PLAYS

Anderson, Maxwell	*Winterset: A Play in Three Acts*
Baldwin, James	*The Amen Corner: A Play*
Beckett, Samuel	*Waiting for Godot: A Tragicomedy in Two Acts*
Brecht, Bertolt	*Mother Courage and Her Children: A Chronicle of the Thirty Years' War*
Chekhov, Anton	*The Cherry Orchard: A Comedy in Four Acts*
Gibson, William	*The Miracle Worker: A Play for Television*
Giraudoux, Jean	*The Madwoman of Chaillot*
Goetz, Ruth, and Augustus Goetz	*The Heiress*
Hansberry, Lorraine	*A Raisin in the Sun*
Heggen, Thomas, and Joshua Logan	*Mister Roberts: A Play*

Hellman, Lillian	*The Little Foxes*
Ibsen, Henrik	*Hedda Gabler*
Kaufman, George S., and Moss Hart	*You Can't Take It with You*
Lawrence, Jerome, and Robert E. Lee	*Inherit the Wind*
Leigh, Mitch, and Joe Darion	*Man of La Mancha*
Lindsay, Howard, and Russel Crouse	*Life with Father*
Lorca, Federico García	*Blood Wedding*
MacLeish, Archibald	*J. B.*
Marlowe, Christopher	*Doctor Faustus*
McCullers, Carson	*The Member of the Wedding*
Miller, Arthur	*Death of a Salesman*
O'Neill, Eugene	*Long Day's Journey into Night*
Rattigan, Terence	*The Winslow Boy*
Rodgers, Richard, and Oscar Hammerstein	*Oklahoma!*
Sartre, Jean-Paul	*No Exit*
Shakespeare, William	*Hamlet*
Shaw, George Bernard	*Pygmalion*
Sheridan, Richard Brinsley	*The School for Scandal*
Sherwood, Robert E.	*Abe Lincoln in Illinois*
Sophocles	*Antigone*
Stein, Joseph	*Fiddler on the Roof*
Synge, J. M.	*The Playboy of the Western World*
Wilde, Oscar	*The Importance of Being Earnest*
Wilder, Thornton	*Our Town*
Williams, Tennessee	*The Glass Menagerie*

1967

Fiction

Austen, Jane	*Pride and Prejudice*
Balzac, Honoré de	*Père Goriot*
Brontë, Charlotte	*Jane Eyre*

Brontë, Emily	*Wuthering Heights*
Buck, Pearl S.	*The Good Earth*
Butler, Samuel	*The Way of All Flesh*
Camus, Albert	*The Stranger*
Cather, Willa	*My Ántonia*
Cervantes Saavedra, Miguel de	*Don Quixote de la Mancha*
Conrad, Joseph	*Lord Jim*
Crane, Stephen	*The Red Badge of Courage*
Dickens, Charles	*David Copperfield*
Dostoyevsky, Fyodor	*Crime and Punishment*
Dreiser, Theodore	*An American Tragedy*
Eliot, George	*The Mill on the Floss*
Faulkner, William	*The Sound and the Fury*
Fitzgerald, F. Scott	*The Great Gatsby*
Galsworthy, John	*The Forsyte Saga*
Golding, William	*Lord of the Flies*
Hardy, Thomas	*The Return of the Native*
Hawthorne, Nathaniel	*The Scarlet Letter*
Hemingway, Ernest	*The Old Man and the Sea*
Hersey, John	*A Bell for Adano*
Hudson, W. H.	*Green Mansions*
Hugo, Victor	*Les Misérables*
Huxley, Aldous	*Brave New World*
James, Henry	*The Ambassadors*
Knowles, John	*A Separate Peace*
Lee, Harper	*To Kill a Mockingbird*
Lewis, Sinclair	*Main Street*
Llewellyn, Richard	*How Green Was My Valley*
Maugham, W. Somerset	*Of Human Bondage*
Melville, Herman	*Moby-Dick*
Mitchell, Margaret	*Gone with the Wind*
Nordhoff, Charles B., and James Norman Hall	*The Bounty Trilogy: Comprising the Three Volumes,* Mutiny on the Bounty, Men against the Sea, *and* Pitcairn's Island
Orwell, George	*Animal Farm*
Page, Elizabeth	*The Tree of Liberty*

Paton, Alan	*Cry, the Beloved Country: A Story of Comfort in Desolation*
Poe, Edgar Allan	*The Complete Tales and Poems*
Remarque, Erich Maria	*All Quiet on the Western Front*
Richter, Conrad	*The Sea of Grass*
Roberts, Kenneth	*Northwest Passage*
Rolvaag, O. E.	*Giants in the Earth*
Salinger, J. D.	*The Catcher in the Rye*
Saroyan, William	*The Human Comedy*
Scott, Sir Walter	*Ivanhoe*
Sienkiewicz, Henryk	*Quo Vadis*
Steinbeck, John	*The Grapes of Wrath*
Stevenson, Robert Louis	*The Strange Case of Dr. Jekyll and Mr. Hyde*
Stone, Irving	*Lust for Life: A Novel of Vincent van Gogh*
Thackeray, William Makepeace	*Vanity Fair: A Novel without a Hero*
Tolstoy, Leo	*War and Peace*
Turgenev, Ivan	*Fathers and Sons*
Twain, Mark	*The Adventures of Huckleberry Finn*
Undset, Sigrid	*Kristin Lavransdatter*
Wharton, Edith	*Ethan Frome*
Wilde, Oscar	*The Picture of Dorian Gray*
Wilder, Thornton	*The Bridge of San Luis Rey*
Wolfe, Thomas	*Look Homeward, Angel: A Story of the Buried Life*
Wouk, Herman	*The Caine Mutiny*

1966

Drama

BOOKS ABOUT THE THEATER

Blum, Daniel	*Great Stars of the American Stage: A Pictorial Record*
	Theatre World
Burns Mantle, Robert	The Burns Mantle Best Plays Series
Cornell, Katharine	*I Wanted to Be an Actress: The Autobiography of Katharine Cornell*

Courtney, Marguerite	*Laurette*
Fowler, Gene	*Good Night, Sweet Prince: The Life and Time of John Barrymore*
Funke, Lewis, and John E. Booth	*Actors Talk about Acting*
Green, Stanley	*The Rodgers and Hammerstein Story*
Harmon, Charlotte	*How to Break into the Theatre*
Hart, Moss	*Act One: An Autobiography*
Prideaux, Tom	*World Theatre in Pictures: From Ancient Times to Modern Broadway*
Ross, Lillian, and Helen Ross	*The Player: A Profile of an Art*
Van Druten, John	*Playwright at Work*

Drama

PLAYS

Anderson, Maxwell	*Winterset: A Play in Three Acts*
Anouilh, Jean	*Antigone*
Beckett, Samuel	*Waiting for Godot: A Tragicomedy in Two Acts*
Besier, Rudolf	*The Barretts of Wimpole Street: A Comedy in Five Acts*
Chase, Mary	*Harvey: A Comedy in Three Acts*
Chekhov, Anton	*The Cherry Orchard: A Comedy in Four Acts*
Connelly, Marc	*The Green Pastures: A Fable*
Coward, Noël	*Cavalcade*
Coxe, Louis O., and Robert Chapman	*Billy Budd*
Frings, Ketti	*Look Homeward, Angel*
Gibson, William	*The Miracle Worker: A Play for Television*
Giraudoux, Jean	*The Madwoman of Chaillot*
Goetz, Ruth, and Augustus Goetz	*The Heiress*
Gordon, Ruth	*Years Ago*
Hamilton, Patrick	*Angel Street: A Victorian Thriller in Three Acts*
Hansberry, Lorraine	*A Raisin in the Sun*
Heggen, Thomas, and Joshua Logan	*Mister Roberts: A Play*

Ibsen, Henrik	*Hedda Gabler*
Kaufman, George S., and Moss Hart	*You Can't Take It with You*
Kesselring, Joseph	*Arsenic and Old Lace: A Play in Three Acts*
Lawrence, Jerome, and Robert E. Lee	*Inherit the Wind*
Lindsay, Howard, and Russel Crouse	*Life with Father*
Logan, Joshua	*The Wisteria Trees*
MacLeish, Archibald	*J. B.*
Marlowe, Christopher	*Doctor Faustus*
McCullers, Carson	*The Member of the Wedding*
Miller, Arthur	*Death of a Salesman*
O'Neill, Eugene	*Ah, Wilderness!*
Patrick, John [pseud.]	*The Hasty Heart: A Play in Three Acts*
Rattigan, Terence	*The Winslow Boy*
Rodgers, Richard, and Oscar Hammerstein	*Oklahoma!*
Rostand, Edmond	*Cyrano de Bergerac*
Shakespeare, William	*Hamlet*
Shaw, George Bernard	*Pygmalion*
Sheridan, Richard Brinsley	*The School for Scandal*
Sherwood, Robert E.	*Abe Lincoln in Illinois*
Synge, J. M.	*The Playboy of the Western World*
Van Druten, John	*I Remember Mama: A Play in Two Acts*
Wilde, Oscar	*The Importance of Being Earnest*
Wilder, Thornton	*Our Town*
Williams, Tennessee	*The Glass Menagerie*

1965

Biography

Adams, Henry	*The Education of Henry Adams*
Anderson, Marian	*My Lord, What a Morning: An Autobiography*
Antin, Mary	*At School in the Promised Land; or The Story of a Little Immigrant*

Bainton, Roland H.	*Here I Stand: A Life of Martin Luther*
Baruch, Bernard M.	*Baruch: My Own Story*
Bell, E. T.	*Men of Mathematics*
Boswell, James	*The Life of Samuel Johnson*
Bowen, Catherine Drinker	*Yankee from Olympus: Justice Holmes and His Family*
Buck, Pearl S.	*My Several Worlds: A Personal Record*
Castelot, André	*Queen of France: A Biography of Marie Antoinette*
Cellini, Benvenuto	*The Autobiography of Benvenuto Cellini*
Chute, Marchette Gaylord	*Shakespeare of London*
Cunliffe, Marcus	*George Washington, Man and Monument*
Curie, Eve	*Madame Curie: A Biography*
Davis, Burke	*They Called Him Stonewall: A Life of Lt. General T. J. Jackson, C.S.A.*
Ferguson, Charles W.	*Naked to Mine Enemies: The Life of Cardinal Wolsey*
Fermi, Laura	*Atoms in the Family: My Life with Enrico Fermi*
Forbes, Esther	*Paul Revere and the World He Lived In*
Frank, Anne	*Anne Frank: The Diary of a Young Girl*
Franklin, Benjamin	*Autobiography*
Grey, Ian	*Peter the Great, Emperor of All Russia*
Guérard, Albert Léon	*Napoleon I: A Great Life in Brief*
Hagedorn, Hermann	*The Roosevelt Family of Sagamore Hill*
Hart, Moss	*Act One: An Autobiography*
Heiser, Victor	*An American Doctor's Odyssey: Adventures in Forty-five Countries*
Jenkins, Elizabeth	*Elizabeth the Great*
Keller, Helen	*The Story of My Life*
Kelly, Amy Ruth	*Eleanor of Aquitaine and the Four Kings*
Kennedy, John F.	*Profiles in Courage*
Krutch, Joseph Wood	*Henry David Thoreau*
Lamb, Harold	*Suleiman the Magnificent: Sultan of the East*
Maurois, André	*Ariel: The Life of Shelley*
Merton, Thomas	*The Seven Storey Mountain*
Morison, Samuel Eliot	*Christopher Columbus, Mariner*
Payne, Robert	*The Three Worlds of Albert Schweitzer*
Pepys, Samuel	*The Diary of Samuel Pepys*
Plutarch	*Lives*

Roosevelt, Eleanor	*This I Remember*
St. John, Robert	*Ben-Gurion: A Biography*
Steffens, Lincoln	*The Autobiography of Lincoln Steffens*
Stone, Irving	*Clarence Darrow for the Defense*
Strachey, Lytton	*Queen Victoria*
Stuart, Jesse	*The Thread That Runs So True*
Taylor, A. J. P.	*Bismarck: The Man and the Statesman*
Terasaki, Gwen	*Bridge to the Sun*
Tharp, Louise Hall	*The Peabody Sisters of Salem*
Thomas, Benjamin P.	*Abraham Lincoln*
Twain, Mark	*The Autobiography of Mark Twain*
Van Loon, Hendrik Willem	*R. v. R.: The Life of Rembrandt van Rijn*
Vining, Elizabeth	*Windows for the Crown Prince*
Washington, Booker T.	*Up from Slavery: An Autobiography*
Wong, Jade Snow	*Fifth Chinese Daughter*

Fiction

Austen, Jane	*Pride and Prejudice*
Balzac, Honoré de	*Père Goriot*
Bellamy, Edward	*Looking Backward: 2000–1887*
Brontë, Charlotte	*Jane Eyre*
Brontë, Emily	*Wuthering Heights*
Buck, Pearl S.	*The Good Earth*
Butler, Samuel	*The Way of All Flesh*
Cather, Willa	*My Ántonia*
Cervantes Saavedra, Miguel de	*Don Quixote de la Mancha*
Collins, Wilkie	*The Moonstone*
Conrad, Joseph	*Lord Jim*
Crane, Stephen	*The Red Badge of Courage*
Dickens, Charles	*David Copperfield*
Dostoyevsky, Fyodor	*Crime and Punishment*
Dreiser, Theodore	*An American Tragedy*
Dumas, Alexandre	*The Count of Monte Cristo*
Eliot, George	*The Mill on the Floss*
Fitzgerald, F. Scott	*The Great Gatsby*

Fuller, Iola   *The Loon Feather*
Galsworthy, John   *The Forsyte Saga*
Glasgow, Ellen   *Vein of Iron*
Guareschi, Giovanni   *The Little World of Don Camillo*
Hardy, Thomas   *The Return of the Native*
Hawthorne, Nathaniel   *The Scarlet Letter*
Hemingway, Ernest   *The Old Man and the Sea*
Hersey, John   *A Single Pebble*
Hudson, W. H.   *Green Mansions*
Hugo, Victor   *Les Misérables*
Kipling, Rudyard   *Kim*
Lewis, Sinclair   *Arrowsmith*
Llewellyn, Richard   *How Green Was My Valley*
Maugham, W.   *Of Human Bondage*
  Somerset

Melville, Herman   *Moby-Dick*
Mitchell, Margaret   *Gone with the Wind*
Monsarrat, Nicholas   *The Cruel Sea*
Nordhoff, Charles B., and   *The Bounty Trilogy: Comprising the Three Volumes,*
  James Norman Hall   Mutiny on the Bounty, Men against the Sea, *and*
                                      Pitcairn's Island

Orwell, George   *Animal Farm*
Page, Elizabeth   *The Tree of Liberty*
Paton, Alan   *Cry, the Beloved Country: A Story of Comfort in*
                                      Desolation

Poe, Edgar Allan   *The Complete Tales and Poems*
Rawlings, Marjorie Kinnan   *The Yearling*
Remarque, Erich Maria   *All Quiet on the Western Front*
Richter, Conrad   *The Sea of Grass*
Roberts, Kenneth   *Northwest Passage*
Rolvaag, O. E.   *Giants in the Earth*
Saroyan, William   *The Human Comedy*
Scott, Sir Walter   *Ivanhoe*
Shellabarger, Samuel   *Prince of Foxes*
Sienkiewicz, Henryk   *Quo Vadis*
Steinbeck, John   *The Grapes of Wrath*
Stevenson, Robert Louis   *Kidnapped*
Stewart, George R.   *Storm*

Stone, Irving	*Love Is Eternal*
Thackeray, William Makepeace	*Vanity Fair: A Novel without a Hero*
Tolstoy, Leo	*War and Peace*
Turgenev, Ivan	*Fathers and Sons*
Twain, Mark	*The Adventures of Huckleberry Finn*
Undset, Sigrid	*Kristin Lavransdatter*
Wharton, Edith	*Ethan Frome*
Wilder, Thornton	*The Bridge of San Luis Rey*

1963

Biography

Adams, Henry	*The Education of Henry Adams*
Anderson, Marian	*My Lord, What a Morning: An Autobiography*
Antin, Mary	*At School in the Promised Land; or The Story of a Little Immigrant*
Bainton, Roland H.	*Here I Stand: A Life of Martin Luther*
Baruch, Bernard M.	*Baruch: My Own Story*
Bell, E. T.	*Men of Mathematics*
Boswell, James	*The Life of Samuel Johnson*
Bowen, Catherine Drinker	*Yankee from Olympus: Justice Holmes and His Family*
Buck, Pearl S.	*My Several Worlds: A Personal Record*
Castelot, André	*Queen of France: A Biography of Marie Antoinette*
Cellini, Benvenuto	*The Autobiography of Benvenuto Cellini*
Chute, Marchette Gaylord	*Shakespeare of London*
Cunliffe, Marcus	*George Washington, Man and Monument*
Curie, Eve	*Madame Curie: A Biography*
Davis, Burke	*They Called Him Stonewall: A Life of Lt. General T. J. Jackson, C.S.A.*
Ferguson, Charles W.	*Naked to Mine Enemies: The Life of Cardinal Wolsey*
Fermi, Laura	*Atoms in the Family: My Life with Enrico Fermi*
Forbes, Esther	*Paul Revere and the World He Lived In*
Frank, Anne	*Anne Frank: The Diary of a Young Girl*
Franklin, Benjamin	*Autobiography*

Grey, Ian	*Peter the Great, Emperor of All Russia*
Guérard, Albert Léon	*Napoleon I: A Great Life in Brief*
Hagedorn, Hermann	*The Roosevelt Family of Sagamore Hill*
Hart, Moss	*Act One: An Autobiography*
Heiser, Victor	*An American Doctor's Odyssey: Adventures in Forty-five Countries*
Jenkins, Elizabeth	*Elizabeth the Great*
Keller, Helen	*The Story of My Life*
Kelly, Amy Ruth	*Eleanor of Aquitaine and the Four Kings*
Kennedy, John F.	*Profiles in Courage*
Krutch, Joseph Wood	*Henry David Thoreau*
Lamb, Harold	*Suleiman the Magnificent: Sultan of the East*
Maurois, André	*Ariel: The Life of Shelley*
Merton, Thomas	*The Seven Storey Mountain*
Morison, Samuel Eliot	*Christopher Columbus, Mariner*
Payne, Robert	*The Three Worlds of Albert Schweitzer*
Pepys, Samuel	*The Diary of Samuel Pepys*
Plutarch	*Lives*
Roosevelt, Eleanor	*This I Remember*
St. John, Robert	*Ben-Gurion: A Biography*
Steffens, Lincoln	*The Autobiography of Lincoln Steffens*
Stone, Irving	*Clarence Darrow for the Defense*
Strachey, Lytton	*Queen Victoria*
Stuart, Jesse	*The Thread That Runs So True*
Taylor, A. J. P.	*Bismarck: The Man and the Statesman*
Terasaki, Gwen	*Bridge to the Sun*
Tharp, Louise Hall	*The Peabody Sisters of Salem*
Thomas, Benjamin P.	*Abraham Lincoln*
Twain, Mark	*The Autobiography of Mark Twain*
Van Loon, Hendrik Willem	*R. v. R.: The Life of Rembrandt van Rijn*
Vining, Elizabeth	*Windows for the Crown Prince*
Washington, Booker T.	*Up from Slavery: An Autobiography*
Wong, Jade Snow	*Fifth Chinese Daughter*

Fiction

Austen, Jane	*Pride and Prejudice*
Balzac, Honoré de	*Père Goriot*

Bellamy, Edward	*Looking Backward: 2000–1887*
Brontë, Charlotte	*Jane Eyre*
Brontë, Emily	*Wuthering Heights*
Buck, Pearl S.	*The Good Earth*
Butler, Samuel	*The Way of All Flesh*
Cather, Willa	*My Ántonia*
Cervantes Saavedra, Miguel de	*Don Quixote de la Mancha*
Collins, Wilkie	*The Moonstone*
Conrad, Joseph	*Lord Jim*
Crane, Stephen	*The Red Badge of Courage*
Dickens, Charles	*David Copperfield*
Dostoyevsky, Fyodor	*Crime and Punishment*
Dreiser, Theodore	*An American Tragedy*
Dumas, Alexandre	*The Count of Monte Cristo*
Eliot, George	*The Mill on the Floss*
Fitzgerald, F. Scott	*The Great Gatsby*
Fuller, Iola	*The Loon Feather*
Galsworthy, John	*The Forsyte Saga*
Glasgow, Ellen	*Vein of Iron*
Guareschi, Giovanni	*The Little World of Don Camillo*
Hardy, Thomas	*The Return of the Native*
Hawthorne, Nathaniel	*The Scarlet Letter*
Hemingway, Ernest	*The Old Man and the Sea*
Hersey, John	*A Single Pebble*
Hudson, W. H.	*Green Mansions*
Hugo, Victor	*Les Misérables*
Kipling, Rudyard	*Kim*
Lewis, Sinclair	*Arrowsmith*
Llewellyn, Richard	*How Green Was My Valley*
Maugham, W. Somerset	*Of Human Bondage*
Melville, Herman	*Moby-Dick*
Mitchell, Margaret	*Gone with the Wind*
Monsarrat, Nicholas	*The Cruel Sea*
Nordhoff, Charles B., and James Norman Hall	*The Bounty Trilogy: Comprising the Three Volumes,* Mutiny on the Bounty, Men against the Sea, *and* Pitcairn's Island

Orwell, George	*Animal Farm*
Page, Elizabeth	*The Tree of Liberty*
Paton, Alan	*Cry, the Beloved Country: A Story of Comfort in Desolation*
Poe, Edgar Allan	*The Complete Tales and Poems*
Rawlings, Marjorie Kinnan	*The Yearling*
Remarque, Erich Maria	*All Quiet on the Western Front*
Richter, Conrad	*The Sea of Grass*
Roberts, Kenneth	*Northwest Passage*
Rolvaag, O. E.	*Giants in the Earth*
Saroyan, William	*The Human Comedy*
Scott, Sir Walter	*Ivanhoe*
Shellabarger, Samuel	*Prince of Foxes*
Sienkiewicz, Henryk	*Quo Vadis*
Steinbeck, John	*The Grapes of Wrath*
Stevenson, Robert Louis	*Kidnapped*
Stewart, George R.	*Storm*
Stone, Irving	*Love Is Eternal*
Thackeray, William Makepeace	*Vanity Fair: A Novel without a Hero*
Tolstoy, Leo	*War and Peace*
Turgenev, Ivan	*Fathers and Sons*
Twain, Mark	*The Adventures of Huckleberry Finn*
Undset, Sigrid	*Kristin Lavransdatter*
Wharton, Edith	*Ethan Frome*
Wilder, Thornton	*The Bridge of San Luis Rey*

1961

Biography

Adams, Henry	*The Education of Henry Adams*
Anderson, Marian	*My Lord, What a Morning: An Autobiography*
Antin, Mary	*At School in the Promised Land; or, The Story of a Little Immigrant*
Bainton, Roland H.	*Here I Stand: A Life of Martin Luther*
Baruch, Bernard M.	*Baruch: My Own Story*

Bell, E. T.	*Men of Mathematics*
Boswell, James	*The Life of Samuel Johnson*
Bowen, Catherine Drinker	*Yankee from Olympus: Justice Holmes and His Family*
Buck, Pearl S.	*My Several Worlds: A Personal Record*
Castelot, André	*Queen of France: A Biography of Marie Antoinette*
Cellini, Benvenuto	*The Autobiography of Benvenuto Cellini*
Chute, Marchette Gaylord	*Shakespeare of London*
Curie, Eve	*Madame Curie: A Biography*
Davis, Burke	*They Called Him Stonewall: A Life of Lt. General T. J. Jackson, C.S.A.*
Ferguson, Charles W.	*Naked to Mine Enemies: The Life of Cardinal Wolsey*
Fermi, Laura	*Atoms in the Family: My Life with Enrico Fermi*
Forbes, Esther	*Paul Revere and the World He Lived In*
Frank, Anne	*Anne Frank: The Diary of a Young Girl*
Franklin, Benjamin	*Autobiography*
Grey, Ian	*Peter the Great, Emperor of All Russia*
Guérard, Albert Léon	*Napoleon I: A Great Life in Brief*
Hagedorn, Hermann	*The Roosevelt Family of Sagamore Hill*
Hart, Moss	*Act One: An Autobiography*
Heiser, Victor	*An American Doctor's Odyssey: Adventures in Forty-five Countries*
Jenkins, Elizabeth	*Elizabeth the Great*
Keller, Helen	*The Story of My Life*
Kelly, Amy Ruth	*Eleanor of Aquitaine and the Four Kings*
Kennedy, John F.	*Profiles in Courage*
Krutch, Joseph Wood	*Henry David Thoreau*
Lamb, Harold	*Suleiman the Magnificent: Sultan of the East*
Maurois, André	*Ariel: The Life of Shelley*
Merton, Thomas	*The Seven Storey Mountain*
Morison, Samuel Eliot	*Christopher Columbus, Mariner*
Payne, Robert	*The Three Worlds of Albert Schweitzer*
Pepys, Samuel	*The Diary of Samuel Pepys*
Plutarch	*Lives*
Roosevelt, Eleanor	*This I Remember*
St. John, Robert	*Ben-Gurion: A Biography*
Steffens, Lincoln	*The Autobiography of Lincoln Steffens*

Stone, Irving — *Clarence Darrow for the Defense*
Strachey, Lytton — *Queen Victoria*
Stuart, Jesse — *The Thread That Runs So True*
Taylor, A. J. P. — *Bismarck: The Man and the Statesman*
Terasaki, Gwen — *Bridge to the Sun*
Tharp, Louise Hall — *The Peabody Sisters of Salem*
Thomas, Benjamin P. — *Abraham Lincoln*
Twain, Mark — *The Autobiography of Mark Twain*
Van Loon, Hendrik Willem — *R. v. R.: The Life of Rembrandt van Rijn*
Vining, Elizabeth — *Windows for the Crown Prince*
Washington, Booker T. — *Up from Slavery: An Autobiography*
White, William Allen — *The Autobiography of William Allen White*
Woodham-Smith, Cecil — *Florence Nightingale, 1820–1910*
Wong, Jade Snow — *Fifth Chinese Daughter*

1959

Fiction

Austen, Jane — *Pride and Prejudice*
Balzac, Honoré de — *Père Goriot*
Bellamy, Edward — *Looking Backward: 2000–1887*
Brontë, Charlotte — *Jane Eyre*
Brontë, Emily — *Wuthering Heights*
Buck, Pearl S. — *The Good Earth*
Butler, Samuel — *The Way of All Flesh*
Cather, Willa — *My Ántonia*
Cervantes Saavedra, Miguel de — *Don Quixote de la Mancha*

Collins, Wilkie — *The Moonstone*
Conrad, Joseph — *Lord Jim*
Crane, Stephen — *The Red Badge of Courage*
Dickens, Charles — *David Copperfield*
Dostoyevsky, Fyodor — *Crime and Punishment*
Dreiser, Theodore — *An American Tragedy*
Dumas, Alexandre — *The Count of Monte Cristo*
Eliot, George — *The Mill on the Floss*

Fitzgerald, F. Scott	*The Great Gatsby*
Fuller, Iola	*The Loon Feather*
Galsworthy, John	*The Forsyte Saga*
Glasgow, Ellen	*Vein of Iron*
Guareschi, Giovanni	*The Little World of Don Camillo*
Hardy, Thomas	*The Return of the Native*
Hawthorne, Nathaniel	*The Scarlet Letter*
Hemingway, Ernest	*The Old Man and the Sea*
Hersey, John	*A Single Pebble*
Hudson, W. H.	*Green Mansions*
Hugo, Victor	*Les Misérables*
Kipling, Rudyard	*Kim*
Lewis, Sinclair	*Arrowsmith*
Llewellyn, Richard	*How Green Was My Valley*
Maugham, W. Somerset	*Of Human Bondage*
Melville, Herman	*Moby-Dick*
Mitchell, Margaret	*Gone with the Wind*
Monsarrat, Nicholas	*The Cruel Sea*
Nordhoff, Charles B. and James Norman Hall	*The Bounty Trilogy: Comprising the Three Volumes,* Mutiny on the Bounty, Men against the Sea, *and* Pitcairn's Island
Orwell, George	*Animal Farm*
Page, Elizabeth	*The Tree of Liberty*
Paton, Alan	*Cry, the Beloved Country: A Story of Comfort in Desolation*
Poe, Edgar Allan	*The Complete Tales and Poems*
Rawlings, Marjorie Kinnan	*The Yearling*
Remarque, Erich Maria	*All Quiet on the Western Front*
Richter, Conrad	*The Sea of Grass*
Roberts, Kenneth	*Northwest Passage*
Rolvaag, O. E.	*Giants in the Earth*
Saroyan, William	*The Human Comedy*
Scott, Sir Walter	*Ivanhoe*
Shellabarger, Samuel	*Prince of Foxes*
Sienkiewicz, Henryk	*Quo Vadis*
Steinbeck, John	*The Grapes of Wrath*

Stevenson, Robert Louis	*Kidnapped*
Stewart, George R.	*Storm*
Stone, Irving	*Love Is Eternal*
Thackeray, William Makepeace	*Vanity Fair: A Novel without a Hero*
Tolstoy, Leo	*War and Peace*
Turgenev, Ivan	*Fathers and Sons*
Twain, Mark	*The Adventures of Huckleberry Finn*
Undset, Sigrid	*Kristin Lavransdatter*
Wharton, Edith	*Ethan Frome*
Wilder, Thornton	*The Bridge of San Luis Rey*

PART THREE

Special Lists

This part contains lists that have been created from the cumulative database of books selected over the years.

The first, the Top Twenty-Four, comprises the titles that have appeared most frequently on the OBCB lists from 1959 to 2004 (annotations for which may be found in part 1). Even though these books were published in the previous two centuries, they have acquired a patina that only enhances their value to the reader. They have been widely read, often imitated, but never replaced. Most of them are found on other recommended reading lists. They are made into movies and television shows. They are cussed and discussed in literary essays and reviews, classrooms, book discussion groups, and among friends and scholars.

The views and interpretations change with each generation, but, as one of the characters says in Karen Joy Fowler's *The Jane Austen Book Club*, "The great thing about books was the solidity of the written word. You might change and your reading might change as a result, but the book remained whatever it had always been."

The books on this list have remained "whatever they have always been." Their appeal remains constant regardless of the news from the NEA that the reading of novels, short stories, plays, or poetry in leisure time is in decline. The good news is that the classics are enjoying a resurgence of interest— even popular talk show host Oprah Winfrey is selecting some of them for her book club.

The second list, Now/Current, is a combination of the Now and the Current annotated lists selected by the 1971 and 1976 committees. Although now of limited value for selection purposes, this list is a fine example of the efforts of these two committees to provide lists that were both relevant and useful to the readers of that period. Unless they were selected by other committees, these titles do not appear in part 1.

THE TOP TWENTY-FOUR: Most Frequent Selections, by Year

	1959	1961	1963	1965	1966	1967	1968	1971	1976	1982	1988	1991	1994	1999	2004
TEN APPEARANCES															
Austen, Jane — *Pride and Prejudice* (1813)	X		X	X		X		X	X	X	X	X	X		
Fitzgerald, F. Scott — *The Great Gatsby* (1925)	X		X	X		X		X	X	X	X	X	X		
Paton, Alan — *Cry, the Beloved Country* (1948)	X		X	X		X		X	X	X	X	X	X		
Twain, Mark — *The Adventures of Huckleberry Finn* (1884)	X		X	X		X		X	X	X	X	X	X		
NINE APPEARANCES															
Brontë, Charlotte — *Jane Eyre* (1847)	X		X	X		X		X	X	X	X	X			
Curie, Eve — *Madame Curie: A Biography* (1937)		X	X	X			X	X	X	X	X			X	
Dostoyevsky, Fyodor — *Crime and Punishment* (1866)	X		X	X		X		X	X	X	X			X	
Keller, Helen — *The Story of My Life* (1902)		X	X	X			X	X	X	X	X			X	
Remarque, Erich Maria — *All Quiet on the Western Front*	X		X	X		X		X	X	X	X		X		
EIGHT APPEARANCES															
Cather, Willa — *My Ántonia* (1918)	X		X	X		X		X	X	X	X				
Crane, Stephen — *The Red Badge of Courage* (1885)	X		X	X		X		X	X	X	X				

EIGHT APPEARANCES (cont.)

	1959	1961	1963	1965	1966	1967	1968	1971	1976	1982	1988	1991	1994	1999	2004
Frank, Anne *Anne Frank: Diary of a Young Girl* (1952)		X	X	X			X	X	X	X	X			X	
Hart, Moss *Act One: An Autobiography* (1955)		X	X	X	X		X	X			X	X			
Poe, Edgar Allen *Collected works in various editions*	X		X	X		X			X	X	X		X		
Steinbeck, John *The Grapes of Wrath* (1939)	X		X	X		X			X	X	X		X		
Wilde, Oscar *The Importance of Being Earnest* (1895)					X		X	X	X	X	X	X	X	X	

SEVEN APPEARANCES

	1959	1961	1963	1965	1966	1967	1968	1971	1976	1982	1988	1991	1994	1999	2004
Golding, William *Lord of the Flies* (1954)						X		X	X	X	X	X	X		
Hawthorne, Nathaniel *The Scarlet Letter* (1850)	X		X	X		X			X	X	X				
Hesse, Herman *Siddhartha* (1951)								X	X	X	X	X	X	X	
Lee, Harper *To Kill a Mockingbird* (1960)						X	X	X	X	X	X	X	X	X	
McCullers, Carson *The Member of the Wedding* (1946)					X		X	X	X	X	X	X	X	X	
Orwell, George *Animal Farm* (1945)	X		X	X		X				X	X		X		
Salinger, J. D. *The Catcher in the Rye* (1951)			X	X		X	X	X	X	X	X	X	X	X	
Williams, Tennessee *The Glass Menagerie* (1945)					X		X	X	X		X	X	X	X	

NOW/CURRENT

Alive: The Story of the Andes Survivors, Piers Paul Read **(1974)**, 1976

Plane crash victims in the Andes, facing sub-zero temperatures and no food, are forced to make a decision—eat their dead comrades or die themselves.

All the President's Men, Carl Bernstein and Bob Woodward **(1974)**, 1976, 1994

Following lead after lead, two *Washington Post* reporters lift the veil of secrecy surrounding the Nixon administration's Watergate cover-up.

The Andromeda Strain, Michael Crichton **(1969)**, 1971

Four scientists must race against time to isolate a deadly microorganism from outer space which has killed all but two in a small Arizona town.

The Astrologer, John Cameron **(1972)**, 1976

By using natal configurations, computers predict malignant and benign potentials of each human birth and are able to herald a Catholic Messiah and a "perfect" world.

The Autobiography of Malcolm X, Malcolm X (as told to Alex Haley) **(1965)**, 1971, 1976, 1982, 1988, 1994, 1999

A great and controversial Black Muslim figure relates his transformation from street hustler to religious and national leader.

The Bell Jar, Sylvia Plath **(1963)**, 1976

No longer able to cope with her feelings of inferiority, Esther Greenwood, a talented college junior, retreats to the protective cover of the bell jar.

The Bermuda Triangle Mystery: Solved, Larry Kusche **(1975)**, 1976

Expert sleuthing and research blast the supernatural explanations for the disappearance of ships, planes, and men within this area of the Atlantic.

Between Myth and Morning: Women Awakening, Elizabeth Janeway **(1974)**, 1976

Believing that the women's movement was inevitable, this journalist explores ways to ensure that women are viewed as equals, not just as "helpmates."

The Biological Time Bomb, Gordon Rattray Taylor **(1968)**, 1971

In the offing are memory-erasing drugs, choice of gender in the offspring, reconstructed organisms, and the indefinite postponement of death.

Black Rage, William H. Grier and Price M. Cobbs **(1968)**, 1976

Two African American psychiatrists tell why African Americans are angry—why some are so angry that they are "compelled to burn, loot, and kill in a rage against white society."

Blackthink: My Life as Black Man and White Man, Jesse Owens and Paul G. Neimark **(1970),** 1971

> Owens argues for dealing with people as individuals and feels that too much concentration on African American studies and "black rage" is over-reaction serving to perpetuate racism.

Bless the Beasts and Children, Glendon Swarthout **(1970),** 1971

> Five misfits in an Arizona boys' camp sneak out on a daring escapade to save a herd of buffalo from bloodthirsty gun-toting tourists.

Body Language, Julius Fast **(1970),** 1976

> One's body unconsciously expresses feelings and emotions.

The Brain Changers: Scientists and the New Mind Control, Maya Pines **(1973),** 1976

> The fact that the mind can be improved or impaired by modern scientific methods has created moral and social dilemmas for modern man.

Buried Alive: The Biography of Janis Joplin, Myra Friedman **(1973),** 1976

> Although adored by her loyal audiences, Janis Joplin is plagued by loneliness and insecurity and seeks an "out" in alcohol and drugs.

Carrying the Fire: An Astronaut's Journeys, Michael Collins **(1974),** 1976

> Mike Collins, astronaut, writes an intelligent, technical, yet personal and breezy account of the education of a space man and what it's like "up there."

Catch-22, Joseph Heller **(1961),** 1971, 1976, 1982, 1988, 1999

> In this satirical novel, Captain Yossarian confronts the hypocrisy of war and bureaucracy as he frantically attempts to survive.

The Chocolate War, Robert Cormier **(1974),** 1976, 1988, 1994

> When Jerry refuses to sell chocolates for a fund-raising drive, he upsets the power structure of his school and becomes the object of a "war" of intimidation and violence.

The Choice: The Issue of Black Survival in America, Samuel F. Yette **(1971),** 1976

> The former *Newsweek* Washington correspondent presents evidence that there is a concerted effort in this country to re-enslave, perhaps even to wipe out, the African American.

The Closing Circle: Confronting the Environmental Crisis, Barry Commoner **(1972),** 1976

> Professor Commoner warns that we are the unknowing victims of smog, nitrate, and waste pollution caused by shortsighted technology and the relentless drive for profits.

Culture and Commitment: The New Relationships between the Generations in the 1970s, Margaret Mead **(1970),** 1971, 1976, 1982

> We need not only to recognize global problems, Mead argues, but also to commit ourselves to solving them.

Custer Died for Your Sins: An Indian Manifesto, Vine Deloria Jr. **(1969)**, 1971, 1976

The author, himself a Standing Rock Sioux, destroys the historical and contemporary misconceptions of Native Americans and discusses the many problems facing them today.

Daybreak, Joan Baez **(1968)**, 1971

An evocative, fragmented, informal autobiography of the folksinging spokeswoman for civil liberties and nonviolent resistance.

Death Is a Noun: A View of the End of Life, David Langone **(1972)**, 1976

"Is abortion murder?" "When is a person dead?" and other moral questions are considered objectively in this "view of the end of life."

The Drug Scene, Donald B. Louria **(1968)**, 1971

The illicit use of dangerous drugs will remain a problem until "this society regains its vigor, direction and integrity."

Dummy, Ernest Tidyman **(1974)**, 1976

A poor African American, Donald Lang, who could not hear, talk, or write, was tried and convicted for the murder of a prostitute purely on circumstantial evidence.

Each Other's Victims, Milton Travers **(1970)**, 1971

Father and son grapple to understand themselves and each other in this graphic account of life in the drug culture.

Eating May Be Hazardous to Your Health: How Your Government Fails to Protect You from the Dangers in Your Food, Jacqueline Verrett and Jean Carper **(1974)**, 1976

Arguing that the Federal Drug Administration does not protect the public, the authors describe chemicals added to the popular foods that have caused cancer, malformed children, and other tragedies.

The Environmental Handbook, Garrett De Bell (comp.) **(1970)**, 1971

The planet Earth needs help! This handbook suggests action that can be taken in any community, by any individual.

Escape from Childhood: The Needs and Rights of Children, John Holt **(1974)**, 1976

Holt argues that the rights and responsibilities of adult citizens be made available to any young person, of whatever age, who wants to make use of them.

Festival! The Book of American Musical Celebrations, Jerry Hopkins **(1970)**, 1971

From the mid-fifties to Woodstock and Big Sur, the successes and failures, the togetherness and excitement of "happenings" are conveyed through text and photographs.

The Fixer, Bernard Malamud **(1966)**, 1971, 1976

> Victim of a vicious anti-Semitic conspiracy, Yakov Bok is in a Russian prison with only his indomitable will to sustain him.

The Foxfire Book, Eliot Wigginton (ed.) **(1972)**, 1976

> Students from Appalachia are turned off by school until a teacher involves them in their heritage—folklore, mountain crafts, and natural medicine— and encourages them to write about it.

Future Shock, Alvin Toffler **(1970)**, 1971, 1976

> This book stimulates discussion of the effects of rapidly accelerating change in our society.

Handbook of Adolescence: A Medical Guide for Parents and Teenagers, Marvin J. Gersh and Iris F. Litt **(1971)**, 1976

> This medical guide focuses on such adolescent concerns as sex, obesity, smoking, drugs, and suicide.

Hatter Fox, Marilyn Harris **(1973)**, 1976

> Having struggled to survive for seventeen years, Navaho Hatter Fox stabs a reservation doctor, gains his attention, and almost starts a new life.

Hey, White Girl! Susan Gregory **(1970)**, 1971

> When her family moves from the suburbs, Susan Gregory attends a Chicago ghetto high school in her senior year and becomes much more than another "whitey."

The House of Tomorrow, Jean Thompson (pseud.) **(1967)**, 1971

> A pregnant twenty-year-old girl writes in her diary during her stay in a Salvation Army home for unwed mothers.

I Never Promised You a Rose Garden, Joanne Greenberg **(1964)**, 1971, 1976

> A sixteen-year-old girl struggles out of the seductive kingdom of her madness and reenters the real world.

I'm O.K.—You're O.K., Thomas A. Harris **(1969)**, 1976

> This popular guide to transactional analysis underscores the elements in each person's psyche and relates them to today's society.

In the Service of Their Country: War Resisters in Prison, Willard Gaylin **(1970)**, 1971

> Six imprisoned war resisters tell their stories as recorded in these compelling case histories by Dr. Gaylin, a psychiatrist.

Journey to Ixtlan: The Lessons of Don Juan, Carlos Castaneda **(1972)**, 1976

> Castaneda breaks away from the use of drugs, is initiated into the world of sorcerers, and learns to "see" rather than merely "look."

Judges, Donald Dale Jackson **(1974)**, 1976

> Postulating that the quality of justice reflects the quality of the judges, Jackson portrays examples of some of the good, the bad, and the indifferent.

La Raza: The Mexican Americans, Stan Steiner **(1970)**, 1971, 1976, 1991

> A study of the problems of "The Race," which includes an account of the journey of Cesar Chavez from the boyhood of a migrant farmworker to the role of leader of his people.

Learning for Tomorrow: The Role of the Future in Education, Alvin Toffler (ed.) **(1974)**, 1976

> The future directions of education and curricula are explored in sixteen essays that question current practices.

Long Time Coming and a Long Time Gone, Richard Fariña **(1969)**, 1971

> Richard Fariña, a young folk hero who lived only a short time, will be remembered through this posthumous collection of his essays, stories, song lyrics, and poems.

The Making of a Counter Culture: Reflections on the Technocratic Society and Its Youthful Opposition, Theodore Roszak **(1969)**, 1971, 1976

> The influence of such personalities as Herbert Marcuse, Allen Ginsberg, Timothy Leary, and Paul Goodman is examined together with the leading causes of youthful dissent in the sixties.

Marijuana, E. R. Bloomquist **(1968)**, 1971

> Through an informal and nonmoralistic approach, and with the use of some excellent cartoons, the author "tells it like it is" about marijuana.

Mr. and Mrs. Bo Jo Jones, Ann Head **(1967)**, 1971

> July and Bo Jo, not yet high school graduates, are already three months into expectant parenthood.

My Lai 4: A Report on the Massacre and Its Aftermath, Seymour M. Hersh **(1970)**, 1971

> A reporter recounts what happens on March 16, 1968, when Charlie Company obliterates the hamlet of My Lai.

The Nashville Sound: Bright Lights and Country Music, Paul Hemphill **(1970)**, 1971

> Country-and-western music begins in Nashville.

No More Masks! An Anthology of Poems by Women, Florence Howe and Ellen Bass (eds.) **(1973)**, 1976

> Women poets drop their masks to reveal their female uniqueness.

Nobody Ever Died of Old Age, Sharon R. Curtin **(1972)**, 1976

> Only the elderly themselves can unite and change our society from one which brings them loneliness, discrimination, and insecurity to one that recognizes their rights.

On Being Different: What It Means to Be a Homosexual, Merle Miller **(1971)**, 1976

> With almost fifty years of pretense behind him, this writer admits his homosexuality and analyzes its effect on his life, both publicly and privately.

On Violence, Hannah Arendt **(1970)**, 1971, 1976, 1991

> The author explores the reasons why violence is so prevalent in modern society.

One Flew over the Cuckoo's Nest, Ken Kesey **(1962)**, 1976, 1982

> An irrepressible rebel leads fellow inmates of a mental hospital in a struggle with tyrannical Head Nurse Ratched.

Open Marriage: A New Life Style for Couples, Nena O'Neill and George O'Neill **(1972)**, 1976

> This modern manual suggests that monogamous relationships are not fulfilling for all couples; rather it is total communication and honesty which are the keys to marriage.

Our Bodies, Ourselves, Boston Women's Health Book Collective **(1973)**, 1976

> The total implications of womanhood, from the physical to the psychological, are frankly examined in this personalized and unique guide written by women.

Our Own Worst Enemy, William J. Lederer **(1968)**, 1971

> A longtime student of Asian affairs observes the complexities of the Vietnam War and offers some possible solutions but no panaceas.

Our Time Is Now: Notes from the High School Underground, John Birmingham **(1970)**, 1971

> Uncensored high school students speak of injustices in the schools and of changes needed.

Peace-Love-Thought-God, Peter Max **(1970)**, 1971

> Peter Max illustrates and enlivens the ideas of his spiritual leader.

A Peck of Salt: A Year in the Ghetto, John T. Hough Jr. **(1970)**, 1971

> Recollections of a young white VISTA volunteer who served in the beleaguered African American ghettos of Chicago and Detroit.

Poetry of Rock, Richard Goldstein **(1969)**, 1971

> Rock and roll lyrics make interesting poetry.

The Population Bomb, Paul R. Ehrlich **(1968)**, 1971

> If population growth continues, Ehrlich warns that the world will experience such horrors as widespread famine and multiplying environmental problems.

The Price of My Soul, Bernadette Devlin **(1969)**, 1971

> A crusading young Irishwoman and member of Parliament is in and out of jail for her political actions in Ulster.

Psychogeist, L. P. Davies **(1967),** 1971

Edward Garvey is reliving a comic book episode involving the character of Angred the Freedman who has grown in Edward's subconscious and now wants a younger, healthier body.

Red Sky at Morning, Richard Bradford **(1968),** 1971

Joshua Arnold, a wise, wry man-child, must cope with an absent father and a sherry-tippling mother while learning to live in a new town, make friends, and finish growing up.

The Right to Privacy, Bill Severn **(1973),** 1976

Innocuous requests for personal information by credit unions and public agencies, as well as illegal wiretapping, result in blatant invasion of privacy.

Rock from the Beginning, Nik Cohn **(1969),** 1971

The personalities, performing styles, and ethos of pop/rock music are described from Elvis to the Jefferson Airplane.

Rock: A Social History of the Music, 1945–1972, Mike Jahn **(1973),** 1976

New York Times rock critic has observed the scene since the early fifties and answers that perennial question: What does it all mean?

Search for the New Land: History as Subjective Experience, Julius Lester **(1969),** 1971

Through "found" poems, news clippings, and war chronologies, a sensitive African American militant documents history as he has lived it since the bombing of Hiroshima.

Serpico, Peter Maas **(1973),** 1976

Serpico tries to be an honest cop in the New York City Police Department but is thwarted by fellow cops, politicians, and criminals.

Sex before Twenty: New Answers for Youth, Helen F. Southard **(1967),** 1971

This book offers practical advice regarding sex and sexuality with emphasis on the total person.

Siddhartha, Hermann Hesse **(1951),** 1971, 1976, 1982, 1988, 1991, 1994, 1999

Emerging from a kaleidoscope of experiences and tasted pleasures, Siddhartha transcends to a state of peace and mystic holiness in this strangely simple story.

The Silent Sound of Needles, Michael Zwerin **(1969),** 1971

Drug addicts undergo rehabilitation at a center in Harlem.

Silent Spring, Rachel Carson **(1964),** 1971, 1976, 1988, 1994, 1999

This landmark book gave birth to the environmental movement.

The Soft Revolution: A Student Handbook for Turning Schools Around, Neil
  Postman and Charles Weingartner **(1971),** 1971

> How can schools be changed and humanized without violence?

Soul on Ice, Eldridge Cleaver **(1968),** 1971, 1994

> Through essays and open letters written while in prison, Eldridge Cleaver
> expresses the inner feelings and drives of the outraged African American
> man.

The Strawberry Statement: Notes of a College Revolutionary, James S. Kunen
  (1969), 1971

> In diary form, Kunen tells of the 1968 Columbia student uprising and says,
> "I'm a 19-year-old civilian and I am tired of fighting."

Students without Teachers: The Crisis in the University, Harold Taylor **(1969),** 1971

> The former president of Sarah Lawrence College writes in detail of the stu-
> dent movement in the United States.

Supership, Noel Mostert **(1974),** 1976

> Supership is a plea for the protection of the ecology of our waterways.

Tell Me That You Love Me, Junie Moon, Marjorie Kellogg **(1968),** 1971

> Junie Moon, an acid-scarred girl; Warren, a paraplegic; and Arthur, a near
> spastic, decide to leave the hospital and set up housekeeping together.

The Terminal Man, Michael Crichton **(1972),** 1976

> Even though his own life is threatened, Benson, an epileptic with a com-
> puter in his brain, sets out to destroy the ruling machines.

To Be Young, Gifted and Black: Lorraine Hansberry in Her Own Words, Lorraine
  Hansberry **(1969),** 1971

> A writer presents a portrait of herself and her view of the human spirit.

**"To My Brother Who Did a Crime . . .": Former Prisoners Tell Their Stories in
  Their Own Words,** Barbara Habenstreit **(1973),** 1976

> After living most of their lives in a world of drugs, crime, and prison, four-
> teen young men struggle to "go straight" at Long Island University.

The Todd Dossier, Collier Young **(1969),** 1971

> Financier Hollis Todd receives a new heart from a young donor whose "ac-
> cidental" death is questioned by Dr. Charles Everett.

Trial, Tom Hayden **(1970),** 1971

> Besides giving a personal account of the Chicago Seven trial, Hayden de-
> scribes the differing politics of the defendants and criticizes the protest
> movement.

Up Your Banners: A Novel, Donald E. Westlake **(1969),** 1971

> Oliver, a young white teacher, struggles with a student strike, an African American caucus, militants, an interracial love affair, and his own self-doubts.

Voices of the New Feminism, Mary Lou Thompson (ed.) **(1971),** 1971

> Twelve women active in the women's liberation movement write on a variety of subjects from "The Liberation of Black Women" to "The Educational Establishment and Women."

Ward 402, Ronald J. Glasser **(1973),** 1976

> Against the wishes of the father and ignoring the implications of their actions, doctors struggle to keep a young leukemia victim alive.

The Weedkiller's Daughter, Harriette Simpson Arnow **(1969),** 1971

> Caught between her outrageously bigoted father and frightened, empty mother, Susan manages to maintain contacts with people who make her world seem real.

The Whole World Is Watching: A Young Man Looks at Youth's Dissent, Mark Gerzon **(1969),** 1971

> In intelligent, reasoned essays on specifics of the youth scene, a Harvard undergraduate presents his generation's concern for the individual and a more psychologically comfortable, humane world.

The Writing on the Wall: 108 American Poems of Protest, Walter Lowenfels **(1969),** 1971

> Martyrdom, inhumanity, war, and death are placed in fierce confrontation with the conscience of the reader.

Your Legal Rights as a Minor, Robert H. Loeb Jr. and John P. Maloney **(1974),** 1976

> What are youths' rights in relation to drugs, driving, sex, work, school, parents, buying, and crime?

Zen and the Art of Motorcycle Maintenance: An Inquiry into Values, Robert M. Pirsig **(1974),** 1976

> Pirsig and his son Chris travel across the country by motorcycle, while the reader travels across the metaphysical puzzle that caused Pirsig's mental breakdown.

Guidelines for the *Outstanding Books for the College Bound* Committee

Charge

To prepare a revised and updated edition of the *Outstanding Books for the College Bound* booklists every five years.

Purpose

To provide reading recommendations to students of all ages who plan to continue their education beyond high school.

Audience

The lists are primarily intended for students in grades 9–12 who wish to enrich and strengthen their knowledge of various subject areas in both classic and contemporary literature.

The lists can be used both by students wishing to round out their reading before entering college and by those taking college entrance examinations such as the ACT and SAT.

The lists can also be used by young adults and adults who are life-long learners wishing to increase or update their knowledge of literature in areas covered by the lists.

Committee Members

The committee will consist of fifteen members who are appointed by the YALSA Vice President/President-Elect for a two-year term beginning immediately after the conclusion of one Midwinter Meeting and ending at the conclusion of the Midwinter Meeting two years later.

Ten members *are required* to attend both the Annual Conferences and the Midwinter Meetings during their term on this committee. As many as *five* members may be "virtual" members. The virtual members will be encouraged to attend the Annual Conferences and the Midwinter Meetings during their term of office but *are not required* to do so. However, they must participate, along with the other committee members, electronically throughout their two-year term on a special electronic list. *Therefore, access to the Internet is a requirement for all committee members.*

Chair

The Chair will be appointed for a two-year term by the Vice President/President-Elect. While the primary role of the Chair is to facilitate the work of the committee, the Chair will have the right to participate in all committee activities. *Access to the Internet and a willingness to communicate continuously and electronically with committee members are requirements for chairing the committee.*

Liaison

The Association of College and Research Libraries will appoint a liaison to serve as a consultant to work with this committee. The liaison will advise the committee on the reading of college students today and will be available to comment on and react to selections of categories and titles.

Committee Organization

The Chair will organize the committee in a way that will get the work done in the most efficient manner. The committee may operate as a committee of the whole or in subcommittees according to categories.

Selection Criteria

Standard selection criteria consonant with the ALA Library Bill of Rights shall be applied.

Although copyright is not a consideration, all titles should be widely available.

Each category may have a special set of criteria.

Books can be in print or out of print, in hardcover or paperback.

Books that have appeared on earlier Outstanding Books lists, including revised editions of books from earlier Outstanding Books lists, are eligible.

Categories

The committee may select up to five categories. The traditional categories for Outstanding Books are the Arts, Biography, Fiction, and Nonfiction. Poetry has sometimes been a separate category, sometimes not. A Now/Current category was used for a time. Plays have been a subcategory of the Arts. There may be some variance in selected categories depending on trends in society and in publishing. There may be subcategories as well.

Suggested Selection Procedures

Determine categories.

Determine criteria, if needed, for selection in each category.

Review titles in the most recent edition of *Outstanding Books for the College Bound* to determine which titles should be reconsidered.

Survey other lists of recommended books and look for titles that are recommended in several sources. The following sources may be helpful:

- *Good Reading: A Guide for Serious Readers,* 23rd ed. (Bowker, 1990)
- *Books for You: An Annotated Booklist for Senior High,* 14th ed. (National Council of Teachers of English, 2001).
- *Senior High School Library Catalog,* 16th ed. (H. W. Wilson, 2002)
- *Best Books for Young Adults: The Selection, the History, the Romance* (ALA, 1994)
- *Best Books for Young Adults,* 2nd ed. (ALA, 2000)
- *Fifty Years of Notable Books* (Booklist Publications, 1996)
- *Reading Lists for College Bound Students,* 3rd ed. (Prentice-Hall, 2000)
- *Recommended Reading: 5000 Classics Reviewed* (Salem Press, 1995)
- *New Lifetime Reading Plan,* by Clifton Fadiman (HarperCollins, 1999)
- Bibliographies from specific subject areas.
- Current reviews and retrospective reviews.
- Annual lists of outstanding and notable books.

Construct a working list of possible titles for study and reading.

Select up to twenty-five titles for each category.

Voting Procedures

The committee will determine its own voting procedure; however, most committees use a simple or a two-thirds majority for their final vote.

Annotations

Using "Procedures for Writing and Publishing Annotations and Bibliographies for Publications by YALSA" (YALSA, *Publications Handbook VII-5,* appendix D, http://www.ala.org/ala/yalsa/aboutyalsa/pubsmanualupdated2004.pdf), determine bibliographic information needed and style required for annotations.

Locate essential bibliographic information according to the "Procedures for Writing and Publishing Annotations and Bibliographies for Publications by YALSA" and verify author, title, and publisher's name.

Write annotations that will appeal to young adults.

The Chair must turn in to the YALSA staff by the end of the 2004 Midwinter Meeting a completed list of "Outstanding Books" by category, arranged alphabetically by author within each category, in hard copy and IBM disk format.

Tips for Using *More Outstanding Books*
for the College Bound

Parents and other interested adults can use this book to guide young adult reading as well as their own. The book is especially suited for book discussion groups because of the wide variety of subjects that are covered. The lists in the book can also be used to begin a discussion (or conversation) about what should be considered an "outstanding book."

As of 2003 there were 1.1 million students being homeschooled in the United States.[1] Providers and students alike will find this book particularly useful both as a historical survey of recommended books for young adults and as a guide to titles for recommended reading lists and for assigned reading.

The lists in this book have a variety of uses. For a firm grounding in the classics use the Top Twenty-Three list in part 3. The 2004 list in part 2 is especially useful because of its arrangement by academic discipline and its currency. If the user has a special interest such as music, the list under that heading will provide a basic foundation for reading in the subject. This book can also be used as a review of titles already read and as a plan for future reading. The 2004 list is especially useful because of its diversity and organization by academic discipline.

Strategies for Readers

Prepare a Reading Action Plan (appendix C).

Keep a reading journal to record author, title, main characters, comments, and observations.

Use Bartleby.com to review characters and content and read biographical information about some of the authors.

Read constantly and steadily.

Read all types of reading materials.

Participate in book discussion groups both in person and online.

Participate in community and state reading programs.

Read Oprah's Book Club classic selections.

Strategies to Encourage Readers

Use *More Outstanding Books for the College Bound* as a resource for

- displays
- book discussion groups
- recommended reading lists
- lists of recommended books
- summer reading lists
- reading camps
- homeschool assignments
- bookmarks

Make copies of the Reading Action Plan available.

Allow reading time in classes and meetings.

Allow self-selection of books to read.

Establish regular reading times at home and school.

Model reading by immersing yourself in a book while others are reading.

Develop an atmosphere that encourages a community of readers.

Encourage writing and talking about books and reading.

NOTE

1. National Center for Education Statistics, *1.1 Million Homeschooled Students in the United States in 2003* (July 2004), http://nces.ed.gov/pubs2004/2004115.pdf.

Reading Action Plan

Time Frame   Month _____ Year _____   *to*   Month _____ Year _____

Name _____ Age _____

Education Level   ____ Middle School   ____ High School   ____ College   ____ Lifelong Learner

Reader Type   ____ Reluctant   ____ Indifferent   ____ Passionate

Reading Speed   ____ Slow   ____ Medium   ____ Fast

Reading Frequency   ____ Daily   ____ Weekly   ____ Monthly

Favorite Reading Materials

____ Books   ____ Magazines   ____ Newspapers   ____ Online   ____ Other _____

READING INTERESTS

Reading Goal

    ____ Read more often   ____ Read for better test scores

    ____ Read faster   ____ Read to prepare for college

    ____ Read a variety of materials   ____ Read to increase knowledge

    ____ Read for pleasure

    ____ Other _____

Books I Have Already Read (*list 5*)

_____

_____

Authors I Want to Read (*list 5 to 10*)

_____

_____

Books I Want to Read (*list 5 to 10*)

_____

_____

Allington, Richard L., and Anne McGill-Franzen. "The Impact of Summer Setback on the Reading Achievement Gap." *Phi Delta Kappan* 85 (September 2003): 68–75.

Bell, Sherri. "Transforming Seniors Who Don't Read into Graduates Who Do." *English Journal* 93 (May 2004): 41.

Center for Applied Research in Education. "Reading List for the College-Bound," in Judie L. H. Strouf, *The Literature Teacher's Book of Lists.* West Nyack, NY, 1993.

College Board. "101 Great Books: Recommended for College-Bound Readers." 2004. http://www.college board.com/article/0,3868,2-8-0-23628,00.html.

Freedman, Samuel G. "To Fire Up Troubled Students, a Program Turns to the Classics." *New York Times,* August 18, 2004.

Good Reading: A Guide for Serious Readers. 23rd ed. New York: R. R. Bowker, 1990.

International Reading Association. "Adolescent Literacy: A Position Statement." *Journal of Adolescent and Adult Literacy* 44, no. 1 (1999): 97–110.

———. *Supporting Young Adolescents' Literacy Learning: A Joint Position Statement of the International Reading Association and National Middle School Association.* 2004. http://www .reading.org/downloads/positions/ ps1052_supporting.pdf.

Modern Library. *100 Best.* 1998. http: //www.randomhouse.com/modern library/100best.html.

Reading Lists for College-Bound Students. 3rd ed. Stamford, CT: Thomson Learning, 2000.

Rosenberg, Merri. "No Required Reading Lists, but Loads of Suggestions." *New York Times,* May 21, 2000.

"Study Cites Most Re-read Books." Associated Press, August 5, 2004. Available at http://www.msnbc.msn.com/id/ 5614141/.

AUTHOR INDEX

Page numbers in bold indicate annotations.

TITLE INDEX

Page numbers in bold indicate annotations.